HOLLIWOOD

Edited by Franco La Polla

Editor-in-Chief
Roberta Busnelli

Translators
David Downie
Emilia Ligniti
David Tabbat

Art Director
Andrea Lancellotti

Photocomposition
Nexus (Michele Olivieri)

Image Sources
Fondazione Alaska/
Archivio Zambetti (Bergamo)
Cahiers du Cinéma (Parigi)
Photofest (New York)

ISBN 88-85982-73-5

*All That Jazz – From New Orleans
to Hollywood and Beyond*
© 2003 Festival internazionale del film Locarno
All Rights Reserved

English Edition
© 2003 Fres srl – Edizioni Olivares
via Pietro Mascagni, 7
I – 20122 Milano
Ph: (39) 02 76001753
e-mail: olivares@edizioniolivares.com
www.edizioniolivares.com

The Locarno International Film Festival is
willing to proceed with licensing (and payment
of the relative usage fee) for those images
with ownership that has not been discovered.

All That Jazz

FROM NEW ORLEANS TO HOLLYWOOD AND BEYOND

Edited by Franco La Polla

56. *Festival internazionale del film Locarno*

This volume is published on the occasion of the retrospective "All That Jazz – From New Orleans to Hollywood and Beyond," organized by the 56th Locarno International Film Festival (6–16 August 2003).

We would like to express our gratitude to:

Robert Altman
Peter Baumann (Columbus AG)
Leo Baumgartner (20th Century Fox)
Bernard Benoliel
(Cinémathèque Française, Paris)
Frédéric Bourboulon
(Little Bear Production)
Hélène Cardis (Monopole Pathé Films)
Gabrielle Claes
(Cinémathèque Royale, Bruxelles)
Piero Colussi
Jean-Louis Comolli
Bryony Dixon (BFI)
Gian Luca Farinelli
(Cineteca del Comune di Bologna)
Michele Fadda
Krin Gabbard
Roger Garcia
Jean-Baptiste Garnero (Archives Françaises du Film, CNC)
Murray Glass
Kanako Hayashi
Roger Huber (Columbus AG)
Shigeki Iwasaka (Shochiku Co. Ltd)
Livio Jacob (Cineteca del Friuli)
Eric Lagesse (Flash Pyramide)
Marc Maeder (20th Century Fox)
Dominique Marti-Dubois (CAC-Voltaire)
Tim McDowell
Antonio Monda
Marina Mottin
Gilles Mouëllic
Yuko Murata
(The Japan Foundation)
Jacques Muyal
Rui Nogueira (CAC- Voltaire)
Roberta Novielli
Claudine Paquot (Cahiers du Cinéma)
Roberta Parizzi
Richard Peña
Baptiste Piégay
Francesco Pitassio
Sydney Pollack
Ishmael Reed
Martin Reinmann
(Monopole Pathé Films)
Paul Richer (Flash Pyramide)
Mandy Rosencrown (Hollywood Classic)
Marc Scheffen (Cinémathèque Municipale, Luxembourg)
Eric Spilker
Melanie Tebb (Hollywood Classic)
Jennifer Teefy
Akira Tochigi (The National Museum of Modern Art, Tokyo)
Tetsuo Tsujimura (The National Museum of Modern Art, Tokyo)
Bernie Uhlmann
(Cinémathèque Suisse, Lausanne)
Arthur Wren
Sandro Zambetti
(Fondazione Alaska, Bergamo)
Theo Zwicky

Satchmo the Great

Contents

8   Jazzing Up
    Irene Bignardi

12 On Cinema & Jazz/Cinema e jazz
    Franco La Polla

18 Laocoon Between Hollywood
    and New Orleans/Laocoonte
    fra Hollywood e New Orleans
    Franco La Polla

ARTICLES

63 The Eye Keeps Watch,
    the Body Listens
    (Filming free jazz)
    *Philippe Carles and
    Jean-Louis Comolli*

73 The Colors of Jazz
    Giampiero Cane

109 Saving It Twice: Preserving Jazz
    in Documentaries, Compilation
    Films, and Short Subjects
    Krin Gabbard

121 The Decline and Fall
    of the Jazz Biopic
    Krin Gabbard

145 Fictional Jazzmen
    Gilles Mouëllic

155 Epiphany and Revelation: Jazz in Film
    Ermanno Comuzio

184 A Date with Jazz: Notes
    on Jazz and Animated Film
    Michele Fadda

194 Documenting Jazz...
    Franco Minganti

INTERVIEWS

219 Ken Burns – Constitution,
    Baseball, and Jazz
    Antonio Monda

221 Alain Corneau – Cinema & Jazz:
    Very Close, Very Far
    Baptiste Piégay

229 Bertrand Tavernier – No Biopics, Please
    Baptiste Piégay

237 Lalo Schifrin – Aleph: Where
    All Music Meets
    Bill Krohn

APPENDICES

255 Cinema and Jazz: Chronology
    Gilles Mouëllic and Michele Fadda

269 Contributors

JAZZING UP

Irene Bignardi

They are almost the same age. They marked a century with their power that is both popular and sophisticated at the same time. They unraveled, during the same years, new rhythms and ways of communicating.

Cinema and jazz belong to the same generation. They are the two art forms that are original to and characteristic of the 20th century (well, we could say that the 19th century saw the first signs of them, but their essence remains bound to the 20th century). They are simultaneously popular and aristocratic. And a common destiny marked them, seeing that the first talkie – or at least the one that is officially recognized as being so – chose precisely jazz (it could have been the melodrama, it could have been the popular music) to make its voice be heard and wed together the two 20th-century art forms in a symbolic manifesto.

Therefore, in the retrospective that the Locarno International Film Festival proposes this year, almost a century of film – or certainly three-quarters of a century – will parade on by upon the silver screen. Over seventy years of cinema that narrated jazz – that exalted it, deprecated it, loved it. Of cinema that recounted its world, that took on the rhythm of its beat, that used it to talk about feelings and contemporary stories, from the United States to Japan, France to Italy. Of cinema that gave us Miles Davis and Bill Evans, Ella Fitzgerald and Count Basie, Charlie Mingus and Duke Ellington with their voices, their music, their stories, and those of the others who went along.

Major and minor jazz legends will pass upon the big screen as characters and musical spirit, as protagonists and moods, with mirth and melancholy – always, however, with that excitement that accompanies and distinguishes the music born in New Orleans but known the world over.

JAZZING UP

Irene Bignardi

Hanno quasi la stessa età, hanno segnato un secolo, lo hanno segnato con la loro forza popolare e sofisticata insieme, hanno scoperto, negli stessi anni, nuovi ritmi e nuovi modi di comunicare.

Il cinema e il jazz sono quasi coetanei, sono le due forme d'arte originali e proprie del Novecento (va be', si può dire che i vagiti li hanno fatti al volgere dell'Ottocento, ma la loro essenza resta novecentesca…), sono due espressioni popolari e aristocratiche insieme. E un destino comune le ha segnate, visto che il primo film sonoro – o almeno quello che ufficialmente è riconosciuto tale – ha scelto proprio il jazz (poteva essere il melodramma, poteva essere la musica popolare) per far sentire la sua voce e saldare le due arti del Novecento in un manifesto simbolico.

Nella retrospettiva che il Festival Internazionale del Film di Locarno propone quest'anno sfila dunque quasi un secolo di cinema – o certamente tre quarti di secolo. Oltre settant'anni del cinema che ha raccontato il jazz, lo ha esaltato, deprecato, amato. Del cinema che ne ha raccontato il mondo, che si è fatto ritmare dal suo beat, che lo ha usato per narrare i sentimenti e le storie contemporanee, dagli Stati Uniti al Giappone, dalla Francia all'Italia. Del cinema che ci porta Miles Davis e Bill Evans, Ella Fitzgerald e Count Basie, Charlie Mingus e Duke Ellington con le loro voci, la loro musica, le loro storie: e quelle degli altri che accompagnano.

I grandi e i meno grandi del jazz passeranno sullo schermo come personaggi e come spirito musicale, come protagonisti e come atmosfera, con divertimento e con malinconia, sempre però con quell'eccitazione che accompagna e contraddistingue la musica nata a New Orleans e diventata di casa in tutto il mondo.

It is certainly not by chance that we say "jazz it up," and therefore "strength," "power," "gaiety." Of the many possible etymologies of the word "jazz" (to chatter, from the French "jaser," as a few sustain? A shortened name of a musician called Chas or Jas? From the expression "jassing it up," which is what was done in the manufacturing industry to enliven perfumes with "jasmine"?), the "jazzing up" is the effect, we expect, this volume, this retrospective, this study will have on the inquisitive reader and the Festival's audience. A probing into and study conducted in a world of cinematic rarities that we wish be translated also and above all in festive merriment – that of music, and of the music of our century.

Irene Bignardi
Artistic Director
Festival internazionale del film Locarno

Certo non a caso si dice "jazz it up", e quindi forza, allegria. Delle tante possibili etimologie della parola jazz (cicalecciare, dal francese "jaser", come sostiene qualcuno? Un diminutivo dal nome di qualche musicista che si chiamava Chas o Jas? Dall'espressione "jassing it up", che era quello che si faceva nell'industria manifatturiera per dare un tocco in più ai profumi con il "jasmine", il gelsomino?), il "jazzing up" è quello che, ci aspettiamo, questo libro, questa retrospettiva, questa ricerca produrranno sul lettore curioso e sul pubblico del festival. Un lavoro di esplorazione e di ricerca condotto in un mondo di rarità cinematografiche che vogliamo si traduca anche e soprattutto in una festosa allegria: quella della musica, e della musica del nostro secolo.

Irene Bignardi
Direttore artistico
Festival internazionale del film Locarno

ON CINEMA & JAZZ

Franco La Polla

This collection of essays, published on the occasion of the "All That Jazz" retrospective organized by the 2003 edition of the Locarno Film Festival, is aimed at accompanying this cinematic event by providing an implicit comment to the movies that will be shown. But its goal is also (and perhaps to an even greater extent) to re-open a discourse on the relationship between these two forms of art and on the idea that the models and procedures pertaining to a particular creative field can be transferred in some way unto a different one (in our case, from music to cinema). An important protagonist is obviously the theme of improvisation – backbone of the entire history of jazz – that at times has found on the silver screen a place in which to experiment in visual and, as we would say today, multimedia terms. But the meeting points between cinema and jazz must not make us forget how the structure of jazz phrasing (whether improvised or not) has revealed itself to the works of a few of the most restless and inquisitive directors in film. Just think of Robert Altman in the United States. But not only: there have even been directors, like Harry Smith, who attempted to realize a "graphic translation" of the original notes of a Dizzy Gillespie or a Thelonious Monk.

All this suffices in making us understand how the juxtaposition of the two terms, the two artistic areas (cinema and jazz) has ushered in a rather impressive quantity of innovations in the broad and varied field of images in motion.

With regards to the structure of this book, the editor has made use of a perhaps artificial (and certainly unofficial) division of the areas of "genre" that characterize the world of cinema and jazz.

Anthologies and shorts, biographies of historical and not-so-historical musicians, cartoons, documentaries of various kinds, films commented by a soundtrack greatly connoted by jazz, and much more. Moreover, what was attempted is to give a full and complete vision of the panorama in question.

CINEMA E JAZZ

Franco La Polla

Questa raccolta di saggi, pubblicata in occasione della retrospettiva "All That Jazz" organizzata dal Festival di Locarno 2003, ha certo lo scopo di accompagnare questa manifestazione fornendo un implicito commento alle pellicole in programma. Ma ha anche, e forse più, l'intenzione di riaprire una discussione sul binomio del titolo, sui rapporti fra l'uno e l'altro ambito artistico, sull'idea stessa che modelli e procedure di un'area creativa possano essere trasposti in qualche modo in un diverso ambito d'operazioni (in questo caso, dalla musica al cinema). Grande protagonista è ovviamente il tema dell'improvvisazione, colonna portante dell'intera storia del jazz, che ha trovato talora nel cinema un terreno di sperimentazione in termini visivi e, come si direbbe oggi, multimediali. Ma gli innesti fra cinema e jazz in questa chiave non devono far dimenticare come la struttura della frase jazzistica – poco importa se improvvisata o no – ha informato di sé l'opera di alcuni fra i registi più inquieti e curiosi del cinema. Basti pensare in America a Robert Altman. Non solo: c'è stato persino chi, come Harry Smith, ha tentato una traduzione grafica delle originali note di un Dizzy Gillespie o di un Thelonious Monk.
Bastano questi accenni a far comprendere come la giustapposizione dei due termini, dei due ambiti – cinema e jazz – è stata foriera di non poche novità nel largo e variegato campo delle immagini in movimento.
Nel pensare la struttura del libro il curatore si è appoggiato a una suddivisione forse artificiale (e certo non ufficiale) delle zone di "genere" che caratterizzerebbero il terreno cinema e jazz.
Antologie e *shorts*, biografie di musicisti storici, biografie di musicisti fittizi, cartoni animati, documentari di vario genere, film commentati da una colonna sonora fortemente connotata in termini jazzistici, ecc. Per quanto possibile si è voluta dare una visione globale di questo panorama.
A corredo, alcune interviste con importanti autori che hanno fatto del jazz parte fon-

In addition, there are a few interviews with important figures that have made jazz a fundamental part of their work. And finally, the reader will find a well-documented film-jazz chronology starting from the first talkies, including a few fundamental cartoons.

The contributors are all prominent experts in the field: from illustrious critics such as Jean-Louis Comolli and Philippe Carles to world-renowned authorities like Krin Gabbard and Gilles Mouëllic, musicologists such as Giampiero Cane and Ermanno Comuzio, trusted jazz critics like Franco Minganti and enthusiastic scholars of cartoons such as Michele Fadda.

At this point, we should close this introduction by allowing the reader to judge for him/herself. But to confirm just how truly problematic this endeavor we are about to embark upon is, perhaps instead of "reader" we should say "listener."

Franco La Polla
Curator of the retrospective and
editor of the volume "All That Jazz"

damentale del loro lavoro. E infine una ricca cronologia del rapporto film/jazz dalle origini del sonoro, compresi alcuni fondamentali *cartoons*.
I contributors sono tutti di primo piano: da grandi critici come Jean-Louis Comolli e Philippe Carles a esperti mondiali come Krin Gabbard e Gilles Mouëllic, a musicologi come Giampiero Cane ed Ermanno Comuzio, provati critici di jazz come Franco Minganti e appassionati cultori di *cartoons* come Michele Fadda.
A questo punto, si dovrebbe chiudere con un "giudicherà il lettore". Ma a riprova di quanto problematico sia il campo che abbiamo davanti, forse dovremmo dire: l'ascoltatore.

Franco La Polla
Curatore della retrospettiva
e del volume "All That Jazz"

St. Louis Blues (Allen Reisner, 1958)
Nat "King" Cole, Eartha Kitt, Cab Calloway

LAOCOON BETWEEN HOLLYWOOD AND NEW ORLEANS

Franco La Polla

Gilles Mouëllic entitled his noteworthy study, of some years ago, *Le Jazz, une esthétique du Xxe siècle*. But the meaning of this title extends well beyond the time period it refers to and beyond the intention of placing jazz in the cultural context in which it was born. "An aesthetics of the 20th century" signifies above all: a way of making art (music, in our case) that is a part of that which characterizes the creative activity of the entire century.
What creative activity?
In order to understand, we need to go straight to the root of a phenomenon, the first signs of which appeared in the poetical revolution of Baudelaire and the great symbolists such as Rimbaud and others – persons believed to have been responsible for the explosion of the historic avant-garde movements in Europe during the 20th century. These movements, as is known, trace back their primary source of inspiration to the so-called "primitive art" (especially African), superimposing the extreme level of intellectual sophistication attained by proto-20th century European art with the primitive component of African and exotic art. "The Negro is a modern savage," wrote in 1924 Harry Farjeon, scandalized, about ragtime. And if this phrase were emptied of its disparaging intent, it could have been seconded by not a small number of artists of the historic European avant-garde movements.
Jazz therefore enters the scene when such signs become unstoppable – when Picasso studies the African masks and Conrad sees in the Dark Continent the evil conscience of Western colonialism.
But the advent of jazz, in addition to being laden with the consequences of an ideological kind of the Old World (so much so that it can be considered the first step towards a rethinking of the shameful prejudices nurtured for centuries by white cultures), had in store other surprises. And this time, which is also clear in the title of Mouëllic's work, surprises of a strictly aesthetic kind.

LAOCOONTE FRA HOLLYWOOD E NEW ORLEANS

Franco La Polla

Gilles Mouëllic intitola un suo cospicuo studio di qualche anno fa *Le Jazz, une esthétique du Xxe siècle*. Ma il senso di questo titolo va ben oltre la circostanza cronologica cui esso allude e oltre la stessa intenzione di situare il jazz nel contesto culturalmente adeguato alla sua comparsa. "Un'estetica del XX secolo" significa soprattutto: un modo di fare arte (musica, in questo caso) che partecipa di ciò che caratterizza l'operare artistico dell'intero secolo.
Quale operare?
Per comprenderlo bisognerebbe andare alla radice di un fenomeno che vide i primi fermenti nella rivoluzione poetica baudelairiana, in quella dei grandi simbolisti come Rimbaud e via dicendo, i quali sarebbero stati alla base dell'esplosione delle avanguardie storiche europee del Novecento. Queste, peraltro, come è noto, rintracciarono nella cosiddetta "arte primitiva" (soprattutto africana) una primaria fonte di ispirazione sovrapponendo l'estremo grado di sofisticatezza intellettuale raggiunto dall'arte europea protonovecentesca alla componente, appunto, primitiva dell'arte visuale africana ed esotica: "the negro is a modernized savage", scriveva Harry Farjeon parlando scandalizzato del ragtime nel 1924, e la frase, svuotata del suo intento denigratorio, avrebbe potuto essere sottoscritta da non pochi artisti dell'avanguardia storica europea.
Il jazz dunque arriva quando tale fermento incomincia a ribollire, quando Picasso studia le maschere africane e Conrad vede nel Continente Nero la cattiva coscienza del colonialismo occidentale.
Ma l'avvento del jazz, pur gravido di conseguenze sul tappeto ideologico del vecchio continente (tanto da poter essere considerato il primo passo verso una revisione dei vergognosi pregiudizi nutriti per secoli dalla cultura dei bianchi), aveva in serbo altre sorprese, e questa volta, come del resto è chiaro nel titolo di Mouëllic da cui siamo partiti, sul versante strettamente estetico.

In America towards the end of the 19th century, ragtime had begun chipping away at the (hypocritically) conscience-stricken and "respectable" characterization of popular music. Preceded by not-so-orthodox sounds taken from outside sources (especially from social dance) just like polka had done fifty years earlier, the rhythm of which, according to Richard Crawford, is believed to have inspired even authentic "cornerstones" of national American music like *Oh, Susanna!* (composed by Stephen Foster), ragtime had, among other things, the "fault" of being a music that was elaborated not by any old culture, like Polish culture (which from Bohemia had spread to Prague then Vienna then Paris), but by black culture. Though more traditionally tied to America, black culture was ideally and socially more distant than any other, even being forced to endure what James Weldon Johnson denounced as a "deracialization" (E. A. Berlin). The culmination of this was the self-proclamation in 1915 of Irving Berlin as one of the fathers of the "ragtime mania in America."

But "chipping away at the conscience-stricken and 'respectable' veneer of popular music" meant at the most an attack on customs and conventional models of socialization that had been acquired some time prior: the *cake walk* and the *turkey trot* derived from ragtime did just this, causing a great stir among the rigid middle class.

Aesthetically speaking, all this is much more important. Ragtime laid the rhythmic foundations so that the jazz and syncopated music yet to come would be able to develop a musical-instrumental approach that was completely different with respect to existing models. Not only: an approach that was extraordinarily close to what the avant-garde movements were formulating for the literature and painting inherited from the preceding century. If we observe the "spots" of any painting by Utrillo, or read a page, chosen at random, of Joyce's *Ulysses*, or read word by word the rarefied verses of e.e. cummings or Apollinaire, we can feel the common ground that these share with the "deconstruction" of a number by Armstrong's "Hot Five" or Beiderbecke's "Wolverines."

The world was coming undone. But not in the literal and Apocalyptic sense that reactionary and conservative thinking – Nazism and Fascism in first place – espoused, denouncing the artistic avant-garde movements and jazz as the expression of a "decadent" or even "degenerate" art form (this last term was unfortunately used by Hugues Panassié in his attack on be-bop). But rather as the object of an observation that was made from a new and very different perspective. As usual, what changed was not so much the world in itself, but the way in which it was considered and looked at, and consequentially, the notion that was provided of it by the new arts.

In America, sul finire del secolo precedente, il ragtime aveva incominciato a sfaldare l'impianto compunto e perbenistico della musica popolare. Preceduto da musiche d'importazione poco ortodosse (soprattutto sul terreno della danza sociale) come cinquant'anni prima la polka, il cui ritmo, secondo Richard Crawford, avrebbe ispirato persino veri e propri capisaldi della musica nazionale americana come *Oh, Susanna!* di Stephen Foster, il ragtime aveva, fra le altre cose, il torto di essere una musica elaborata non tanto presso una cultura genericamente "altra" come la polacca (che peraltro dalla Boemia era giunta a Praga conquistando Vienna e poi Parigi), ma addirittura negra: più tradizionalmente collegata alla terra americana, dunque, ma idealmente e socialmente molto più lontana di qualunque altra, tanto che dovette subire quella che James Weldon Johnson denunciò come una "deracialization" (Edward A. Berlin), culminata nell'autoconsacrazione (1915) di Irving Berlin come uno dei padri della "ragtime mania in America".

Ma "sfaldare l'impianto compunto e perbenistico" significava al massimo un attacco al costume, a modelli convenzionali di socializzazione da tempo acquisiti: il *cake walk* e il *turkey trot* derivati dal ragtime fecero proprio questo, con grande scandalo dell'azzimata comunità borghese.

Esteticamente, tuttavia, il discorso è molto più importante. Il ragtime pose le basi ritmiche perché il jazz e la musica sincopata a venire potessero sviluppare un discorso musicale strumentale del tutto innovativo rispetto ai modelli imperanti. Non solo: un discorso che si avvicinava straordinariamente a quel che le avanguardie stavano compiendo sul corpo della letteratura e della pittura ereditate dal secolo precedente. Osserviamo la "macchiatura" di un qualunque quadro di Utrillo, leggiamo una pagina a caso dell'*Ulisse* joyciano, compitiamo i rarefatti versi di e.e. cummings o di Apollinaire e sentiremo quale comune terreno essi condividono con la "decostruzione" non dico di un brano del più tardo be-bop, ma degli "Hot Five" di Armstrong o dei "Wolverines" di Beiderbecke.

Il mondo si stava sfaldando. Ma non nel modo letterale e apocalittico che il pensiero reazionario e conservatore – nazismo e fascismo in prima fila – allora intese, denunciando avanguardie artistiche e jazz come espressioni di una non meglio definita "arte decadente" o addirittura "degenerata" (un termine, quest'ultimo, in seguito impiegato purtroppo anche da Hugues Panassié nel suo attacco al be-bop); bensì come oggetto di un'osservazione compiuta attraverso lenti diversissime da quelle con cui esso era stato osservato in passato. Come al solito, non era tanto il mondo a essere cambiato quanto il modo di guardarlo e conseguentemente la nozione che di esso fornivano le nuove arti.

New arts. Actually, painting and literature could hardly be defined as "new." What could be called new was perhaps the canons adopted by these art forms for the creation of a different, original and innovative artistic product. The music provided by jazz used the usual scale (in the same years it was rather Schoenberg – and in a non-popular musical field – to break with the traditional model). The radical novelty belonged exclusively to cinema.

Cinema was such a breakthrough that many went out of their way to transform it into theater. Or rather, of a deteriorating and imperfect theater. In fact, the linguistic and expressive potential of this new medium, which Majakovskij understood so well, was indeed revolutionary. But what interests us here is that the *fragmentation*, pivotal point of the entire cinematic process, is the link that unites the new medium with the other arts that were contextually operating in the direction of a cultural renewal of the entire Western world.

There is no doubt that these new arts upset the ordered framework of 19th-century culture. The *stream of consciousness* of Woolf and Joyce can after all be defined as the fragmentation of the logical and reassuring thought construction. In theater, Pirandello's game of deformed identities (not to mention the declared avant-gardisms, from Jarry to Artaud) also operated in the same direction: that of a fragmentation of the reference points created by the certainties of middle-class culture. But perhaps poetry was the area in which such a characteristic became the most pronounced. If considering only the United States, let us recall the opposition of even the most sophisticated critics to America's most intricate of poets, Wallace Stevens. T.S. Eliot himself, who enjoyed favor among the critics, speaks in *The Waste Land* of "these fragments I have shored against my ruins."

The newly-born psychoanalysis also played its part in chipping away the old world by creating a precise and rational place for a few taboos up to that moment banished to the "Bogeyman's dark room," and by seeing under the seemingly reassuring middle-class reality a world of unmentionable shames, of transgression and secrets, thus rendering an image of the world that was anything but solid and unitary. And moreover at the center of its interpretation of the world there was fragmentation.

An entire culture, as we were saying, was coming undone. Its "legibility" was no longer the same. Its values had become tarnished and its structures, wavering. It was not over but was undergoing, to paraphrase Shakespeare, "a sea-change into something rich and strange." The material was the same, but the combinations of its ele-

Nuove arti. In realtà, pittura e letteratura potevano difficilmente essere definite "nuove". Nuovi semmai erano i canoni da esse adottati per la creazione di un diverso, originale, innovativo prodotto artistico. La musica stessa fornita dal jazz si muoveva sulla usuale scala tonale (contestualmente a essa fu piuttosto Schoenberg – e in ambito di musica non popolare – a rompere con il modello tradizionale). La novità radicale sul terreno popolare fu invece appannaggio del cinematografo.

Il cinema fu una novità così radicale che non pochi si industriarono per ridurlo ai termini del teatro. O per meglio dire, di un teatro imbastardito, decaduto, imperfetto. In effetti, le potenziali novità linguistiche ed espressive del nuovo mezzo, che Majakovskij colse così bene, erano davvero rivoluzionarie. Ma quel che qui ci interessa è che la *frammentazione*, centro pivotale dell'intera operazione cinematografica, è l'anello che lega il nuovo mezzo alle altre arti che contestualmente stavano operando nella direzione del rinnovamento culturale dell'intero Occidente.

Non c'è dubbio che il Moderno abbia operato uno *scramble* nel quadro ordinato della cultura ottocentesca. La *stream of consciousness* della Woolf e di Joyce è in fondo definibile come la frammentazione della costruzione logica e rassicurante del pensiero nella sua traduzione in espressione sociale convenzionale (in particolar modo in un ambito anch'esso convenzionale come il discorso letterario). In teatro il gioco di specchi pirandelliano (per non dire delle avanguardie dichiarate, da Jarry a Artaud) operava dopotutto nella stessa direzione: quella di una frammentazione delle strutture di riferimento costruite dalle certezze della cultura borghese. Ma forse la poesia fu l'ambito nel quale tale caratteristica acquistò una visibilità quasi insostenibile. Per rimanere nella sola produzione americana, si pensi alla resistenza che anche la critica più sofisticata oppose al più intricato dei suoi poeti, Wallace Stevens. Lo stesso T.S. Eliot, che peraltro godette di ben altra accoglienza, parla in *La terra desolata* di "frammenti messi a puntellare le mie rovine".

A sua volta, la neonata psicanalisi aggiungeva i suoi colpi trovando un luogo preciso e razionale per alcuni tabù fino a quel momento relegati nella stanza oscura del babau e leggendo in genere sotto la tessitura rassicurante della realtà borghese un mondo di vergogne inconfessabili, di trasgressioni e segreti, rendendo il riflesso di un'immagine del mondo tutt'altro che solida e unitaria; e inoltre imperniando anch'essa sulla frammentazione e non sul quadro generale d'insieme la sua rilettura del mondo.

Un'intera cultura, dicevamo, si stava sfaldando. La sua leggibilità non era più quella d'un tempo, i suoi valori si erano appannati, le sue strutture vacillavano. Non era fi-

ments were countless and ushered in unpredictable and never-before-seen forms. It is what Glauco Cambon called "the struggle with Proteus." The struggle of Joyce and Rilke, yes, but also of Buñuel and Vertov, Armstrong and Beiderbecke (Leonard Feather once defined Leo Watson, one of the fathers of *vocalese*, as the "James Joyce of jazz"). Jazz and cinema are born not only at the same moment but also into the context of the great upheaval we are discussing, and they become its symbol, though not fully aware of it. Yes, because unlike literature and painting of the age, these *new* art forms possess no pre-existing structures they can turn to – they have no reference point that can indicate the place from whence they came and where they are headed to. These, simply put, *are*. And their existence is in itself a clear testimony of the very reason why they *are*.

And yet, the points where they meet with the traditional arts (in the presence of which these new forms were to be regularly labeled as "popular" during most of the 20th century) do indeed exist. Thirty years ago Neil Leonard pointed out a few in a rather convincing way: T.S. Eliot, with regards to the birth of poetry, admitted that it began "with a savage beating a drum in the jungle, and it retains the essential of percussion and rhythm" and the antiphonal techniques, associated with jazz and African music, which he himself used for his 1930s poetical creations; the contextual performances of different instruments in jazz bands are equivalent to the contextualization of the different voices in *The Waste Land*; the observations of Vachel Lindsay on the relationship between his *Daniel* and Irving Berlin's *Alexander's Ragtime Band*; the centrality of the pictorial and color effect in the composition process of Duke Ellington (something this jazz great himself affirmed, even because as a boy he had studied drawing and graphic arts); the affirmation of the painter Stuart Davis, Ellington's friend, that the geometric forms and colors of his paintings echoed the rhythm and tempo of jazz, and his use of color is like the use a musician makes of his own instrument.

But there is more. Davis himself once stated:

The eye travels through a picture in a period of time just as the ear follows the tonal intervals in music as they are progressively played in a sequence of time.

This is an extremely important phrase because it opens up a theoretic horizon that is much broader than the one suggested by the preceding examples. The affirmation identifies a temporal space that employs two senses (sight and sound). But how do

nita, ma stava subendo, per parafrasare il Bardo, "a sea-change into something rich and strange". Il materiale è lo stesso, ma le combinazioni dei suoi elementi discreti sono incalcolabili e portano a forme imprevedibili, inedite. È quella che Glauco Cambon chiamò "la lotta con Proteo": la lotta di Joyce e di Rilke, sì, ma anche quella di Buñuel e Vertov, di Armstrong e Beiderbecke (Leonard Feather aveva definito Leo Watson, uno dei padri del *vocalese*, "il James Joyce del jazz"). Il jazz e il cinema nascono non solo contemporaneamente, ma contestualmente al grande rivolgimento di cui stiamo parlando, e ne divengono l'ignaro simbolo. Sì, perché, a differenza della letteratura e della pittura dell'epoca, queste *nuove* arti non hanno strutture di riferimento cui rivolgersi, non hanno una storia che dica loro da quale direzione provengono e dove vanno. Esse, semplicemente, sono. E il loro esserci è di per sé chiara testimonianza della ragione stessa per cui esistono.

Pure, i punti di incrocio e di raccordo con le arti tradizionali (davanti alle quali per gran parte del XX secolo esse verranno regolarmente etichettate come "popolari") non mancarono. Trent'anni fa Neil Leonard ne indicava alcuni in modo molto convincente: l'ammissione di T.S. Eliot in merito alla nascita della poesia, che incominciò "with a savage beating a drum in the jungle, and it retains the essential of percussion and rhythm" e le tecniche antifonali, associate al jazz e alla musica africana, da lui usate nella sua produzione degli anni Trenta; le esecuzioni contestuali di diversi strumenti nelle bande jazz equivalenti alla contestualità delle diverse voci in *La terra desolata*; le affermazioni di Vachel Lindsay sul rapporto fra il suo *Daniel* e *Alexander's Ragtime Band* di Irving Berlin; la centralità dell'effetto pittorico e del colore nel processo compositivo di Duke Ellington, per esplicita dichiarazione dell'autore (che del resto da ragazzo aveva studiato disegno e arti grafiche); l'affermazione del pittore Stuart Davis, amico di Ellington, per il quale le forme geometriche e i colori dei suoi quadri echeggiavano il ritmo e il tempo della musica jazz, e il suo uso dei colori equivaleva all'uso che un musicista fa del proprio strumento.
Ma c'è di più: lo stesso Davis ha affermato:

The eye travels through a picture in a period of time just as the ear follows the tonal intervals in music as they are progressively played in a sequence of time.

Si tratta di una frase estremamente importante perché apre un orizzonte teorico ben più ampio di quello suggerito dagli esempi precedentemente indicati. L'affermazione identifica uno spazio temporale che impegna due percezioni sensoriali (visiva e audi-

we interpret the phrase if in the place of a painting, a photograph, or a picture we have figures in motion? It is probable that at this point the relationship in perception becomes dynamic in the sense that the succession of images of which a film is composed of (but even one sequence would suffice) places itself before an onlooker's gaze asking it for a quick and continuous repetition of the specific perceptive model. This is a little like what, though from a different perspective, Arthur Knight comments on when speaking about *Jammin' the Blues*, the example that is still the most celebrated of a *jazz short*. *Jammin' the Blues* separates itself from the genre it belongs to, abandoning the rhetorical construction that 1940s Hollywood imposed upon the *jazz short*: no set design, alternation of long, medium and extreme close-up shots, editing cuts that, by uniting them, present different members of the band or which starting from a detail shot re-elaborate the image by enlarging it. Knight says that the organizing principle of that film is "addition," expressed both with the sound and the images, and that to an increase of the soundtrack tempo there corresponds an increase in the rhythm of the editing. And so Stuart Davis' intuition pertaining to gaze (image) and hearing (music) finds in cinema an excellent example of development in the direction he had indicated.

But we can even go one step further. Balàzs did not fully appreciate the importance of a rhythmical-musical and rhythmical-decorative editing – an embellishment, an ornament (in his own words) of a film. The history of cinema however has shown us what can happen when the editing does not limit itself to dressing-up the film with a juxtaposition of secondary elements, but rather when it establishes its own rhythm on the basis of the music – at times of the music developed by the soundtrack (e.g. cartoons) or in other instances of the models provided by a musical genre (opera, symphony, and even jazz).

Nonetheless, in addition to fragmentation, the central concept and heart of the problem relating to the relationship between jazz and cinema is indicated by some as being *improvisation*. In jazz, improvisation is, as we all know, fundamental and essential. And in cinema? With regards to this the bibliography agrees, at least, on one point: directors of improvisation are very few and, not by chance, the studies in this direction have centered around the first, Cassavetes (especially the Cassavetes of *Shadows*) and on a limited number of other anti-Hollywood directors.

But are we really certain that for "improvisation" in cinema we only mean the practice of a director who lets his/her actors improvise lines and gestures on the basis of a pre-established rough script?

tiva). Ma come dobbiamo leggere la frase se al posto di un quadro, di una foto, di un'immagine fissa (*picture*) noi avessimo figure in movimento? È probabile che a quel punto il rapporto percettivo si faccia dinamico, nel senso che la teoria di immagini di cui è composto un film (ma basta l'esempio di una sequenza) si pone davanti allo sguardo chiedendogli una ripetizione veloce e continua dello specifico modello percettivo. È un po' quel che, sia pure da una diversa prospettiva, commenta Arthur Knight parlando di *Jammin' the Blues*, l'esempio a tutt'oggi più celebrato di *jazz short* mai girato.

Jammin' the Blues si distacca dal genere cui appartiene abbandonando la costruzione retorica che negli anni Quaranta Hollywood imponeva al *jazz short*: niente scenografia, alternanza di piani lunghi, medi e ravvicinatissimi, tagli di montaggio che presentano, collegandoli, diversi membri del gruppo, o che partendo da un dettaglio rielaborano l'immagine allargandola. Knight dice che il principio organizzativo di quel film è l'addizione, espressa sia auralmente che visualmente, e che a un aumento del tempo sulla colonna sonora corrisponde un aumento del ritmo del montaggio. Ecco dunque come l'intuizione di Stuart Davis relativa a sguardo (immagine) e udito (musica) trova nel territorio cinematografico un ottimo esempio di sviluppo nella direzione da lui indicata.

Ma si può andare anche più in là. Béla Balàzs si era limitato in poche righe a parlare di un montaggio ritmico-musicale e ritmico-decorativo, un abbellimento, un ornamento – nelle sue parole – di un film ben altrimenti eloquente. La storia del cinema però ci ha mostrato quel che può avvenire quando il montaggio non si limita a ornare il film con una giustapposizione di elementi secondari, ma stabilisce il proprio ritmo sulla base della musica: talvolta della musica sviluppata dalla colonna sonora (ad esempio, i *cartoons*), talaltra dei modelli forniti da un genere musicale (opera, sinfonia, ma anche jazz).

Tuttavia, oltre a quello di frammentazione, il concetto centrale e insieme il nodo del problema relativo al rapporto fra cinema e jazz viene da alcuni indicato nell'*improvvisazione*. Nel jazz essa è, come sappiamo, fondamentale, irrinunciabile. E nel cinema? La bibliografia sull'argomento concorda perlomeno su un punto: i cineasti dell'improvvisazione sono molto pochi, e non a caso gli studi in questa direzione si sono appuntati sul primo Cassavetes (soprattutto quello di *Shadows/Ombre*) e su pochi altri registi anti-hollywoodiani.

Ma siamo davvero certi che per "improvvisazione" al cinema dobbiamo intendere unicamente la pratica di un regista che lascia liberi i suoi attori di recitare improvvisan-

Let us take for example Robert Altman, an anti-Hollywood director (even though not strictly avant-garde) known for the freedom he allows to his actors on the set. His type of freedom consists in sincerely considering the suggestions proposed by the actors regarding their parts and the course of the film itself, but always *before* the shooting. In other words, Altman, in a strict sense, does not "improvise," but easily changes scene and dialogue components on the basis of his occasional reflections, or those of others. Now, everyone sees that in jazz, which is also what Ted Gioia affirms, improvisation is strictly identified with the present, and with that particular moment of the performance ("What jazz has to offer, then, is a plethora of immediacies, a sequence of present moments"), and where in the case of Altman openness to new ideas, to the unpredictable, to the non-established requires nonetheless a negotiation and an agreement between the parties involved (the person who suggests and the person who considers that suggestion). Would we therefore deny to the creator of *California Split* (in my opinion one of the most constructed films in terms of jazz structure in all of American cinema, and without even a single note of jazz) the characteristic of maestro of improvisation, and of improvisation in terms of jazz?

In order to make myself be better understood I would like to use a classical text of almost half a century ago: *The Book of Jazz* (1957) by Leonard Feather. In the chapter he dedicates to improvisation, the author writes that there are three types: a) the kind that fully respects the original melody; b) the kind that limits itself to changing, by lengthening or shortening, a few notes, repeating others and using tonal variations which become a vehicle of the performer's personal touch, but which overall re-creates a melody that can still be easily recognized; and finally c) the kind characterized by total improvisation, which in turn is divided into three categories: x) the one with notes which are absolutely and instantaneously improvised, y) the one with notes which have been in some way predetermined in the sense that they follow a natural order (arpeggio, chromatic sequence, etc.), and finally z) the one with the notes that are played automatically, without any reflection, because they are readily available and perhaps because they are part of a sequence that had already been played and which remained in the mind of the performer. At this point Feather provides precise examples of legendary jazzmen who performed within this third category: Armstrong, Gillespie, Ellington (who firmly believed that pure improvisation did not exist and that a certain degree of predetermination was inevitable with every musician).

do battute e movimenti sulla base di un canovaccio rozzamente prefissato?

Prendiamo ad esempio Robert Altman, un autore anti-hollywoodiano (anche se non strettamente d'avanguardia) noto per la libertà concessa sul set ai suoi attori. La libertà altmaniana si riassume nella più larga considerazione concessa ai suggerimenti proposti dagli attori in merito alle loro parti e all'andamento del film stesso, ma sempre e abbastanza rigorosamente *prima* delle riprese. Voglio dire: Altman, in senso stretto, non "improvvisa", ma cambia facilmente componenti di sceneggiatura e dialogo sulla base di occasionali riflessioni sue o di altri. Ora, non è chi non veda che nel jazz, come del resto dice anche Ted Gioia, l'improvvisazione si identifica strettamente col presente, con l'attimo di quel particolare momento della *performance* ("What jazz has to offer, then, is a plethora of immediacies, a sequence of present moments"), laddove nell'esempio altmaniano la disponibilità al nuovo, all'imprevisto, al non prefissato richiede tuttavia una negoziazione e un accordo fra le parti in causa (chi suggerisce e chi recepisce il suggerimento). Negheremo per questo all'autore di *California Split/California Poker* (a mio avviso uno dei film più costruiti in termini di struttura jazzistica dell'intero cinema americano, e senza una sola nota di jazz) la qualità di maestro dell'improvvisazione, e dell'improvvisazione in termini jazzistici?

Per far comprendere meglio quanto sto tentando di dire vorrei ricorrere a un testo classico di quasi mezzo secolo fa: *The Book of Jazz* (1957) di Leonard Feather. Nel capitolo che dedica all'improvvisazione l'autore scrive che ve ne sono di tre tipi: a) quello che rispetta completamente la melodia originale; b) quello che si limita a mutare, ampliandole o accorciandole, alcune note, che ne ripete altre, che usa variazioni tonali le quali si fanno veicolo del personale mondo artistico del *performer*, ma che nell'insieme propone una melodia ancora facilmente riconoscibile; e finalmente c) quello della piena improvvisazione, a sua volta suddivisa in tre categorie: x) quella le cui note sono assolutamente e istantaneamente improvvisate, y) quella le cui note sono in qualche misura predeterminate nel senso che seguono una sequenza naturale (arpeggio, sequenza cromatica, ecc.), e infine z) quella in cui le note sono suonate automaticamente, senza riflessione di pensiero, perché sono a portata di mano e forse perché fanno parte di una sequenza già suonata che è rimasta inconsciamente nella memoria del *performer*. A questo punto Feather fornisce esempi precisi di grandi jazzisti che hanno operato all'interno della terza categoria sino a far diventare talune loro frasi ricorrenti dei *clichés*: Armstrong, Gillespie, Ellington (il quale credeva fermamente che l'improvvisazione pura non esistesse e che un certo grado di predeterminazione fosse inevitabile in ogni musicista).

Now, it would be certainly risky to affirm that, at least as far as American cinema is concerned, any director who more or less slavishly films the subject provided to him/her by the production in no way considers improvisation, while a director who makes no variation on the subject but furnishes it with small formal details (of editing, set design, etc.) that make the final product more complete and eloquent can be ascribed to a); a director who, like Orson Welles before his last works, follows a recognizable narrative thread, but varied in its particulars, can be ascribed to b); a director like the Cassavetes in *Shadows* is without a doubt identifiable with case x); the Warhol in *Chelsea Girls* (this is only one example) is identifiable with case y); that in the last case, z), the most varied directors fit in here, from *auteurs* like Minnelli, Ray and Sirk to *underground* visionaries like Kenneth Anger (a good example in Italy could be Carmelo Bene).

It is evident: in all these cases it is not the term "improvisation" that is the most suitable to the circumstance, but rather and to different extents, creativity, initiative, innovative spirit, etc. It would seem impossible to classify Altman's work in some of his movies in any one of the categories mentioned above. Actually, as Comolli also writes, "the *cinema-machine* is more rigid and heavier than, in comparing the two, the musician's instrument." In other words, the directorial and generically technical mediation that characterizes a film – any film – makes it impossible for a comparison between the improvisation of a jazz solo and any movie (or even just one sequence). At the most, we can resort to the term and concept of *structure*, that is to say, of a collection of components that possess a method of assembling which may to a certain extent be compared with the sequence of sounds in a solo. In the already-cited *California Split* the basic narrative thread (a fervid gambler meets another person like him and they join up, continuing to go to casinos to satisfy their pathological desire to risk it all) expands in a seemingly casual and haphazard manner that is not unlike what we perceive in a Charlie Parker solo where every space seems to be independently traversed by the awareness that the listener has or does not have of its presence. The spaces of Altman's film emerge to the eyes of the spectator without providing the correlatives of a pause, of a logical intuition of why these are being presented. In the film all the women are called "Barbara," like a *riff* that runs through the entire movie, heedless of everything that is not its calm rhythm, its structure that expands trying to absorb the most space possible and adapting it to its own pace, to the metronome that silently governs its elusive form.

Ora, sarebbe certo azzardato affermare che, quantomeno nel cinema americano, un qualsiasi regista che gira più o meno pedissequamente il soggetto fornitogli dalla produzione sfugga del tutto, ovviamente, all'idea di improvvisazione, mentre un regista che non opera alcuna variazione su di esso ma che lo guarnisce di piccoli dettagli formali (di scenografia, di montaggio, ecc.) tali da renderlo più pieno ed eloquente è ascrivibile ad a); un regista che, come Orson Welles prima delle sue ultime cose, segue una linea narrativa riconoscibile, ma variata nei suoi tratti discreti, è ascrivibile a b); che un regista come il Cassavetes di *Shadows* è senz'altro identificabile col caso x); che il Warhol di *Chelsea Girls* (è solo un esempio) è identificabile col caso y); che nell'ultimo caso z) rientrano i registi più diversi, da *auteurs* come Minnelli, Ray, Sirk a geni visionari dell'underground come Kenneth Anger (un buon esempio in Italia potrebbe essere Carmelo Bene).

È evidente: in tutti i casi suddetti non è il termine "improvvisazione" il più adatto alla circostanza, ma piuttosto, e in vari gradi, quello di intraprendenza, creatività, spirito innovativo, ecc. Non a caso, sembrerebbe impossibile classificare all'interno di uno qualunque dei casi sopra indicati il lavoro compiuto da Altman in talune sue pellicole. In realtà, come scrive anche Comolli, "la machine-cinéma est-elle plus rigide, plus lourde, que ne l'est, outil pour outil, l'instrument du musicien". Vale a dire che la mediazione registica e genericamente tecnica che caratterizza il film – qualunque film – rende impossibile un'equiparazione fra l'improvvisazione dell'assolo jazz e una qualsiasi pellicola (o anche solo una sua sequenza). Tutt'al più è lecito ricorrere al termine e al concetto di *struttura*, vale a dire di un insieme di componenti il cui modo di assemblaggio può in certa misura essere comparato con la sequenza dei suoni in un assolo. Nel citato *California Split* la linea narrativa di base (un giocatore incallito ne incontra un altro e i due si uniscono continuando a recarsi nelle sale da gioco per soddisfare il loro morboso desiderio di tentare la sorte) si espande secondo un'apparente casualità – che ovviamente rimanda a quella che presiede al modello del gioco – non diversa da quella che si percepisce in un assolo di Charlie Parker, nel quale ogni spazio sembra essere percorso indipendentemente dalla coscienza che l'ascoltatore ha o non ha della sua presenza, della sua potenziale indagabilità. Gli spazi del film di Altman emergono agli occhi dello spettatore senza fornire i correlativi di un'attesa, di una logica intuizione del perché essi vi vengono presentati. I nomi delle donne del film sono tutti "Barbara", come un *riff* che percorre la pellicola, incurante di alcunché che non sia il suo calmo ritmo, la sua struttura che si espande a macchia d'olio, cercando cioè di assorbire il maggior spazio possibile adeguandolo al proprio passo, al metronomo che silenziosamente ne governa la struttura inafferrabile.

In the same way, it is not easy to find in cinema a model of poíesis comparable to the one, typically of jazz, that calls for an improvisation based not on melody but on the structure provided by the chords that every jazz historian and critic frequently speaks about – from Nat Hentoff to Leonard Feather. What is the (visual) model of the "chord" in cinema? At the most, we could mean as a chord a specific situation of composition: who knows?, three persons sitting in a room who just found out they won a lottery. At this point, improvisation can be identified in their excited and agitated gestures or in the words they say to one another: gestures and words that the director does not suggest, thus leaving them free to invent as they go along. But this, as can be understood well, does not have much to do with cinema as a language, and in particular as a language that is inspired by musical models of expression. The editing, the camera movements and even the lighting are some of the elements of this language. But where does improvisation (not to mention the solo) fit in? However much invented at the last minute, these always have a "before," a deciding moment that is not identified in the very act of the performance, but which, as we have already discussed, requires nonetheless negotiation not only with the director but also with the technical support on the set. Once again, Comolli:

The risk that is necessarily accepted in improvisation is not paid with the same price in both cases, seeing that the lightness of the musical instrument (in jazz, the improvisation space is often the place where there is the closest relationship among musicians: duos, trios, quartettes) allows the musician to pick the motif up again, to record one, two, ten variations of it and to choose (or not) among these – something that a director, like a matador in an arena, cannot greatly practice.

Besides, it is Mouëllic himself who cites the eloquent, in this sense, words of Cassavetes: "For me, improvisation means that there is such spontaneity in the work that one can believe that nothing has been prepared." And it is Mouëllic himself who, always with regards to Cassavetes in relation to jazz, speaks about "means used to achieve an impression of improvisation that reveal themselves as essential." Or rather, limiting the observation to the quite particular field of *vocalese*, we even push the confrontation with jazz up to affirming with Barry Keith Grant that:

Like Eisenstein's montage, the music, the lyrics and the performance of vocalese

Allo stesso modo, non è facilmente rintracciabile nel cinema un modello poietico comparabile a quello, tipicamente jazzistico, che vuole l'improvvisazione basata non sulla melodia, ma sulla struttura fornita dagli accordi di cui parla regolarmente qualunque storico e critico del jazz, da Nat Hentoff allo stesso Leonard Feather. Qual è al cinema il modello (visivo) dell'"accordo"? Tutt'al più si potrà intendere come accordo una situazione compositiva specifica: che so?, tre persone sedute in una stanza che hanno appena appreso di aver vinto a una lotteria. A quel punto, l'improvvisazione può identificarsi nei gesti concitati di qualcuno di loro o nelle parole che essi si scambiano al riguardo: gesti e parole che il regista non suggerisce, lasciandoli liberi di inventarseli. Ma questo, lo si comprende bene, non ha molto a che fare con il cinema come linguaggio, e in particolare come linguaggio che si ispira a modelli musicali di espressione. Il montaggio, l'angolazione, il movimento di macchina, persino l'illuminazione sono alcuni degli elementi di questo linguaggio: ma in quale luogo potrebbe stare l'improvvisazione (per non dire l'assolo) nel momento della loro pratica? Per quanto inventati all'ultimo momento, essi hanno pur sempre un "prima", un momento decisionale che non si identifica nell'atto stesso della *performance*, ma che, come si diceva, richiede comunque una negoziazione non solo con il regista ma anche con i supporti tecnici del set. Per dirla ancora con Comolli:

Le risque nécessairement accepté dans l'improvisation ne se paie pas du meme prix ici et là, tant la légèreté de l'appareil musical (en jazz, l'espace de l'improvisation est souvent le lieu de la plus proche relation des musiciens entre eux: duos, trios, quartettes) permet au musicien de revenir sur le motif, d'en enregistrer une, deux, dix variantes, et de choisir (ou non) entre elles, ce que le cinéaste, comme d'ailleurs le matador dans l'arène, ne peut guère pratiquer.

Del resto, è lo stesso Mouëllic a riportare le eloquenti, in questo senso, parole di Cassavetes: "Pour moi, l'improvisation veut dire qu'il y a un telle spontaneité dans le travail qu'on pourrait croire que ça n'a pas été préparé". Ed è lo stesso Mouëllic che, sempre a proposito di Cassavetes in rapporto al jazz, parla di "moyens utilisés pour parvenir à une impression d'improvisation qui se révèlent alors essentiels". Oppure, restringendo l'osservazione al campo alquanto particolare del *vocalese*, si può anche spingere il confronto col jazz sino ad affermare con Barry Keith Grant:

Like Einstenian montage, the music, the lyrics, and the performance of vocalese are

are parts that exist independently, but together they are capable of expressing something more than the parts individually.

But not much more.
It is therefore true that in *performance* not little is entrusted to haphazardness, and it is also true that the aesthetic goal of the jazzman is to "organize the haphazardness" and this is what unites him with the director (or at least, with a director like Cassavetes). But it is also true that rarely any sequence, any *take* (and even more so, an entire film) can be compared to an improvised solo. In a certain sense, we are still within the area discussed by Lessing in *Laocoon* when he urges not to confuse different materials of expression (in his case painting and poetry). His observations on painting and space on the one hand and poetry and time on the other disclose extraordinary analogies, respectively, with cinema and jazz.
At the basis of the idea that unites the jazz improvisation with possible analogous attempts in cinema is a kind of unrecognized contradiction. It is Mouëllic who cites an extremely important phrase of Charlie Mingus, who Cassavetes called to collaborate on the soundtrack for *Shadows* because of his well-known talent as a jazz improviser. Mingus, having seen a part of the film on the film-editing machine, burst out, "This is going to take me a lot of time, you know. I went to Julliard." And he said that he intended to *write* all the music for that film beforehand.
Now, that a great jazz improviser is surprised that a director would ask him to improvise a soundtrack is something that also causes great surprise. But it reveals something extremely important. Mingus' reaction shows us in fact that improvisation is not one of the many ways that a jazz musician can choose to realize a work. To make music, professionally, means to write it, perhaps after having studied at a top-notch school like Julliard. Improvisation in jazz is the result of an exercise of the soul, the consequence and the equivalent of the "urgency of personal discovery that's jazz" (Hentoff). A director cannot request an improvisation, and when it does indeed happen, it happens because the performer has something to say and not because he was asked to say something. One has all the right to think that a celebrated musician like Mingus has in any case something to say, but we cannot push our request on the musician to create that special something. The most that we can do is to ask the musician for some music: at the right moment it will be the performer who decides how to give it in the most personal and inspired way, which is precisely what happened in *Shadows*. And before that

parts that exist independently, but together they are capable of expressing something more than the parts individually.

Ma non molto di più.

È vero dunque che in un'arte di *performance* non poco è affidato al caso (*hazard*), ed è vero che il fine estetico del jazzista è di "organizzare il caso" e che questo è ciò che l'accomuna al regista (o almeno, a un regista come Cassavetes), ma è anche vero che difficilmente una qualunque sequenza, un qualunque *take* (e ancor meno un intero film, naturalmente) è comparabile a un assolo improvvisato. In certo senso siamo ancora nell'ambito denunciato da Lessing nel *Laocoonte* quando questi esorta a non confondere differenti materiali d'espressione (nel suo caso pittura e poesia). Le sue notazioni sulla pittura e lo spazio da un lato e sulla poesia e il tempo dall'altro dispiegano straordinarie analogie, rispettivamente, con cinema e jazz.

Alla base dell'idea che accomuna l'improvvisazione jazzistica a eventuali analoghi tentativi in sede cinematografica sta una sorta di contraddizione non riconosciuta. Proprio Mouëllic riferisce una frase estremamente importante di Charlie Mingus, che Cassavetes aveva chiamato a collaborare alla colonna musicale di *Shadows* per il suo ben noto talento di improvvisatore. Mingus, avendo visto una parte del film alla moviola, sbottò: "Ca va me prendre beaucoup de temps, vous savez. Je suis allé à la Juilliard". E disse che aveva l'intenzione di *scrivere* in anticipo tutta la musica per quel film.

Ora, che un grande improvvisatore del jazz si meravigli che un regista gli chieda di improvvisare una colonna sonora è cosa che a sua volta suscita meraviglia. Ma è anche qualcosa di estremamente rivelatore. L'atteggiamento di Mingus ci dice infatti che l'improvvisazione non è un modo fra i tanti che un jazzista può scegliere per confezionare un lavoro. Fare musica professionalmente vuol dire scriverla, magari dopo aver studiato a una scuola qualificatissima come la Juilliard. L'improvvisazione in jazz è il risultato di un moto dell'animo, la conseguenza e il corrispettivo dell'"urgency of personal discovery that's jazz" (Hentoff); essa non fa parte di ciò che il committente può richiedere, e quando avviene avviene perché il *performer* ha qualcosa da dire, non perché gli è stato chiesto di dire qualcosa. Si ha tutto il diritto di pensare che un formidabile musicista come Mingus abbia comunque qualcosa da dire, ma non si può spingere la propria richiesta fino a commissionargli quel qualcosa. Il massimo che ci è concesso è chiedergli della musica: al momento opportuno sarà lui stesso a darla nel modo più

special moment Mingus (and anyone else) is "only" a musician who studied music.
But then, what kind of improvisation are we talking about? Is it really possible to reunite under the same meaning a solo by Armstrong and one by Coltrane? Jazz, as we all know, had a vast and precise historical evolution and to such a degree that even within it, as was also the case with literature a few centuries ago, there were disagreements between traditionalists and modernists. It is no secret that Armstrong hated be-bop, even expressing himself in public. Therefore, when we speak about solos and improvisations do we mean those of the leader of the "Hot Five" or those persons who in a popular classical piece insert two or three new chords that substitute the original ones in a way that changes the number and which is even presented sometimes with another title – something that Gillespie, Monk and even George Shearing are known to have done? And what shall we do about the fact that (these are the words of LeRoi Jones – this is how he called himself back then – a critic that was anything but soft and accommodating):

[…] *Eckstine's orchestra clearly demonstrated that be-bop could be written, and even as a score for large bands; moreover, it made us understand that that music was not simply a whim or an affectation, but rather a serious and important musical language.*

I am certainly not denying the existence and importance of an essential and conspicuous tradition of improvisation in jazz. But I simply wish to remind that it is just *one part* of the big picture and that therefore reducing the relationship between jazz and cinema to a comparison regarding this single aspect greatly limits our research.
Frederick Garber, for example, proposes a different but important problem pertaining to biopics about famous jazz musicians (more specifically, Michael Curtiz's Bix Beiderbecke), stressing how these movies – and they are indeed many – revolve around a contradiction. Or rather: an oxymoron. On the one hand, these films attempt to re-create the specific aura of the musician in question and the uniqueness of the musician's performance. And on the other hand, these movies bow down to the Hollywood cliché of the artist – more or less unhappy and always searching for his/her art (in the biography of Glenn Miller, directed by Anthony Mann, the wife of the musician, June Allyson, continues to reassure him that one day he will find his

ispirato e personale, come del resto è infine avvenuto con *Shadows*. Prima di quel momento Mingus (e chiunque altro) è "soltanto" un musicista che ha studiato musica.
Ma poi, di quale improvvisazione stiamo parlando? Davvero è possibile riunire sotto lo stesso significante un assolo di Armstrong e uno di Coltrane? Il jazz, lo sappiamo, ha avuto un'evoluzione storica ampia e precisa: tanto che anche in esso, come del resto qualche secolo fa in letteratura, non è mancata una *querelle* fra tradizionalisti e modernisti. Non è un segreto il fatto che Armstrong disprezzasse il be-bop, contro il quale a suo tempo si espresse pubblicamente. Dunque, quando parliamo di assolo e di improvvisazione intendiamo quelli del *leader* degli "Hot Five" o quelli che su un brano popolare classico inseriscono due o tre accordi sostitutivi al posto di quello originale in modo da mascherare il brano stesso, che viene presentato addirittura con un altro titolo, come hanno fatto Gillespie, Monk e persino George Shearing? E d'altra parte, come la mettiamo col fatto che (sono parole di LeRoi Jones – allora si chiamava così – vale a dire di un critico tutt'altro che tenero e accomodante):

[...] *Eckstine's orchestra clearly demonstrated that be-bop could be written, and even as a score for large bands; moreover, it made us understand that that music was not simply a whim or an affectation, but rather a serious and important musical language.*

Non sto certo negando – incredibile assurdità – l'esistenza e l'importanza di una grande tradizione improvvisativa nel jazz, ma semplicemente ricordando che essa è *una parte* della più larga storia di quella musica e che quindi ridurre il rapporto fra cinema e jazz a un'eventuale comparazione in relazione a quel singolo aspetto riduce in certa misura il campo dell'indagine.
Frederick Garber, per esempio, pone un diverso ma pur sempre importante problema relativo ai film biografici su jazzisti famosi (nel caso specifico si tratta del Bix Beiderbecke di Michael Curtiz) sottolineando come queste pellicole – e sono moltissime – ruotano attorno a una contraddizione. Meglio: a un ossimoro. Esse da un lato cercano di ricostruire l'*aura* specifica della figura in questione e l'irripetibilità di questa o quella sua esecuzione, e dall'altro obbediscono al *cliché* hollywoodiano dell'artista, infelice o meno, sempre comunque alla ricerca della sua arte (nella biografia di Glenn Miller diretta da Anthony Mann la moglie del musicista, June Allyson, continua a dirgli che un giorno egli troverà il suo "stile" senza farci capire alcunché in merito a che

"style" but without making us understand what exactly she means by this). What is more: the cliché is regularly the way in which the film attempts to present the aura of the musician. Or rather: that which is the most irreducible and undefinable in the artistic activity of a person is outlined by using a standard model of presentation that can be applied to anyone.

The question is therefore: Why is cinema (at least Hollywood cinema) not able to – or perhaps does not want to – portray a sincere and convincing image of the jazz musician (and probably of the artist in general)?

But this question becomes dangerously vast if we consider that the relationship between biopics about white and black musicians is completely in favor of the first category. If we take out William C. Handy not a whole lot of black is left in classical Hollywood cinema on jazz. And it is symptomatic that the various copies of the script of *New Orleans* by Lubin increasingly cut the roles of Louis Armstrong and Billie Holiday, who at the beginning were supposed to be the film's protagonists (in this sense *Shadows* is once again an anti-Hollywood and anti-mainstream work).

LeRoi Jones affirms that the word "art" is one of the most looked down upon in the American language. And in fact the treatment that cinema has reserved for the artist is one of misunderstanding. A practical and pragmatic culture like American culture cannot easily find a place for those who have made a career from their own thinking and feeling. American suspicion towards art – when not an outright censure – has age-old roots in the prohibitions sanctioned, for theological reasons, by the first colonists. But when the artist is not simply a white person (that is to say a "dissident" who in some way separated him/herself from his/her own social context by means of his/her thoughts – and at times even by lifestyle – considered unsuitable to mainstream) but rather a black person (or rather, someone who is not different from anyone else but unlike others had his/her place in the social context imposed), the matter is quite different. The racism that legally governed for a few centuries and that continued to do so even illegally for other centuries cannot be but the evil conscience of the past that still conditions the present. We prefer to believe that jazz is a phenomenon that is white for the most part, or however an area in which Whites ruled over Blacks. This is what we see in Hollywood cinema: reassuring black and white jam sessions where the black musician pays his respects to the bravura of his white colleague, like for example in *The Five Pennies* by Shavelson. It is unavoidable that

cosa ciò significhi). Di più: il *cliché* è regolarmente il modo in cui il film tenta di presentare l'aura del musicista. Ovvero: ciò che vi è di più irriducibile, irraccontabile, indefinibile nell'attività artistica di una persona viene tratteggiato attraverso un modello standard di presentazione applicabile a chiunque.

La domanda è dunque: perché mai il cinema (almeno quello hollywoodiano) non riesce – e forse non vuole – rendere una sincera e convincente immagine del musicista jazz (e probabilmente dell'artista in genere)?

Ma la domanda si amplia pericolosamente se pensiamo che il rapporto fra *biopics* girati su musicisti bianchi e neri è schiacciante a favore dei primi. Se si toglie William C. Handy non rimane granché di nero nel cinema hollywoodiano classico sul jazz, ed è sintomatico che le varie stesure della sceneggiatura di *New Orleans* di Lubin abbiano via via sempre più ridotto ed emarginato le parti di Louis Armstrong e Billie Holiday, che inizialmente avrebbero dovuto esserne i protagonisti (in questo senso *Shadows* è ancora una volta un'opera anti-hollywoodiana e controcorrente).

LeRoi Jones afferma che la parola "arte" è fra le più disprezzate della lingua inglese d'America. E in effetti il trattamento che il cinema ha riservato all'artista è eloquente, a dir poco, di un'incomprensione. Una cultura pratica, pragmatica come quella statunitense non può trovare facilmente posto per chi ha fatto del proprio pensare e sentire, nonché della loro espressione, una professione. Il sospetto americano verso l'arte – quando non una vera e propria censura – ha radici antiche, nelle proibizioni stesse sancite, per ragioni teologiche, dai primi insediamenti religiosi. Ma quando l'artista non è semplicemente un bianco, vale a dire un dissidente che si è in qualche misura distaccato dal proprio contesto sociale attraverso un pensiero (e talvolta anche uno stile di vita) inadeguato alle direttive della maggioranza, bensì un nero, cioè qualcuno di non diverso dall'altro, che però a differenza da questi non ha scelto il proprio luogo nel contesto sociale ma se l'è trovato imposto, allora le cose cambiano. Il razzismo che ha governato legalmente per un paio di secoli il paese e che in seguito ha continuato a farlo senza alcuna legittimità per quasi altrettanto tempo non può che essere la cattiva coscienza del passato che ancora condiziona il presente. Non si toccano tasti sgradevoli, spiacevoli e in ultima analisi non poco compromettenti come questo: si preferisce fingere che il jazz sia un fenomeno in buona misura bianco, o comunque un ambito nel quale i bianchi hanno primeggiato sui neri.

È quel che vediamo nel cinema hollywoodiano: rasserenanti jam miste nelle quali il nero porge i suoi ossequi ammirati alla maestrìa del collega bianco, come ad esem-

all this brings about a radicalization of the differences. And it is also unavoidable that as a reaction the absolute "Negro-ness" of jazz is affirmed, forgetting about the other ethnic contributions that are at the very basis of its birth. That jazz is an exquisitely black form of expression there is no doubt. That its origins found fertile terrain in the ethnic-cultural melting-pot of late 19th-century New Orleans is something that must be reminded every time. We must also remember that the initial idea was to insert heterogeneous elements of disturbance in the rhythmical-musical structure of the Napoleonic European march that soon arrived even in Louisiana (Jones) and which was already quite diffused, with the brass bands before the Civil War up to becoming, with the new century, profoundly rooted in Afro-American tradition. Regarding that period Joyner observes:

In New Orleans, spirituals and blues from the plantations rubbed shoulders with opera and concert music, ragtime and brass bands with French, Spanish and Caribbean folksongs and dances. It was, in New Orleans terms, a rich gumbo.

How much this melting-pot was indeed alive and vital is objectively testified by the incredible fact that the first white band to play jazz there was, in 1888, Papa Jack Laine's "Ragtime Band" and that the use of mixed bands continued up to 1902, the *annus horribilis* of segregation.

We can in any case understand well that jazz tickled the fantasy of critics, causing writers and theorists to move in the direction of a comparison between jazz and cinema (or better, a few of its less regimented products). The greatest dream and aesthetic aspiration of the West in the modern age was and is the free, instinctive and inspired creator who does not have to endure any canon. Rather, he/she expresses an art that is already inside – an inborn vocation and not something that needs to be developed or corrected over the course of time. Jazz, as any jazz musician or critic can tell you, expresses the *hic et nunc* of a feeling, an emotion – it is direct communication of sensations and feelings that does not pass through any filter instituted by Western musical culture. The difference is precisely this: as with every kind of music, jazz is the expression of states of mind, of moods. But while the mood of any of Chopin's *polinaises* is entrusted to the interpreter – to the way in which he/she "reads" the original music – the jazz player's mood has nothing to base itself upon (if not jazz itself). The jazzman creates not only the performance

pio in *The Five Pennies/I cinque penny* di Shavelson. È inevitabile che tutto questo porti a una radicalizzazione delle differenze. È inevitabile che in controtendenza si affermi la assoluta "negritudine" del jazz dimenticando gli altri apporti etnici che sono all'origine della sua nascita. Che esso sia una forma squisitamente nera d'espressione non v'è alcun dubbio; che le sue origini abbiano trovato linfa nel crogiuolo etnico-culturale della New Orleans di fine Ottocento è cosa che ogni volta va ribadita, ricordando, fra l'altro, come l'idea iniziale fu quella di inserire eterogenei elementi di disturbo nella struttura ritmico-musicale della marcia europea napoleonica giunta presto anche in Louisiana (Jones) e già molto diffusa, con le *brass bands*, prima della Guerra Civile fino a diventare, al volgere del secolo, profondamente radicata nella tradizione afro-americana. Charles Joyner afferma, anzi, a proposito di quel periodo:

In New Orleans, spiritual and blues from the plantations rubbed shoulders with opera and concert music, ragtime and brass bands with French, Spanish and Caribbean folksongs and dances. It was, in New Orleans terms, a rich gumbo.

Quanto tale crogiuolo fosse vivo e vitale è oggettivamente testimoniato dall'inimmaginabile fatto che la prima banda bianca a suonare jazz laggiù fu, addirittura nel 1888, la "Ragtime Band" di Papa Jack Laine e che l'uso delle bande miste continuò fino al 1902, *annus horribilis* del rigurgito segregazionista.
Si può tuttavia ben comprendere che il jazz solletichi le corde della fantasia critica spingendo scrittori e teorici nella direzione di una comparazione fra esso e il cinema (o meglio, alcuni suoi prodotti meno irreggimentati). Il maggior sogno e il maggior mito estetico occidentale dell'età moderna è stato – ed è – quello del creatore libero, istintivo, ispirato che non deve sottoporsi ad alcun canone normativo, ma che esprime un'arte già in lui, una vocazione immediata e non qualcosa che va coltivato, curato e spesso anche corretto lungo l'intero arco di una vita. Il jazz, vi dirà qualunque jazzista e qualunque critico, esprime lo *hic et nunc* di un sentimento, di un'emozione, è diretta comunicazione di sensazioni e non passa attraverso alcuna mediazione istituita dalla cultura musicale occidentale. La differenza è proprio questa: come ogni musica, il jazz è espressione di stati d'animo: la differenza è che mentre, poniamo, lo stato d'animo di una qualunque polacca chopiniana è affidato all'interprete, al modo in cui egli "legge" l'originale testo dell'autore, quello del jazzista non ha nulla su cui fondarsi, cui rifarsi, rapportarsi (se non il jazz stesso), egli crea non solo l'esecuzione

but also the notes each time. Now, that this process can find an equivalent in any cinematic practice remains quite dubious, even if Gerry Mulligans' affirmation sounds a bit excessive:

I do not think that a direct bond between jazz and cinema can exist. In general, the directors who use jazz do so in order to give a particular mood to the images and to the story.

Jazz is one of the few kinds of music that does not obey to a pre-established pattern but to chords that do not necessitate writing (even if, as we have seen, it may be written out), that in some way gives an idea of the artistic product as something that is extemporaneous and outside the realm of studying – discipline – rehearsals – corrections. It comes out perfect, as a director would say, on the first *take*. For this reason the Beat Generation was so fascinated by jazz, making its musicians – indiscriminately, it must be admitted – into teachers, cult figures and even gurus, and inventing (though pushing it a bit, in LeRoi Jones' words, even if he too was part of this group) ideas and terms as "bop prosody."
In a certain sense, jazz becomes the evil conscience not only of American racism but also of the anti-Establishment aspirations of Western post-War bohemians – the proof that art is identified with the inspiration of the moment and flows from the heart without passing through any sort of filter. A step ahead, and it is unavoidable to begin thinking that both literature and cinema (or any other artistic field) can enjoy this state of grace, thus canceling centuries of intellectual elaboration or age-old debates.
And yet, the numerous things that cinema and jazz have to say to each other, that is, their meeting ground – the fusion of music and movement, the heightening of a mood created by the images, the memorial function even in the worst biopic, the obsession of a sad human condition, the pathology of a psychological weakness, the simple testimony of a unique spirit tied to an era that no longer exists – all this and much, much more is certainly a testimony of an unavoidable, essential negotiation between these two arts that, born at the same moment and both representative of a few fundamental characteristics of 20th century *poíesis*, are after all traversing the same path towards a destiny in their evolution that perhaps has already come to be.

ma anche le note ogni volta. Ora, che questo processo possa trovare un corrispettivo in qualunque prassi cinematografica resta cosa alquanto dubbia, anche se forse suona eccessiva l'affermazione di Gerry Mulligan:

I do not think that a direct bond between jazz and cinema can exist. In general, the directors who use jazz do so in order to give a particular mood to the images and to the story.

Il jazz è una delle poche musiche che non obbedisce a uno schema prefissato ma a un impianto di accordi, che non esige scrittura (anche se, come abbiamo visto, può essere scritto), che insomma propone un'idea del prodotto artistico come qualcosa di estemporaneo, estraneo allo studio, alla disciplina, alle prove, alle correzioni, esibendolo come perfetto, direbbe un cineasta, al primo *take*. Per questo la Beat Generation ne subì tanto il fascino e dei jazzisti fece – indiscriminatamente, bisogna dire – dei maestri, figure di culto, saggi sacerdoti e addirittura guru, giungendo a inventarsi, "un po' azzardatamente" secondo LeRoi Jones (che pure era stato alquanto vicino al loro gruppo), idee e termini come "prosodia bop".
In certo senso il jazz diventa la cattiva coscienza non solo del razzismo americano, ma anche delle aspirazioni anti-Establishment del *bohémien* occidentale postbellico, la prova che l'arte si identifica con l'ispirazione del momento e sgorga dal cuore senza passare attraverso alcun alambicco depuratore. Un passo avanti, ed è inevitabile incominciare a pensare che sia la letteratura che il cinema (o qualsiasi altro ambito artistico) possano godere di questo stato di grazia, cancellando in tal modo secoli di elaborazione intellettuale o comunque dibattiti annosi e complessi tentativi normativi.
Pure, le mille cose che cinema e jazz hanno da dirsi, cioè i terreni d'incontro delle loro rispettive prassi: la fusione – o l'accordo – della musica e del movimento, l'esaltazione di un'atmosfera creata dalle immagini, la funzione memoriale anche del peggior *biopic*, l'ossessività di una lamentevole condizione umana, la morbosità di una debolezza psicologica, la semplice testimonianza di un'atmosfera irripetibile legata a un'epoca che non è più, tutto questo e molto, molto di più sono certo testimonianza di un'imprescindibile, irrinunciabile negoziazione fra ambiti artistici che, nati contemporaneamente, e insieme rappresentativi di alcune fondamentali caratteristiche della poièsi novecentesca, stanno in fondo percorrendo lo stesso cammino verso un destino evolutivo che forse si è già realizzato.

BIBLIOGRAPHY

The title of the work of Gilles Mouëllic from which stems my reflections is *Le Jazz, une esthétique du Xxe siècle*. Presses Univérsitaires de Rennes, Rennes, 2000. The disparaging remark by Harry Farjeon on the Negro as a "modernized savage" is cited by Edward A. Berlin in his excellent *Ragtime. A Musical and Cultural History*. University of California Press, Berkeley-Los Angeles-London, 1980 in which the "deracialization" committed by white culture against ragtime, and denounced by James Weldon Johnson, is also discussed. That the rhythm of the polka, arrived in America towards the mid-19th century, influenced even the celebrated *Oh, Susanna!* by Stephen Foster is affirmed by Richard Crawford in his impressive volume *America's Musical Life. A History*. W.W. Norton & Co., New York-London, 2001. The definition of Leo Watson as the "James Joyce of jazz" on behalf of Leonard Feather is cited by Barry Keith Grant in his essay "Purple Passages or Fiestas in Blue? Toward an Aesthetic of Vocalese" in Krin Gabbard (ed.), *Representing Jazz*. Duke UP, Durham-London, 1995, and also the comparison to Eisenstein's montage is made. A few examples of the relationship between jazz and other arts, as well as the affirmations of Stuart Davis, are found in Neil Leonard's essay "Jazz and the Other Arts" in Charles Nanry (ed.), *American Music: from Storyville to Woodstock*. Transaction Publishers, New Brunswick, 1972. The organizing principle of "addition" and the equivalence between musical rhythm and the rhythm of film editing in *Jammin' the Blues* was expressed by Arthur Knight in his essay "*Jammin' the Blues*, or the Sight of Jazz" in Krin Gabbard (ed.), *Representing Jazz* (cited above). On the indeed very restrictive idea of rhythmic-musical and decorative editing please see the innovative study of Béla Balàzs, *Theory of the Film: Character & Growth of a New Art*. Ayer Company Publishers, Manchester, 1978, towards the final pages of Chapter X dedicated to editing. Ted Gioia speaks about jazz as an art of the "present moment" and is cited by Frederick Garber in his interesting essay "Fabulating Jazz" in Krin Gabbard (ed.), *Repre-

RIFERIMENTI BIBLIOGRAFICI

Il titolo del volume di Gilles Mouëllic da cui partono le riflessioni di questo brano introduttivo è *Le jazz, une esthétique du Xx.e siècle*, Rennes, Presses Univérsitaires de Rennes, 2000; la sprezzante frase di Harry Farjeon sul negro come "selvaggio modernizzato" è riportata da Edward A. Berlin nel suo ottimo *Ragtime. A Musical and Cultural History*, Berkeley-Los Angeles-London, University of California Press, 1980, nel quale si parla anche della "deracialization" operata dalla cultura bianca nei confronti del ragtime e denunciata da James Weldon Johnson; che il ritmo della polka, giunta in America verso la metà dell'Ottocento, abbia influenzato anche la celeberrima *Oh, Susanna!* di Stephen Foster è affermato da Richard Crawford nel suo imponente volume *America's Musical Life. A History*, New York-London, W.W. Norton & Co., 2001; la definizione di Leo Watson come "James Joyce del jazz" da parte di Leonard Feather è riportata da Barry Keith Grant nel suo saggio "Purple Passages or Fiestas in Blue? Toward an Aesthetic of Vocalese", in Krin Gabbard (ed.), *Representing Jazz*, Durham and London, Duke UP, 1995, dove si rintraccia anche il paragone con il montaggio eisensteniano; alcune esemplificazioni dei rapporti fra il jazz e altri ambiti d'operazione artistica, nonché le affermazioni di Stuart Davis, si rintracciano nel saggio di Neil Leonard, "Jazz and the Other Arts", in Charles Nanry (ed.), *American Music: from Storyville to Woodstock*, New Brunswick, N.J., Transaction Publishers, 1972, mentre sul principio organizzativo dell'addizione e sulla corrispondenza fra il ritmo musicale e quello del montaggio in *Jammin' the Blues* si è espresso Arthur Knight nel suo saggio "*Jammin' the Blues*, or the Sight of Jazz", in Krin Gabbard (ed.), *Representing Jazz*, cit.; sull'idea, invero molto restrittiva, di montaggio ritmico-musicale e decorativo si veda il pionieristico studio di Béla Balàzs, *Il film. Evoluzione ed essenza di un'arte nuova*, Torino, Einaudi, 1955, verso le pagine finali del cap. X dedicato al montaggio; del jazz come arte del "momento presente" parla Ted Gioia, citato da Frederick Garber nel suo interessante

senting Jazz (cited above). The classification of the different types of jazz improvisation is in the still admirable work of Leonard Feather *The Book of Jazz*. Laurel, New York, 1976, but originally published in 1957, and in which Feather also discusses improvisation based on the chords and not only the melody – a classic topic that Nat Hentoff also treats in his essay "Paying Dues: Changes in the Jazz Life" which can be found in *American Music: from Storyville to Woodstock* (cited above). In this essay, the phrase "urgency of personal discovery that's jazz" is also found. On the rigidity of cinema with respect to the musical instrument and on the various risks connected to improvisation in cinema and in jazz please see Jean-Louis Comolli, "Passages entre musique et cinéma" in "Cahiers du Cinéma," special issue "Musique au cinéma," 1995. Both the words of Cassavetes and Mouëllic on improvisation as an impression of spontaneity and the remarks regarding the "organization of the haphazard" in the art of performance are in Gilles Mouëllic, *Jazz et cinéma*. Editions Cahiers du cinéma, Paris, 2000.

In fact, Mouëllic dedicates the entire second part (four chapters) to analyzing *Shadows* in relation to jazz and in which there is also the comment of Charlie Mingus on the Julliard School. The phrase of LeRoi Jones on the possibility of writing be-bop and its importance, as well as the allusion to American disdain for the word "art," the reference to the European marches and the enthusiasm of the Beat Generation for jazz are in the classic *Blues People: Negro Music in White America*. Morrow, New York, 1963. The information on the brass bands tradition and the musical melting-pot in late 19th-century New Orleans, as well as the first white bands like the one of Papa Jack Laine, are from Charles Joyner "African and European Roots of Southern Culture: The *Central Theme* Revisited" in Richard H. King and Helen Taylor (editors), *Dixie Debates. Perspectives on Southern Cultures*. New York UP, New York, 1996. The affirmation of Gerry Mulligan on the absence of a relationship between jazz and cinema is cited by Claudio Donà in his essay "Dalla parte del jazz" in Ermanno Comuzio and Roberto Ellero (editors), *Cinema & Jazz*. Municipal Government of Venice, Council on Culture Publications, Venice, 1985.

saggio "Fabulating Jazz", in Krin Gabbard (ed.), *Representing Jazz*, cit.; la classificazione dei tipi di improvvisazione jazzistica è nell'ancor oggi ammirevole studio di Leonard Feather, *The Book of Jazz*, New York, Laurel, 1976, ma originariamente pubblicato nel 1957, nel quale si parla anche dell'improvvisazione fondata sugli accordi e non sulla melodia, classico argomento su cui ritorna anche Nat Hentoff nel saggio "Paying Dues: Changes in the Jazz Life", in *American Music: from Storyville to Woodstock*, cit., saggio dove si rintraccia anche la frase sulla "urgency of personal discovery that's jazz"; sulla rigidità del cinema rispetto allo strumento musicale e sui rischi diversi connessi all'improvvisazione nel cinema e nel jazz si veda Jean-Louis Comolli, "Passages entre musique et cinéma", in "Cahiers du Cinéma", numéro spécial "Musique au cinéma", 1995; sia le parole di Cassavetes che quelle di Mouëllic sull'improvvisazione come impressione di spontaneità e quelle relative all'"organizzazione del caso" nell'arte di *performance* sono in Gilles Mouëllic, *Jazz et cinéma*, Paris, Editions Cahiers du cinéma, 2000, che dedica l'intera sua seconda parte (ben quattro capitoli) alla lettura di *Shadows* in relazione al jazz, e nel quale figura anche la frase di Charlie Mingus sulla Juilliard School; la frase di LeRoi Jones sulla possibilità di scrittura del be-bop e sulla sua importanza, nonché l'allusione al disprezzo americano per la parola "arte", il riferimento alle marce europee e al talvolta azzardato entusiasmo Beat per il jazz, sono nel classico *Il popolo del blues*, Torino, Einaudi, 1968, mentre le notizie sulla tradizione delle *brass bands* e sul crogiuolo musicale della New Orleans di fine secolo, nonché sulle prime bande bianche come quella di Papa Jack Laine, vengono da Charles Joyner, "African and European Roots of Southern Culture: The *Central Theme* Revisited", in Richard H. King e Helen Taylor (editors), *Dixie Debates. Perspectives on Southern Cultures*, New York, New York UP, 1996; l'affermazione di Gerry Mulligan sull'assenza di rapporti fra cinema e jazz è riportata da Claudio Donà nel suo saggio "Dalla parte del jazz", in Ermanno Comuzio e Roberto Ellero (a cura di), *Cinema & Jazz*, Quaderno del Comune di Venezia, Assessorato alla Cultura, Venezia, 1985.

Madamu to nyobo/The Neighbor's Wife and Mine
(Heinosuke Gosho, 1931)

Hollywood Hotel (Busby Berkeley, 1938)
Conducting: Benny Goodman. Piano: Teddy Wilson.
Drums: Gene Krupa. First trumpet: Harry James.
Fourth trumpet: Johnny (Scat) Davis (actor, singer. Not in band)

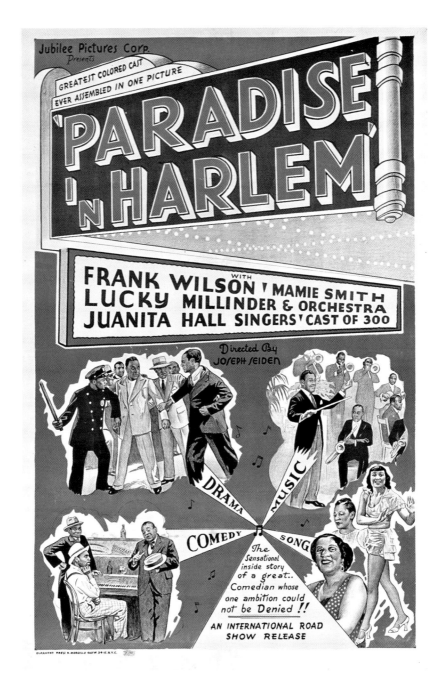

Paradise in Harlem
(Joseph Seiden, 1939)
Original poster

Broken Strings (Bernard B. Ray, 1940)
Clarence Muse and William Washington

Birth of the Blues (Victor Schertzinger, 1941)
Mary Martin and Bing Crosby

Syncopation (William Dieterle, 1942)
Bonita Granville and Jackie Cooper

Stormy Weather
(Andrew L. Stone, 1943)
Fats Waller

Jam Session (Charles Barton, 1944) Teddy Powell and his orchestra

Jammin' the Blues
(Gjon Mili, 1944)

Hi-De-Ho (Josh Binney, 1947)
Cab Calloway and his orchestra

New Orleans
(Arthur Lubin, 1947)
Louis Armstrong,
Billie Holiday, Woody Herman

The Fabulous Dorseys
(Alfred E. Green, 1947)
Tommy Dorsey, Janet Blair,
Jimmy Dorsey

Articles

THE EYE KEEPS WATCH, THE BODY LISTENS
(Filming free jazz)

Philippe Carles and Jean-Louis Comolli

The explosion of free jazz in the mid-1960s, like that of a volcano long believed dormant, pushed the eternal question of jazz as "improvised music" in the direction of a certain violence or vehemence. To play "free" was explicitly to go beyond the framework, the pre-established framework (particularly the ideological and commercial framework of the musical show and the record industry); and this escape could not but violate something of the traditions and even of the fantasies connected with the jazz life. Free improvisation, if one may say so, declares itself from the outset as an excess, if not an abuse: the rupture or the distortion of previously encoded and shared musical forms and stylistic givens: gaiety, vivacity, the very length of the improvisations. We need not go back over all of this, which is well known: Ornette Coleman's *Free Jazz* represents a rupture.[1] There is a before and an after. And from this point of rupture, the entire history of jazz comes back for a fresh reading.

Let us take improvisation, for example. Without a doubt it is both a practice and the matrix of an infinite variety of forms; nor is there any question that the irresistible desire to improvise remains jazz's most singular characteristic. What was at stake in free jazz was even more basic: a decisive test in which what had been created was in danger of destroying itself. With free jazz, improvisation becomes almost a matter of life and death. The song of the soloist carries within itself the hints of its own ruin. The performer's solitude is exposed as never before to the phantoms which inhabit jazz. There explodes the possible impossibility of the articulation of each musician with his team-mates, with the ensemble that they form. Ensemble, association, community, family, melting-pot, this whole *collective* dimension, which *free* musicians do not reject – quite the contrary – which they recover from its own ashes; for, in the earlier ages of jazz, the question of the ensemble had found other solutions than that of the parade of soloists, lined up like figurines in a collection. Here, free, the musicians are

[1] Cf. J.P. Moussaron, *Feu le free*. Ed. Belin, 1990; Alexandre Pierrepont, *Le Champ jazzistique*. Ed. Parenthèses. And we hope we may be allowed to refer back to our own book: *Free Jazz/Black Power*. Ed. Champ Libre, 1971; repub. Folio, 2000.

in the arena of music in crisis, at the decisive moment. The challenge to death depends on the slightest gesture, and what is at stake is the decomposition of the ensemble. At the same time, free jazz challenges every display of mastery; and those who take up the challenge renounce their most celebrated qualities, abandoning the very idea of performance.[2] Free improvisation is Penelope speeded up. It condenses within itself the double gesture of both weaving and destroying the musical fabric. It is as if the music responded to the improvisational gesture of the musicians by improvising, in and of itself, their coming to pieces.

How can one film that which undoes itself and threatens to collapse in the very act of constructing itself? Rather than observing the rarity of aleatory jazz encounters, let us say that this terrible free jazz, along with the films that were not afraid of it,[3] is the occasion for observing what cinema can and cannot do when faced with the great free game of improvisation. How can one film that which is unknown? That which moves forward with no warning, with no beginning nor end? That which announces only something already begun, and which will never be other than the suspense of the annunciation itself? Or rather: how to maintain the surprise, to exist vis-à-vis something fugitive; that is to say, something that, at its very birth, has already taken place? Yet again: is not the gaze a kind of delay? Is not vision some sort of inevitable after-fact of listening?

This gap between the eye and the ear plays itself out at an entirely different level: that of our own mercantile societies. It is enough to note that, at the moment when free jazz arises, two forces begin to extend their domination: on the side of the visible, above all as a result of the insistence and the success of television, the show-business side of performance becomes more powerful, the show becomes more generalized, and this also marks the moment of its wider commercialization; where the soundtrack is concerned – and in keeping with this "spectacularization" – background music or *Muzak* begins to proliferate in public spaces, in the streets with their "business weeks," department stores, restaurants, etc.: once again, music linked to trade. We might even venture to suggest that the irruption of free jazz is not unconnected with the conjunction of these two phenomena: we are in the United States, and even the revolt of black America winds up conforming to the mercantile consensus. It is as though free jazz refused to cooperate with the great American show. Free musicians are less picturesque than boppers; the music they play does not lend itself to

[2] It is precisely on this point of the outright display of instrumental virtuosity that a line divides free jazz from what has been called, over the past decade, "free revivalism." One might even refer to "free sic" when the reproduction of "free" traits becomes the business of a virtuoso performance. Let us restate the case: the lamenesses of free jazz are, above all, the signs of a crisis or of a laceration which are anything but an affectation. It is the double body of the musician and the music which is showing signs of difficulty.

[3] In the first rank we must cite Michael Snow's film, *New York Eye and Ear Control* (1964, music by Albert Ayler, Don Cherry, John Tchicai, Roswell Rudd, Gary Peacock, Sunny Murray). Some years later, Pier Paolo Pasolini brought together Gato Barbieri, Don Moye, and Marcello Mellis for *Appunti per un'Orestiade africana* (*Notes Towards an African Orestes*, 1970). Of these two films, which are as different as could be, one might say that cinema leaves the field free for music, as it has rarely yielded to a force stronger than itself. One must also cite Jerzy Skolimowski's very fine film *Le Départ* (1967, for the music of which the composer Krzysztof Komeda brings together Don Cherry, Gato Barbieri, René Urtreger, Jacques Thollot, Jean-François Jenny-Clark, Jacques Pelzer, Eddy Louiss, and Philip Catherine).

showbiz exhibitions – with the exception of Sun Ra, who lucidly played with the fascination of the American "revue." Moreover, despite the resonance between free jazz and Black Power, free jazz refuses to have anything to do with the over-the-top scenes staged by the Black Panthers. To be sure, it displays itself in public, but without the emphasis that increasingly characterizes the U.S. show. How can we fail to deduce that free jazz is secretly tempted to restore the power of listening, to the detriment of the seductions of the visible, and that this may be one of the reasons why so few films dared to seize upon this music – a music too rough to be flattered by the caress of a camera.

Was it a matter of countering the mercantile spectacularization of all kinds of music, including jazz, by restoring the power of listening? All that it took was a kind of music that affirmed the violence of risking the whole of the body in listening. The listener's body, the musician's body: free jazz gambles them to excess, so as to bring them to the crisis point. If one may speak of a violence of free jazz, this is because it tears the body up. As we know, the ear is a constantly open breach: sound enters the hollow of the body, the skin is a vibrating membrane, the belly a resonating body, the heart a percussion instrument, the lungs a bellows, the organs timpani: in short, the body hears, listens, accompanies, and plays at the same time as the music which enters it. The body receives and produces the sonorous manifestations of the world. Music travels through the body. Fragility, violence, openness, abandonment: the body, open to sounds, possesses these qualities which pretty much sum up the range of free jazz. This is the opposite of what happens in terms of the gaze in which – as is also known – the eye is more like a control tower, the organ of ordering (perspective) and surveillance (the Panopticon[4]). The beyond-the-frame as against the frame, the off-stage (the world) as against the stage-set. It is precisely to the extent that free jazz – more explicitly than other stages of jazz – makes a musical assault on the entire body, the body-as-world, that it poses for film the twin problems of staging and framing. Let us look into this paradox. Cinema can film (at least) three states of the body with regard to music: the body dancing, the body playing, the body listening.

[4] Bentham's "Panopticon," as commented on by Michel Foucault in *Surveiller et punir*. Ed. Gallimard, 1975.

With jazz, the body dances; but with free jazz, dancing ceases. What was true in ballrooms is even truer on the screen: no musical film takes this music on board. Documentary cinema on the one hand, experimental cinema on the other. Between the two, nothing, or almost nothing. Nonetheless, well before free jazz, and having little to do with jazz (their contemporary) in general, the great Hollywood musical comedies (from *Brigadoon* – Vincente Minnelli – to *Party Girl* – Nicholas Ray – by way of *Gentlemen Prefer Blondes* – Howard Hawks) had developed a certain *magic of improvisation.* Dancing bodies, moving images, and the movements of the music seemed to get along effortlessly, in the grace of happy meetings. The painstaking work of composition, rehearsal, adjustments, editing seemed to disappear as if by magic; what had been prepared vanished in what came out; bodies and music seemed to spring forth, the one from the other; the shifts from spoken dialogue to singing, from walking to dancing were little miracles which may never, perhaps, be reproduced. The effect was that of a slight threat hanging over the perfection of the performance: a suspense which made the performance seem incomplete at the very moment when it achieved its resolution. Jazz improvisation plays marvelously on this suspense: think of Jimmy Giuffre and André Jaume.[5] It is as if the innumerable rehearsals necessary to achieve such a perfect harmony of bodies, music, and cinematic image were suddenly, magically abolished, in a sort of "first time"; an unrepeatable occasion. Let us look at this point: a filmed dance number is, beyond any doubt, the outcome of a terrific amount of hard work, of harsh constraints imposed on dancing bodies and on teams of technicians – exercises, rehearsals. But to dance – especially in the movies – is also to evoke the appearance of an even freer figure of liberty: though subject to weight, these bodies break free of it. The screen is the site *par excellence* of brilliance, of luminous lightness. Onscreen, the light steps of the dancers – who seem, through some state of grace, to be born and to evaporate as we watch – free us from a jubilation which is, first and foremost, an impulse towards a utopia, a dream of freedom. This *effect of freedom* is all the more exciting in that it can only come into being by dissimulating the effort and discipline which are its preconditions. The system of rehearsals used in the movies (long refinements involving performers and technicians) seemingly calls for twice the rehearsal time needed to perform musical scores or choreographic spectacles. All these teams rehearse endlessly, so it seems, to create, with gestures, settings, and music, perfect mechanisms which give the illusion of the natural, masterpieces of control and synchronization that produce the effect of spontaneity. Thus, as a first lesson, cinema is able to produce – laboriously, but hiding the labor – a sovereign spontaneity, while jazz improvisation as exalted in free jazz remains, essentially, a leap into the void, with or without a rebound, an approach; an open work site, a series of imperfections, a throw of the dice. The work that precedes

[5] There are innumerable examples. One will suffice: *Three Way Split* in "River Station" by Jimmy Giuffre-André Jaume with guest Joe McPhee (Celp C26/Harmonia Mundi).

improvisation is none other than a whole lifetime of music, a sorting-out of all the music one has encountered, a dissatisfied making and unmaking. The same happy game of chance seems to unite the two sorts of improvisation, but this is not so. Improvisation in jazz is not an effect but a condition; it is undergone, not dominated. How can one bring off successfully the improbable meeting between a camera which is directed and a music which is not?

When it is not the dancing body which must be filmed, but the playing body – i.e., the musician's gestures – what happens? Obviously, there is no common denominator between the movements appropriate to a given music, whatever it may be, jazz or something else, and the movements of the musician's body that produces this music.[6] The very gestures of a figure beating time, for example, for all that they are, beyond any doubt, the most figurative of all,[7] have only the slightest of relationships with the musical nature of the sounds produced. It is an illusion (and a widely shared one[8]) to believe that one can film music by filming the gestures that bring it forth from the instrument. Gestures can be visible, seen, filmed. Music, no. Music is, for example, that invisible, unfilmable bond that connects, through simultaneous listening and action, the bodies and the gestures of the musicians who are producing it at that instant… Music: what is *in between* that which is filmable. Probably the makers of instruments did not imagine – it was before the movies – that one day we would see in a frightening close-up Armstrong's twisted mouth as he blows into the mouthpiece of his trumpet to produce the subtlest of held notes, and even less would they have envisaged Gillespie's cheeks puffed out like tennis balls as he reaches a high note. Gestures often denote the effort, the pain, almost the suffering that playing music entails; this terrible mimicry, these contractions, these bent-over bodies display nothing of the serenity or grace of the musical sequences emitted. Let us call it distortion, disharmony, discord. The synchronized image and the recorded sound grow apart. Synchronism has nothing to do with it: the image pulls in one direction, the sound in another. Let us ask ourselves what it means to film this effort of playing bodies, and sometimes this suffering, with such insistence, for the entire duration of a concert for example, as television stations specializing in music do *ad nauseam.* Only a view of the ensemble might permit an image of the invisible factors that go sounding between the bodies; but a shot of the ensemble never lasts long and very quickly, as if impatient, avid, the camera draws near to film close-up, very close-up, cutting the bodies

[6] The Straubs have given much importance to this distance between body and music in their *Chronik der Anna Magdalena Bach (Chronicle of Anna Magdalena Bach,* 1968).

[7] There is no doubt that the gestures of certain conductors, expressive to the point of emphasis, have been influenced by television which gives a privileged place – following the line of least resistance – to the most spectacular gestures.

[8] The difficulty is no less great if we leave behind the playing body and, instead, let the music flow over images – which may be more or less felicitous, but which will always seem less necessary than the music itself. This is a doubly dangerous shoal. Long after Gianni Amico's *Appunti per un film sul jazz* (1965, with Mal Waldron, Don Cherry, Johnny Griffin, Ted Curson, Steve Lacy, Annie Ross, Pony Poindexter, Gato Barbieri, Karl Berger), Laurence Petit-Jouvet's *Off the Road* (2002), with Peter Kowald, combines the two modes: "in" and "on."

(and with them the music) into small pieces, exaggerating the filmed parts of the playing body in a hyper-realist effect which becomes the hyper-spectacular itself. Let us put it differently: to film in close-up musicians who are playing jazz in a concert or in the studio is to resign oneself to reducing the infinity of music to a rosary of images of the body which becomes more repetitive and less inventive than the music being played, poorer, more conventional, and, in the end, tiresome – it is suddenly to postulate a listener-spectator with weak desires, who is condemned to visual boredom. Film the body that makes the music? Yes; but without yielding to the illusion that the body takes the place of the music it plays; without seeking at all costs to single out the parts of the body as though they contained the hidden secret of the music played. All too often, the musical body is the victim of an extortion of images which are expected to fill the void in the visible world opened up by music: there is nothing to see. And yet, no, we can catch a glimpse of something all the same, filling the screen to drive away that void which the music does not cease to hollow out. In fact, we have entered the empire of visible things. To see, to see everything, to see despite everything, to see when it is not a question of seeing – all this is an obligation, a sort of bargain we strike. There is no doubt that it holds true for filmed jazz. Nothing else happens in filmed free jazz, beyond this important nuance: here it is the music that obliges us to listen in a widely framed shot. More than ever, it would be a question of filming the invisible or the immaterial: music as ensemble, the relationship between the players. To define free jazz as something that takes place between two players (or three, or ten) is also to suppose that only by listening can it be described: through the mental play of a listener, or another musician. To listen/to play: it is the same thing. To listen is the very gesture of playing. Sound travels faster than light: free improvisation. Music covers and stirs up the bodies in their play. And it very often happens that the music is more tormented than the bodies it torments. An uninterrupted musical letting loose overflows in its violence and suddenly renders all the imagery of the body insipid, however free those bodies themselves. It has been said: an excess of sound with respect to the visible. A revenge. We are immersed in free jazz. What is this freedom, what is this violence? The violence born of leaving the framework, the stage-set, behind, and of canceling all past contracts, beginning with all contracts involving listening. The immediate, the instantaneous, the unforeseen and unforeseeable: this is what we must discover and face up to.
One might say of free improvisation that it radicalizes every principle of improvisation

while trying – desperately – to maintain an absolute present. What I hear presents itself to me as always in movement, indefinable, unguessable. It is played without anyone's (not the musicians, not the listeners) having the slightest inkling as to where what is taking place is headed – in their presence and involving them – an ever-problematic process of becoming, but separately. It may happen, or not. It may last, or not. It may cease, or not. How can one film something which is in flight, we were asking? How to film musicians who are themselves being improvised by their improvisations? The answers offered by Pascale Ferran's recent film, *Quatre jours à Ocoee,* shed some light on these challenges. The film deals with four days spent in a studio by Sam Rivers (flute, saxophones) and Tony Hymas, recording a number of pieces for a CD produced by "nato" (Jean Rochard).[9] Some of these pieces are written out; others are improvised. This is no doubt what has been called "post-free," but it is also true that the two musicians say "play *free*" when they are talking of improvisation. Separated by the exigencies of studio recording, these two musicians have nothing more vital at stake than to play "together" in the written-out pieces (and it is not so simple) and in the improvisations (where it is not to be taken for granted). The filming of this "ensemble" is the whole story. As it was not possible to frame the two together in a single shot, and as it would have been even less possible to ask them to begin their improvisations over again, the only solution was to film them with two cameras, one for each musician. Filmed simultaneously by the two cameras, the two musicians are always shown in an appropriate frame – every detail that might count, the body of the instrument and the body that plays, are shown in a relationship that is never fragmentary. Nonetheless, a split remains. When you listen to the sound, they are indeed "together" (and how hard they work to achieve this!); in the image, they are not. The two cameras frame two distinct angles of the studio: close to each other, assuredly, but separate. The two shots, that of Rivers and that of Hymas, are not visible "together," but separately, in accordance with that iron-clad law of film editing which decrees that, cut separately, simultaneous actions become successive – let us say, more precisely: successively visible, because edited in successively, so that it falls to the viewer to unite them and to imagine their simultaneity by superposing them after the fact on his/her mental screen. So it is that, paradoxically, of two voices taking part in the same improvisation, to the point where they blend into a single voice for the listener, the film makes two "images," as the term goes, which are necessarily disunited. Once again – let us repeat – we have a delay of the images with respect to

[9] "Winter Garden."

the sounds, of the gaze with respect to the ear. Pascale Ferran's film frankly admits this delay: where the image is concerned, to play is to be out of sync; when one listens, they are together. It sometimes happens in the course of these four filmed days that the editing (always the editing!) invites us to make the leap (through a jump-cut) from the shots of the musicians playing, separated by the image, to a shot of the musicians listening, united by the image, seated side by side on the same couch. This is perhaps the principle of their being an *ensemble of musicians in the invisible* which is achieved at the very moment when the cinema comes up against that which limits it (but also represents its very foundation) in the visible world. Or rather: is it not through the arrangement which permits this manifestation of invisibility (when Rivers plays for the image, Hymas is playing only on the soundtrack, and vice versa) that cinema, losing its grip, allows the music to be heard more than "seen"? Or yet again: is it not the case that, in order to hear, we must give up seeing?

Another question remains: how to film improvisation? To film is to establish a framework, and thus to wait, in the sense of foreseeing what will be captured by the "take"; but to wait might equally well mean an inability to capture what might occur with no warning, not taking place, perhaps, exactly where the view-finder is focused. When a musician plays and a camera films him, the body being filmed is right where it is (as is the cameraman, too). So it becomes a question of awaiting the event, in the place where one already is; an event, however, of which one does not know the nature, or how or precisely where it will occur. Let us say that to frame a shot boils down to assigning a body, a place, a site, a setting, a duration, a lighting arrangement, to what, in the case of improvisation, ought to be the least controllable, the most sovereign factor: that which takes place outside the frame. The invisible is, precisely, what occurs outside the frame. The slowness of images: it is only in the invisible world that cinema moves with the speed of music. There, nothing is foreseen, nothing is framed, nothing is ready. To film music would be to capture in the visible world the trace of what has gone before. Improvisation, as the most intense moments of free jazz have – finally – let it be heard, or rather, revealed it to itself, is that which escapes. It escapes beyond scenarios, scores, programs, frames, rehearsals, contracts; beyond gesture itself. It is what escapes us.

Duke Ellington (late 1940s)

A Song Is Born (Howard Hawks, 1948)
Tommy Dorsey and his orchestra

THE COLORS OF JAZZ

Giampiero Cane

All-Negro (who knows when it became *all-Black*, *all-Afro-American*, *all-African-American*?) is, in any event, a constant that in the course of America's racial conflict made its mark on the country after the Civil War in a more or less visible way when the slaves were to become full-fledged citizens.

Even if the willingness to distinguish/separate is not blatantly declared in the artistic productions of the period, it is nonetheless an ever-present component, the evidence of which can be detected. The "Colored American Opera Company," founded in Washington in 1872, the year after staged *Doctor of Alcantara* by Julius Eichberg, a mediocre composer who arrived in the United States in 1859 from Germany. Philadelphia's "All-Day City Item" reviewed the performance and stated that the troupe was entirely composed of amateurs – "the first colored opera-troupe in existence." Actually, perhaps the term *all-Negro* cannot be applied in this particular case seeing that a German wrote the opera, but it surely would be asking too much that only ten years after the close of the Civil War learned black composers were already in circulation. Moreover, if a distinction does indeed exist, there is however no contrast. The Blacks are still considered *Sambos* and therefore not hostile or dangerous – just plain old simpletons. In order for things to clear up these Sambos must start publicly manifesting their own thoughts on their *ol'massas*, and without any *double talk*; in other words, the expression of black nationalism must come forth.

However, it is not our intention here to outline the history of the nationalistic movement in the United States or the development of *all-Negro* productions. Others have already seen to this. The *Dictionary of the Black Theatre* by Allen Woll[1] offers lists and descriptions of performances, interpreters, organizers, bibliography, a chronology and a discography for a quantity of material that starts with fourteen titles between 1898 and 1919 and finishes with the eleven titles from 1980-1981. It is incomplete, but more than sufficient for a start.

[1] Greenwood Press, Westport (Connecticut)-London, 1983.

Instead, what interests us is that the mix of Blacks and Whites in musical performances is something rare even in the cases where there seems to be no reason for keeping these two communities distinct and separate – especially during a time when the political tension fueled by racism was not yet particularly visible.

This trend, in any case, emphasizes how the history of jazz, Afro-American music *par excellence*, is witness to the division of its musicians on the basis of their skin color – Blacks separate from Whites – already during the years in which the enthusiasm for this musical *hapax* brought Mezzrow to define himself as a "Negro" at City Hall's registry office. Published almost fifty years ago, *A Pictorial History of Jazz* by Orrin Keepnews and Bill Grauer, Jr.[2] offers, despite the hundreds of photos included, only very rare images in which musicians identified in different ways according to American racial laws perform together. We see a drummer from New Orleans, Sidney Arodin, described in the caption as "one of the very few musicians who plays with both black and white bands"; Juan Tizol, who is white but Latin-American, is shown in Ellington's band; a few encounters among musicians in unofficial photos (not for publicity or for play-bills); Joe "Flip" Phillips in Frankie Newton's group at Kelly's Stable – and nothing else before Benny Goodman breaks this segregation in the second half of the 1930s in the ensemble, but not in the big band he also performs in.

Since there are no intellectual reasons to support this segregation of Whites and Blacks into two separate entities, the causes are of a social-political kind.

The different roles pertain first to the musicians, then the audience and finally the organizers – everything within a cosmos profoundly blemished by racial ideology. This ideology, united with increased economic competition, alters the ideological identity of liberalism by introducing the Hobbesesque characteristics of the *homo homini lupus*.

In fact, we should ask ourselves if an aversion of white musicians to their black counterparts, or vice versa, existed or exists and manifests itself in the world of jazz.[3] The answer is, overall, negative but especially with regards to the era in which jazz first made its appearance. In the early years of the 20th century imitation was the model that worked, and without a doubt white imitation of black music was dictated by appreciation and not by considerations of an economic kind. And yet, the musical life of the city center and of Storyville was separate. *All-White* and *all-Black* appear as the natural conditions of this form of musical entertainment. The film *New Orleans* by Lubin proposes black production to imitation and use on the part of Whites by

[2] Crown Publishers, Inc., New York, 1955.

[3] The terms "White" and "Black" do not mean absolutely anything in this field, but we will use them for the sake of brevity and because they are commonly used when speaking. "Black American" and "White American" would not explain anything either. The term "Afro-American" is for us, as we will attempt to demonstrate, a false cultural label if referred to jazz as a whole, even though it is a legitimate invention of the tradition – a taking root in a land of origin that was chosen arbitrarily and for various goals (for example, Mussolini's Rome of Caesars and the Renaissance of S. Bussotti).

means of a not-so-credible entrepreneur who in his gambling house unites and at the same moment keeps distinct the gambling tables of the Whites and the music of the Blacks. But the time has not yet arrived for big money to be made from black music – only modest gains from the *race records* in which the identification of race regards the Blacks. In the film, the interest of white musicians for the music created and characterized mostly by blues is alluded to, showing us an orchestra conductor and an opera singer enchanted by the freshness of this new sound. And this is precisely what happens with, for example, Ansermet, Ravel, Gershwin and Antheill, who was able to syncretize jazz with Futurism.

The artists, therefore, are not insensitive to the non-academic qualities of this kind of music. It is only natural: creative minds have always been open to the new possibilities offered by instruments. The general audience does not nurture great interest for this, but feels both the pleasant and unpleasant effects. In the absence of racist prejudices, the audience is not so interested in the fact that an exciting effect was created by a black person, instead of a white person.

In conclusion, therefore, neither audience ostracism nor academic criticism is particularly damaging to the evolution of art – of any art. For our art (which for many is not an art but only an instrument of evasion or, why not?, a money-maker) the places where it manifests itself reveal themselves as being deciding factors for its fortune and formation. Probably, therefore, it is the nature of the setting that constitutes the discriminating factor.

Naturally this setting is not the actual physical space, but the type of club and the function that it is given. In general, we can mention two types of jazz hang-outs: the first, not so common, where the management dedicates itself with passion and devotion to the music it offers. The second kind is where the music is used as an instrument for economic gain. In the first kind of club the law of art reigns supreme, even though the economic aspect cannot be neglected. Generally in these places there are no components of racism: a racially-mixed ensemble should not create problems if not perhaps for the presence of Whites, since jazz audiences are generally inclined to attribute black supremacy in this musical genre. But if Charlie Parker includes someone like Robert "Red" Rodney in his combo no one should object. Instead, the attitude of the general public, even in 1950 and at least in America's South, is not so open to the idea if Parker prefers to publicize the trumpeter Robert "Red" Rodney as "Albin Red," trying to pass him off as a black albino.[4] This kind of

[4] This anecdote is documented by photos of posters that announced the evening's event. In a book (the title slips my mind) we read that Parker told this fib to two policemen who were about to interrupt the preparations for a concert. But according to Ross Russell (*Bird Lives!*. Quartet Books Ltd., London, 1976) the lie was born from the discussion between the sax player and Billy Shaw at the time plans were being made for the performances. We cite a part of Russell's text because it is quite indicative of the times:

Billy Shaw asked Charlie if he would like to go on tour in the South. "(…) You'll make a lot of money. (…) You decide." "I've already been there. Alright," Charlie said. "Naturally, you mustn't bring that white trumpeter with you," Shaw said. "I don't understand." "You can't risk going down there with a mixed band." "Haven't you ever heard about black albinos?" Charlie asked. "(…) We'll present Rodney as Albin Red."

Announced as "Albin Red, an exclusive of the Charlie Parker Quintet," Rodney had to take part in all the performances and sing the blues. Seeing that Rodney was not familiar with authentic blues, one of Gene Krupa's old hits was taken out of the closet – The Boogy Blues. Rodney conscientiously sang it while Charlie played bold musical clichés in the background. If the Blacks in the South did or did not fall for it, no one ever found out. In any case, they were too polite and did not complain. With regards to the Whites, no doubt was possible… who would ever want to be considered a Black in the South? (…) And Rodney dragged himself, uncertain, to the microphone to sing "his" blues. When the black club managers would say to him, "Mr. Parker, you're most certainly the king of be-bop up there in the North, which is probably very beautiful, but us folks down here want…" "But of course, friends," Charlie would interrupt. "Don't worry. We won't give you anything but good old mu-

attitude would seem typical of audiences that frequent jazz clubs that are less attentive to the music. In those of the United States, up until a rather recent period, there was a clear-cut division. If the white audience, the Manhattan snobs, were already going to Harlem during the "Black Renaissance" years, the opposite was certainly not true. Not even the artists appreciated in the black neighborhoods had the chance to freely go to, for example, the Cotton Club where only at a certain point, according to what LeRoi Jones tells us, they were admitted in limited numbers and relegated to the back. Moreover, if it is true that the tastes the managers of these clubs attribute to the audience correspond to mainstream tendencies, it is also true that in general their musical initiatives tend to block its evolution and innovation, since these places are strictly concerned with making a profit, which is often interrupted by new things that are not simply ornamental and secondary.

Detailed histories of jazz clubs do not exist, but we can, by analogy, obtain information from record production, in which only the initiatives, though very few, of minor record companies promoted artists open to new musical scenes. It was then this same audience, upheld as being anchored to the forms of success, to show (perhaps a bit late) its own interest for the new musical creations that had been acquired, at this point, from the major record companies. And it is this type of company that is the most reluctant to innovation. As Jean Cocteau once said: "The artist is the true rich man. He travels by automobile. The audience follows by bus. So how can we be surprised that they follow at a distance?"[5] At a distance, it is true, but they follow nonetheless. And at an even greater distance, and at a slower pace, follow those who are busy trying to transform art into money.

The Wall Street crisis at the beginning of the 1930s created havoc but at the same time cleared things up. In the field of music the work opportunities were reduced, especially with a hard blow to Blacks whose music, hang-outs and audience were certainly of a superior quality, but less interesting in the eyes of politics and the economy. Naturally, given the constant factor of racism, the cultural reconstruction and promotion put into action by the New Deal (and, more specifically, by the Federal Music Project), promoted art for society but completely neglected, even though it favored creations that were somewhere between democratic and populist, the existence of a music that in the United States had had a therapeutic role against social frustration and disheartenment – against the feeling of inferiority and inadequacy, prejudice and identification according to skin color. In other words, it neglected that jazz which in

sic so you can all dance (...)." At the beginning, this promise was kept (...) but then the band would gradually slide into its own repertory – that of 52nd Street (with the most famous be-bop clubs). In any case, anything they played, for a black or white audience, the music worked like a charm and it made their feet move. Charlie had already learned the trick of making himself be liked by the dancers."

[5] Jean Cocteau "Cock and Harlequin: Notes on Music, 1918" in *A Call to Order*. MSG Haskell House, New York, 1974.

the black world was one of the very few instruments useful in the struggle against a fate that was decided by skin color. To these new American citizens it seemed impossible to not be able to achieve deserved recognition by applying themselves in those areas particularly valued by Whites – that is, in culture and art. Literacy, which was a collective struggle that the Blacks embarked upon immediately, was given such importance that it became a theme-principle in the work of Scott Joplin for his *Tremonisha*. Even the theme of cultural identity, developed around the repertory of the "Fisk Jubilee Singers," was alive and kicking, characterized by the heated confrontation between those who refused the spirituals for their references to slavery and those who instead considered them as a symbol of black creativity even in the worst imaginable conditions. We would not know how to establish the extent to which the compositions of Harry Burleigh or Clarence Cameron White effected the image of the black man. But we do know that the creativity of Oliver, Morton or Armstrong did not obtain for these musicians a place in Osgood's *So This Is Jazz* (1926).

Therefore, in the 1930s, faced with a new incomprehensible poverty, the racist fracture within American society grew deeper, despite the increase in solidarity among the white population. Even the secondary areas of the musical world, dedicated up to then to jazz, became appealing. It is the time when black music becomes fully aware of itself, translating the difference sustained by racial ideas into a distance created by quality.

Probably the white musicians were not aware of this phenomenon, or they preferred to hide reality behind easily recognizable ideological pretenses. The first is undoubtedly the one that considers black music as a generous and indefatigable creative reservoir that the Whites are able to purge with their musically polished abilities in formal constructions. This approach had already been implicit in the definition of "symphonic jazz" used by Paul Whiteman. It would later disappear in ridiculousness with the dizzying performances of Gillespie and Parker; it would reveal its academically weak and tired character when faced with the simplicity of Thelonious Monk; it would rise again as the ideal theme in the "Birth of Cool" orchestra, but return to its ornamental, decor function with the new sounds of the West Coast.

This superior quality of composition is taken on as a completion and substitution of the musical knowledge that Blacks do not possess. White musicians who feel the need to take up jazz, however, cannot help but consider the art of the Blacks, in their eyes more spontaneous, as being in many respects superior to theirs. We see this, for example, in the concert with Benny Goodman and his band at Carnegie Hall on January 16th, 1938 where not only the music this clarinettist composed with Gene Krupa, Teddy Wislon and Lionel Hampton (these last two are black musicians) was presented, but even an entire section entitled "Twenty Years of Jazz" was organized and which included a jam session on *Honeysuckle Rose* (an idea of Irving Kolodin). This hosts the best of the best of the orchestras of Duke Ellington and Count Basie – orchestras that were already making their mark on the history, notion and identity of jazz.

In any case, there are still heterophony purists that do not consider Ellington's orchestra as exemplary of jazz. But between the musical world that adheres more spontaneously to blues (Basie) and the more sophisticated art oriented towards a search in the potential of the timbres (Ellington) there is no conflict that instead begins to take shape at the time between black and white orchestras. In fact, these black bands had the feeling that they were being replaced by their white counterparts with a cheap imitation of their own music. This aversion is born where jazz is transformed into a business, into casual entertainment. It would otherwise not have been averted.

In many cases this antagonism does not derive from the personal ideologies of the black musicians, nor probably of the white musicians. Instead, it is the racism of the populations and the states, especially in the South, that is imported into the bands. The example of "Albin Red" is a confirmation of this, just as the rare recordings of Charlie Parker together with Lennie Tristano are. In any case, the prohibition of integration in musical bands was on the decline: the "Birth of Cool" orchestra puts black and white musicians together and on the West Coast a quintet with two co-leaders (one black, one white) is born – the "Jay and Kay" band of the trombone players Johnson and Winding.

This however does not mean that the problems fomented by racism have disappeared. It is without a doubt though that the theme of identity passes from a phase in which the decisions are in the hands of the members of the white community to that in which black musicians take clearer positions that are in line with their political leaders and the relatively new perspectives that they propose as solutions to their state of being.

The situation, in itself complicated, becomes even more so with the arrival of jazz in the Western world (outside the United States), especially in Atlantic, central European countries.

In Europe the word "jazz" does not possess markedly negative connotations. Actually, after the period of the "degenerate" and "Negroid" arts an atmosphere that was decidedly favorable to *art nègre* began to take shape. The center of this trend was Paris where the influence of African primitivism and the community of Afro-American musicians residing there continued. Further stimulus was given by the orientation of the critics and which, promoted by Hugues Panassié, was reflected in the ideas, even those not in agreement with his, of Lucien Malson and André Hodeir. Paris, a cosmopolitan and international city, offered therefore an extremely positive setting for the flourishing of this new music. But even the other European States, in a more or less similar fashion, welcomed and applauded jazz music after World War II. Favored by a more profound aesthetic opinion, the new forms of jazz did not have to face the intense resistance of traditionalists, who were more numerous in the United States where old jazz had a folklore sound that did not unsettle the people but rather created a feeling of security and reassurance.

The problem of identity was less urgent especially in Europe, which in that period promoted among the Afro-Americans a growing self-awareness in a setting that was attentive to their African origins.

This theme of anchoring oneself to the past, though it appears completely reasonable with regards to a few aspects of social life (for example, a language that is adopted in order to communicate, like the mother tongue of a host country) also takes on superficial and ridiculous aspects right where it intends to direct consciences. If it is right to have and feel as one's own a tradition of belonging to a certain land, it is also fair to take a step away from it and look elsewhere, in a foreign country, for affinities in ways of thinking and in lifestyles. The polemical aspect that brought the majority of Blacks in America to consider Africa as a symbol of their identity is evident. Paradoxically, in this way the superficial aspect upon which racism is based (that is, skin color) was interiorized. And this was not such a wonderful result. This orientation constitutes nonetheless a strong point in the invention of one's own traditions.

If we stop and observe black pride in the movement called the "Harlem Renaissance," when this New York neighborhood could be considered the largest and most populated black city in the world, we find practically nothing neither in music nor in literature nor painting that speaks about Africa, about the Dark Continent. But gradually, starting with the exotic *A Night in Tunisia*, one of the most famous examples in be-bop history, references and titles alluding to Africa begin to appear. This phenomenon is an almost sudden turning point, seeing that the re-birth we are referring to did not take place centuries ago, but is rather limited to a lapse of time between 1919 and 1929, and therefore separated only by one generation from be-bop.

The be-bop movement did not involve the entire black community. Actually, its members simply constituted a clan – a group that expressed itself by means of labyrinthine allusions, hints, references, words that are attributed meanings that are the opposite of canonical definitions. It is a group that selected others on the basis of their elasticity in making be-bop language their own and in creating within its "hermetism." An allure that is more Arabian than African runs through some of its melodies.

There is no need to think of a strongly characterized cultural determination in order to explain the presence of this *melos* in be-bop music. With the war that brought Africa to the Pacific islands and to Europe and military troops to Asia, the exotic taste could be a justification in itself. Even the policy of cultural promotion could offer some explanations, as is the case with the band created around Dizzy Gillespie to demonstrate a few qualities of Cuban music. Moreover, the cinema of the age is teeming with Arabian exoticisms like Hedy Lamarr, Sabu, a Thousand and One Arabian Nights, Sinbad and so on.

However, it is quite interesting to note that in the black world conversions to Islam take place. These are signs of an anti-Western, and therefore anti-Christian, ideology that gradually grows and which is nurtured even by the experience of the war, if it is true that, differently from what we see portrayed on the silver screen, the hardest fighting and greatest dangers were reserved for the Blacks. Given, however, that the crime attributed to the white population by black Americans remained slavery, the fact that the Arab world was indicated as exemplary is perplexing seeing that even before European slave-traders Arabian slave-merchants had plundered the human resources of Africa.

Even though the distance continues to grow between the mythical framework that sustains Afro-American ideology (there are examples of this in the speeches of Malcolm X held in the Audubon Hotel that cause a great stir, as well as in *Mumbo Jumbo* by Ishmael Reed) and the ideology of white Americans, for black musicians the racial unity of the band is not as important as the music, the role and the specific qualities of each single musician. There is also a usage that favors onstage integration. And so for a while *all-Negro* productions become rarer: between the 1939-1940 and 1962-1963 seasons, in 24 years only fifty-two theatrical works of Black Theater are staged in the United States and for a few years nothing new is presented with this characteristic.

The attempt to integrate, at least symbolically, the black population and the white community does not bring great results because starting in the 1960s there is a rise in opposition to moderate reformism, as well as anti-capitalistic and anti-racist unrest.

Even the search for aesthetic quality is abandoned. Presenting his theatrical work, *Blues for Mr. Charlie* (April 1964), James Baldwin declared that he was not particularly interested with the success of the drama. "I want to shock the people," he said. "I want to see them jump to their feet. I want them to think, to follow me in an experience that I believe is important." Even *Dutchman* (March 1964) by Imamu Amiri Baraka (born as LeRoi Jones) has a clear political agenda and an expressive power that can be assimilated only over time. The shock and the uneasiness caused at the première would give way to appreciation only five years later when Clayton Riley of "The New York Times" (August 1969) defined this as the "most beautiful theatrical piece that has ever been written for American theater."

But these were already the years in which the lessons of Ornette Coleman, John Coltrane, Cecil Taylor, Albert Ayler and Archie Shepp had energized the African-American musical world and shocked white audiences.

First of all, it would be useful to emphasize that the identity of African-American music during the 1960s, also known as free jazz, was not determined by a new political approach that was carried over into music. Instead it is true that the numerous innovations brought to artistic production by the musicians whose guiding and avant-garde roles would be recognized as important in defining this musical genre are the result of other motivations, in which it is right and proper to recognize a fertile terrain that is more poetical than political.

For convention, the birth of free jazz is dated May 17th, 1960 when Ornette Coleman and seven other musicians entered the Atlantic Records recording studios to create the work "Free Jazz." But this is only a convention because by the second half of the 1950s signs of renewal were already present on the African-American musical scene, thus preparing for that "tornado" of innovation that a few years later was to traumatize music. These signs were particularly evident especially in the ethically *engagée* music of Charlie Mingus, but also in the works of two musicians dedicated to new musical approaches: Max Roach and Sonny Rollins (the former, protagonist of the post-Parker evolution of be-bop, would always stress the collective nature of black American musical creation, and would always be fully aware of its political resonance). John Coltrane's contribution must also be added here – a musician who came from the "low" layers of music (that is, from the generic rhythm'n'blues that nurtured the popular side of black expression) – and demonstrated his own creative identity in the quintet of Miles Davis during the mid-1950s. He then set out along a transcendentalist course that carried him away from the mannerism of be-bop (that is, the music played even in commercial jazz clubs – the "training ground" of virtuosic forms that had by then become conventional).

During the mid-1950s in the area of internal conflict produced by Yankee racism against the more than fair requests on the part of the black community to gain access to a real equality in the use of public places and services, and after the ruling on the unconstitutionality of segregation in public schools, the United States Supreme Court decision to quickly proceed with desegregation provoked not only a reaction of a strong Southern group in Congress, who invited its citizens to fight against this decision, but also a new outbreak of the Ku Klux Klan. The means used were not limited to "micro-terrorism" consisting in the use of dynamite to blow up homes, churches and schools in the black community, but involved even homicides. For example, there was the killing of three Civil Rights workers that inspired the film *Mississippi Burning* and the homicide of Viola Liuzzo (evidently of Italian origin) who was "guilty" of having "discredited the white race by frequenting and assisting people of the black race." It was the comeback of the "Strange Fruit" – those hanging from the trees of the "gallant South," as Abel Meerpol's song sung by Billie Holiday says – of the bodies of black men and women where blood trickles forth onto the leaves and roots of the poplar trees. Of "a pastoral scene of the gallant South. Bulging eyes and twisted mouth. Scent of magnolias sweet and fresh. And the smell of burning flesh."

Because this conflict showed no signs of placation, it was necessary for President Eisenhower to intervene. At that time the incarnation of white racism was Orval Faubus, Governor of Arkansas, who, in response to the Federal Court decision against the segregation in the schools of Little Rock, called upon the National Guard to impede nine African-American students admission in the public school. At that point Eisenhower took control of those troops and sent federal troops to enforce the decision. Faubus, though, had the electors on his side, who later re-elected him, thus allowing the Governor to resist the decision of the President and Congress. Six years after the Supreme Court ruling the schools in Louisiana, South Carolina, Georgia, Mississippi and Alabama were still completely segregated, thus fueling a tension that was already present for many other reasons.

On December 23rd, 1955 Charlie Mingus recorded *Haitian Fight Song*. It is a bitter blues theme that he would take up again less than fourteen months later in the recording entitled "The Clown." In the album jacket the musician wrote that the title could well have been "Afro-American Fight Song," explaining that the double bass solo responds to "prejudice and hate and persecution, and how unfair it is." Mingus adds, "And it usually ends with my feeling: 'I told them! I hope somebody heard me.'" The work of Mingus is particularly important for the meeting points between music and *polis*. Even if the perspective gradually becomes black – a thing that in the titles happens in an explicit manner only in 1959 with the *Fables of Faubus* recorded in "Mingus Ah Um." His civil activism is evident in the recording of *Pithecanthropus Erectus* (January 1956). Here, the theme of a search for greater freedom in expression is fused with themes of social identity. This music, a rather vast work, lasts for over ten minutes, and is rather surprising in jazz music production. Firstly for its format because the advent of long-play records was rather recent. It was not that African-American musicians felt the necessity to end their numbers within the times established by the old-format records – this is demonstrated not only by the famous concert of Parker, with Gillespie, Powell, Roach and Mingus at Toronto's Massey Hall (which we can listen to because Mingus had a tape-recorder with him) but also by the work documented in other records released more than ten years after they were recorded, like in the 1946 concert of Charlie Parker, with Dizzy Gillespie and Lester Young (it is a Fantasy record entitled "Early Modern" which has a complicated story of re-issuing and transfer of ownership). But the three minutes of the by then quasi-extinct short-playing records had profoundly influenced, even though they did not constitute a rule, the format of the music that would be recorded. But the dimension of *Pithecanthropus Erectus* is in some way new not so much for its length (because jazz music assures that, by making a display of its solo performances, the instruments can remain on one theme even for much longer times), but rather for the fact that it was conceived by Mingus as a work that, with its four movements, necessitates such duration. The movements are entitled "Evolution," "Superiority Complex," "Decline" and "Destruction" and offer themselves as the musician's personal description of the affirmation, decline and self-annihilation of the species born from *pythecanthropus erectus* or rather, humanity.

It must be noted that the theme-subject of this work has a humanistic value that was not able to have any effect on the guilty racist conscience of Americans. Records do not offend American consciences and social relationships. We do not know if Mingus had already created songs that, like *Fables of Faubus*, explicitly commented on the themes of internal American conflict. And it is impossible to say what were the preceding intentions of the musician, whose relationship with record companies led him to create his own label, "Debut," against all forms of censure and violence imposed upon the musicians with the excuse of catering to the audience's tastes.

But even if the ideology of the jazz fans may exact that this music adapts itself to certain formal narrative requests, the bitterest tension, with consequent rigid oppositions, dates back to 1945: innovators and traditionalists, "cool" and "hot" were confronted (when the term "cool" still meant the be-bop that was slowly taking shape and "hot" referred to the "hot clubs" of amateur revival).

In *Pithecanthropus Erectus* the music moves through phrases that, especially in the written parts, show originality – a new harmonic suspension – meters that appear stolen and accelerations of intense expression.

It is probable that the strong growth of the black movement, with its non-violent resistance, the boycotts of public services (the first was in Montgomery, Alabama and led by the charismatic Martin Luther King), the sit-ins, the growth of the NAACP (National Association for the Advancement of Colored People) energized the patient black rebellion. The absence of a strategic pragmatism, however, worsened the situation and, faced with the continuous increase in the number of African States that were attaining their independence (between 1957 and 1965 there were 36), in the United States it seemed as though nothing had changed. In fact, among the youth impatience and hatred grew, thus causing violent rebellions to increasingly find greater consent.

Africa, which over time had lost, for many, its role as Motherland, was increasingly enshrouded with mythical allure and the invention of a tradition anchored to the Great Black Mother continued to find new converts. It is a black interiorization of racism that identifies pigments and color – an attitude Mingus did not approve of.

His roots are American, as say the titles and the images he alludes to in "Blues and Roots," recorded in 1959. It is in the *meeting prayers* on Wednesday evenings, in blues, in Jelly Roll Morton, alongside Ellington, Lester Young, Charlie Parker, Thelonious Monk – maestros of that which Mingus considers as being the great American music. Increasingly less attentive to the academic component that he had been close to only a few years prior (for example, in the "Jazz Experiments" of 1954), Mingus, faced with a black community that was evolving towards a New-Africanism and free jazz (which he considered anarchist), increasingly became rooted in an American and black context. Not considering the unreleased recordings, there exist on various records 13 versions of *Fables of Faubus* – the first in 1959 and the last in 1977. The words, characterized by a didactic realism, say: "Oh Lord, don't let them shoot us/Oh Lord, don't let them stab us/Oh Lord, don't let them tar and feather us/Oh Lord, no more swastikas/Oh Lord, no more Ku Klux Klan/Name me someone ridiculous/Governor Faubus/Why is he sick and ridiculous?/He won't permit integral schools – Then he is a fool/Boo! Nazi Fascist supremacists/Boo! Ku Klux Klan/Name me a handful that's ridiculous/Faubus, Rockefeller, Eisenhower/Why are they so sick and ridiculous?/Two, four, six, eight. They brainwash and teach you hate." Mingus' attention is therefore concentrated on the Unites States; in his music there is no reference to Africa.

Not even Max Roach, the other leading figure in black music during that period profoundly influenced by civil activism, is attracted by the forms of African music. Two personalities – that of Mingus and of Roach – formed in the context of be-bop and in a kind of exaggeration of the idiom and therefore aware of the value of the idiolects in artistic creation. It would have been difficult for them to be influenced by folk constructions, which were ideologically retrospective and idiomatic. But that which Mingus takes from folklore is greatly transformed and thus loses its distinctive characteristics. On the other hand, Roach, a drummer, is intimately tied to an instrument that does not exist in folklore – an instrument that is such an accumulation of percussions that only a group of three or four traditional musicians would be able to create what Roach does by himself. But Roach demonstrates an internationalist interest more than Mingus. In "We Insist! Freedom Now Suite" of 1960, Roach uses the myths of humanity's African origin (*All Africa*), concentrating however on the martyrdom of Afro-Americans (*Driva' Man, Triptych*), on Martin Luther King's "Dream" (*Freedom Day*) and on his present-day political struggle (he takes up *All Africa* and connects it to *Tears for Johannesburg*). Here, Roach stresses the absence of a broader emotional involvement – of pity, of tears, even if in the sounds rebellion and rage surface in an evident manner. The suffering of the Afro-Americans is immense, as the Sharperville massacres in South Africa give proof to this. And this suffering is equally immense among the Afro-Americans, as can be seen in the perpetuation of the racial conflict.

Even though it is true that jazz musicians, by *forma mentis* inclined to performances and entertainment, are mostly indifferent to politics, or at least in certain situations pretend to be, the taking of sides of Duke Ellington, Count Basie, Art Blakey, Charlie Mingus and Roach himself in favor of sit-ins and passive (non-violent) resistance (Mingus in 1960 dedicates a page in jazz history to this, *Prayer for Passive Resistance*) stirs up this existing political apathy during the course of the second half of the 1950s.

Music is not a language and its syntax can be defined only through similarities. Seeing that it does not possess lexical elements (in music there are neither single sounds nor combinations of sounds that function like words), it carries conceptual meaning by means of the scene space and the gestures of the musicians. In fact, at times there are decidedly explicit moments – essential elements of a clear meaning that is cried out can be gathered – that is, the exact vanishing point that reveals the intentions from which a significant episode in music history is born. And therefore if Mingus raises the double bass and places it horizontally, pretending to be a person who is about to fire (which is what he actually did in one of his concerts in Bologna in 1964) – something that is impossible to understand by listening to a recording – and a synchronous "shot" of the drums follows (in the Bologna concert, his devotee during those years was the drummer Dannie Richmond), the meaning and interpretation cannot be misunderstood (the quality of the music, obviously, is separate from the quality of the surroundings).

In the early 1960s, the jazz scene presents as its most important players a well-nurtured line of musicians that had achieved complete musical maturity right in those years. Among these there are Miles Davis, Charlie Mingus, Max Roach, Horace Silver, Sonny Rollins and Thelonious Monk who, born in 1917 and therefore a bit older than the others, had been a protagonist of be-bop in the first half of the 1940s (later, because of his involvement with drugs, he was excluded for years from the public scene). Once again going to clubs and recording studios in the mid-1960s, he attained good success even though a bit late, thanks to his instrumental voice that expresses a strong musical originality. Actually, since his music is rooted in a musical area that had been up to then only vaguely explored, it continued to live on up to the end of the decade in the music of Cecil Taylor. Taylor was a pianist at the start of his career but would later become one of the first three voices (together with Ornette Coleman and John Coltrane) of free jazz.

We have already mentioned the fact that the evolution of free jazz was due to reasons of a musical kind rather than a social kind.

We also discussed that the birth of the free jazz movement is conventionally given a precise date – 1960 – the year Coleman's "Free Jazz" was recorded. And in fact, with the releasing of "Free Jazz" there explodes something that had already been present two or three years prior, thus arousing curiosity and interest among the audience and other musicians.

In the first place we must remember the attention given to the modal concept as an alternative to the tonal concept within which black American music settled in to. In music there does not exist an irremediable contrast between modes and tones: the tones are born from the modes and preserve in the modes much or little "memory" of their origin. Thanks to tonality, the elaboration of that form of syntax typical to music has brought a few achievements that, also translated into habits, transferred themselves, even though in a rather limited way, to jazz and to its twin – popular music. Blues, a black American folk form, incorporates into jazz a touch of modalism (which we find only rarely in popular music products) with its blue notes, the intonation of which does not come under the tonal scale.

When, in the 1970s, it was understood that the blues scale must be considered as a scale of four notes and three intervals that repeat themselves at every fifth (for example: do, re, mi blue note, fa and scale identical one fifth above, sol, la, si blue note, do), this treatment of the sound, especially melodic, was combined with the harmonic progressions, which were more rigorously tonal, without creating any problem for the successive generation of musicians. We must also remember, however, that during the second half of the 1950s modalism begins to impose itself with greater force. This is theorized by George Russell in *The Lydian Chromatic Concept of Tonal Organisation for Improvisers* – a work that leaves the world of performance quite indifferent. But by following different paths, modal music begins to be heard in the ensemble put together on occasion of the concert of Bill Evans with Miles Davis, and on the music of Cannonball Adderley and of John Coltrane with Miles Davis in 1958. Modal music is not an invention, but rather the sign of an explicit distancing from the centrality of European tradition that emphasizes the musical contribution of Third-World countries – the object of ethnomusicology. We could therefore argue that internationalism, expressed in the interest towards Africa, together with the assimilation of sub-Saharan Africans and other populations and territories oppressed by American capitalism and imperialism, finds its musical expression in this modal concept that manifests itself as an alternative to the tonal concept (for example, in his hymns John Philip Sousa gave voice to the euphoric American march with music like *Stars and Stripes Forever* or *Hand Across the Sea*). This is a change in perspective that, not yet evident in the first music in which modalism affirms itself, would fully manifest itself over time (from the second half of the 1960s) in the period of full free jazz (for example, in the music of "Art Ensemble of Chicago"). In fact, this internationalism is demonstrated by the scene masks that first Malachi Favors (the double bassist of the ensemble) and then Don Moye, the drummer, wore.

This is not the perspective John Coltrane operates in – the sax player that made modalism familiar to an entire generation of soloists. His music is rather permeated with a transcendentalism in the search for Truth-Good-Beauty, by means of a process in which the artist finds the sign of his own personal god. In Coltrane, who died when he was only 40 years old in 1967, a progressive and gradual distancing from the contingencies manifested itself – a complete indifference to the musical agenda that was taking shape. He is a traveler like Rudhyar or Cage and like them he arrives in those areas of the Asian sub-continent that inspire the Western anti-capitalistic movement (even "The Beatles" travel to India). But he takes a different course than the one followed by the West. First he goes to Africa and the Nile.

In the same years, Cecil Taylor penetrates in the folds of the dissonance of Thelonious Monk by organizing a piano performance that was intentionally free within spatial structures created from a theatrical perspective. The keys appear to him like a large stage upon which his hands and fingers move in a way that is inspired by classical ballet. Gestures and images mix together but Taylor knows that this whole, even if seemingly haphazard, will stimulate the listeners to unite everything according to the meaning that each single person attributes to the music. The keys seem to him, above all, like an orchestra of drums where the accent of each single note is more important than its pitch. It becomes increasingly difficult to perceive the piano as a source of melody, even if at times fragments of it appear.

Ornette Coleman, in turn, was "arguing" with intonation; seeing that the world had accepted the blue notes (the third and seventh notes on the scale) as the main sign of blues, which for him is the same thing as jazz, he proceeds in "blues-izing" all the notes and intoning them in the way he deems fit. An initial anchoring to be-bop models (people began talking about Coleman as the new Parker), he puts in difficulty the whole, overall sound. His blues is radical and does not accept the piano, thus forcing him to give it up back in 1959 when he recorded "The Shape of Jazz to Come" and "Tomorrow Is the Question" for Atlantic Records.

The transition from hard-bob to free jazz is not determined by social issues, but by a process closely related to the music that these artists were interpreting. Behind them there is unhappiness that soon would bring this search for freedom to unite with the eternal struggle of populations and find liberty once and for all from slavery and subjection. If there is a meaning in writing this history, like every other history in the field of art, it is also to see how the artists, who are born already mature from a creative point of view, operate among worldly things and remain indifferent to the reasons that created them and which in turn they also create.

The meeting points of free jazz with the social rebellion of the 1960s are decidedly posterior to the appearance of this music, and perhaps are even a bit late. It is however clear that looking at things after they have taken place, in their blending and overlapping we can recognize artistic foresight. Therefore, looking back, the same artists that composed music on the basis of mainly formal motivations can recognize the component relating to the subject that others saw in their works. In this way, Cecil Taylor can admit that his own fantasies about the tutus and red ballet shoes were actually placed in a framework where the very existence of jazz is something revolutionary. Defining in this way his own music and at the same time, for example, taking a step away from John Cage meant that Cecil Taylor had decidedly wanted to separate himself from the usual jazz interpretation in the United States. Or rather, from the idea that jazz is a hobby for Blacks, that it is simply a natural inclination to rhythm attributed to the race, a virtuoso performance added to American (or international) pop music. There is also this last aspect when, for example, a sax quartet – splendidly inserted in the musical corpus conceived by Mingus in the perspective of free jazz – performs as a curtain call *O sole mio* or *Volare*, for the delight of the audience. But this same circumstance may be the example of how a music realizes the aspiration of becoming familiar

– an aspiration that is perhaps common to every musical form – a sort of vocation of transforming itself into a sonorous tapestry – whatever the intention of the creator may be.

The encounter of the "new thing" (like many musicians loved calling their music, preferring this definition to "free jazz") with the social-political movements occurs with the second free jazz generation – with musicians like Archie Shepp and Bill Dixon, Frank Kofsky, A. B. Spellman and LeRoi Jones, who later changes his name to Amiri Baraka.

At the beginning, labor union issues are mixed with anti-racial themes. In "Down Beat" (1972) Ornette Coleman remembers a very "open" record company producer who sustained that musicians should not expect to earn enough to get by with their music. "Strange, because he seemed to have a good quality of life thanks to the records musicians made for him," Coleman commented.

"The drama of jazz composers and musicians, and with musicians in general, is that we musicians are the ones who greatly suffer the management of the music business that depreciates our production," he comments. Moreover, Coleman was fully aware that "in jazz, the Negro is the product." He also said this same thing five years earlier in "Down Beat," sustaining that the publicity that accompanied his records was centered around him and his atypical qualities.

Charlie Mingus, who had already understood that producing records on his own was probably the only thing that could safeguard himself and musicians from the economic speculation of the record companies, founded his "Debut" label in 1953. But producing is one thing – and being on the market is another.

What had to occur was a joining of the impatience of professional musicians with the impatience of the public so that both could do without the distribution of the product. Therefore the music could only benefit from the movement that continued to grow around the issues of identity and social justice.

While the notes of *Free Jazz* (Coleman), *Impressions* (Coltrane), *Pots* (Taylor) were a-flutter, the movement was still involved in sit-ins, wade-ins, stand-ins and even kneel-ins, initiatives that attracted an increasingly broader approval and which could last even for an entire season, which is what happened in Nashville where for the entire spring of 1963 protests were organized in favor of the desegregation in all public places and services. The Southern Christian Leadership Conference (SCLC) and the NAACP worked together, promoting action even within the Christian community, especially among Black Christians who had adhered to preceding protests with scarce enthusiasm. With the protests growing and increasing, the pressure of the police became more visible: 1963 is blemished with much bloodshedding in Birmingham and Danville, for example, and by political crimes, lynchings and assassinations – though not reported as such. But at this point, the Afro-Americans no longer felt or were alone and isolated because a visible part of WASP children began seeing them as human beings not different from people of the white race.

The jazz of the times – the music of Taylor, Coltrane and Coleman – had not yet encountered this political movement. The music comes before, without expecting to ever be caught up with. It is an art music – whatever personal opinion may be – that reveals its own necessity by refusing the success and models that record companies tend to impose. The audience interested in these musicians was still decidedly limited. Coleman had difficulty in communicating his own identity with regards to those who wanted to see in his music a proletarian folk version of Parker's jazz. Perhaps Coltrane attracted an audience that was a bit broader because of his old militancy in rhythm'n'blues that still came forth, and for the transcendental aspects that can be heard in his music. Taylor was undergoing an intense psychological crisis. Even Mingus, who was winning over an increasingly wider audience, had his own identity problems which he confronted, filling in his notebooks with a vital frenzy that would later give birth to *Beneath the Underdog* – a sort of expressionist autobiography published in 1971. But the need to create and the growing approval of the public brought him on the scene – a scene that he needed in order to pour forth the power and energy of his own carnality.

When free jazz – anarchist and open to emotional excesses – begins to excite the fantasies for freedom of the younger generations, Mingus decidedly distances himself, using the norms as instruments of liberty through which he can fully and clearly mold his thoughts. Probably free jazz seems dangerous to him because it easily transmits generic excitement and rage, but it moves away from form: from free jazz he sees poor, vulgar and primitive acts come forth and all is translated in the language of hate and rebellion. Even the music of Albert Ayler, which is particularly paradoxical and Rabelaisesque, is interpreted as an expression of antagonistic fury.

The American scene was changing and contributed to definitively loosening the knots in America's guilty conscience. Malcolm X and the Black Panther Party emerge. The themes of civil struggle are muddled with those on the war in Vietnam.

This situation is so exasperating that LeRoi Jones begins treating as "symbolisms" the positions that the black exponents are able to obtain in institutional life, while James Baldwin writes his *Blues for Mr. Charlie* (1964). The music of Archie Shepp is probably the one that is the most able in uniting the most advanced research of Coleman, Coltrane and Taylor with the political movement. It is his encounter with Coltrane's music in 1960 that decides his future. For Coltrane, politics and theater were very important, but he is led to music, the tenor sax, perhaps at the beginning with a certain shyness in which his music is characterized by a "classical" sound, all his attention turned to the audience. This is revealed both in the collaborations with Bill Dixon in "New York Contemporary Five" and with Don Cherry and John Tchicai. But from 1964 he begins to aim his sonorous arrows at the political world with "Malcolm Semper Malcolm" (1965), "The Magic of Ju-Ju" (1967) and "Attica Blues" (1972). This music, which is still rightly called jazz, is completely different from the jazz of the preceding periods. It no longer has any relationship with dance (this had already set in during the World War II years) and it is no longer an esoteric music, destined to the acolytes of be-bop clubs, but rather is able to invade the streets and involve thousands of people. The fact that many youth movements identify themselves in this sound (a phenomenon that also occurred by chance, which is precisely the case with the unexpected and exceptional first edition of Italy's "Umbria Jazz Festival" in 1973) plays to its advantage, but it also constitutes a misunderstanding. For a few years the "age of jazz" mania spreads – so much so that Ishmael Reed writes his *Mumbo Jumbo* (1972) as the jazz fever rises, opposed in vain by the top institutions.

But the political characterization also causes resistance in the old jazz audience a little because they are close and similar to their idols who refrain from getting involved in politics and political issues, and because they are used to be-bop and its exclusivity. The red shirt that Sonny Rollins, one the greatest sax players matured during the 1950s, often wears unites just about everyone but erects almost a wall that defines the space of free jazz. Moreover, the antidotes of music-goods against the infection of the music-art take giant steps: even the "Umbria Jazz Festival" welcomes South American dance tunes while the most generic r'n'r (not the rock of Frank Zappa or the Rolling Stones) conquers youths in their angst.

Though continuing in part to be intimately political, jazz, in so far as it was absolutely convinced of the relationship between African-American music and the industry that turns it into a sellable product [the writings of A.B. Spellman (*Four Lives in*

Be-bop Business), Frank Kofsky (*Black Nationalism and the Revolution in Music*), LeRoi Jones (*Blues People*) and the more didactic and less militant Neil Leonard (*Jazz and the White Americans: The Acceptance of a New Art Form*) had already taken root in the self-awareness of black musicians], and though locking itself up again on the inside of its artistic search, it reaped the fruits of that age. Actually, the most important voices that from the 1980s have characterized the history of jazz descend for the most part from Coltrane, Coleman and Taylor (these last two greats are still fresh and active as artists rather than political leaders). The *all-African-American*, therefore, is a consequence of the technical abilities and of the passion for the themes and issues of black life rather than an ideological choice. And the fact that there are numerous white musicians and social rebels alongside black musicians in recordings proves this.

And cinema – the most effective instrument of ideological and popular divulgation before the advent of television – what image has it given to all this? To what extent and in what way has it treated all this? What has it shown?
It is not easy for a musicologist to answer these questions. Moreover, how can we understand if the creator is black or white if in the credits we only see this person's name? Of course, it should be this way. But if we were to discuss figurative art or the promotion and success of an artist (let us take Andy Warhol, for example) within the context of racial conflict that took place and which continues to exist in the United States, it would certainly be important to know what community (black or white) this artist comes from.
Black films and *Blacks in films* are two different matters. Limiting this discussion only to actors, the second, *Blacks in films*, could be carried out easily enough. But the first, *black films*, is much more difficult also because little or indeed nothing has arrived in our movie theaters (not only Italian but European as well) regarding things we could call *race films*, even if the label used in the record company industry was probably different from the one used in cinema.
Today, the image of the African-American movie has a name – Spike Lee. But everything else, if it does indeed exist, has not reached us or has not been distributed.
With regards to African Americans in films, the classic ones are well known. These were written and filmed by Whites. And the Blacks were forced to take on the racial stereotype of the Sambo (happy slave, devoted servant, superstitious and

bigot buddy), arriving at *The Birth of a Nation* (1915, D.W. Griffith) which gives us "an impassioned and persuasive recognition of the inferiority of the Negro," as Lewis Jacobs once said.[6]

After *The Jazz Singer* (1927), an irreparable idiocy with a "Negro-ized" Al Jolson, a couple of songs and a little synagogue music, we should mention *Hearts in Dixie* and *Hallelujah!* (both from 1929), the first Hollywood films interpreted by black actors. The characters are the 19th century slaves, with an outpouring of cotton fields, psalms and spirituals. The comment of Paul Robeson, five years later, was that "the insistence in always representing […] Blacks as clowns" had ruined both films and that "in *Hallelujah!* the Blacks and their religious services became ridiculous."[7]

For a realistic vision (black characters who also possess loyalty, courage and understand the meaning of friendship) we have to wait for two films: *I'm a Fugitive from a Chain Gang* (1932, Mervyn LeRoy) and *Fury* (1936, Fritz Lang – a non-American director). Strangely enough, these films give an image of the African American that is even more human than the image provided by *all-Negro* films, like *Cabin in the Sky* (1943), in which the characters still appear bound to a magical world, even though in their dreams. What begins to pop up in large quantities are movies with actual Jazz musicians – appreciable and at times even brilliant in their roles – but they always interpret parts that lie outside that of the musician and their image is always veiled with the Sambo connotation. We see this once again in *New Orleans* (1947, Arthur Lubin) in which there also appears Armstrong and Billie Holiday (she plays a maid and he is a jazz trumpeter who rolls his eyes and is amazed at everything). Here even the music leaves something to be desired with *Do You Know What It Means to Miss New Orleans*, the main tune repeated ad infinitum. The shorts filmed on occasion of the performances of each single artist are better: Duke Ellington, Bessie Smith and all the musicians who appear on the series "The Sound of Jazz." But here we are in fact dealing with jazz, actors that coincide with the characters they portray, and without probing into their human side.

The little that we know of black cinema does not seem to have been able to even begin to chip away at the typical Hollywood stereotypes. Jazz is the only creative/artistic field where African Americans proposed alternatives to white creativity, always finding (up till now) the way of both affirming their own originality and re-affirming their own identity in the face of the attempts of imposing on their music a deviation that would allow for greater use on the part of an audience, learned or popular, linked

[6] L. Jacobs, *The Riser of American Folk*. Harcourt Brace, New York, 1939.

[7] "Film Weekly" (September 1st, 1933), cited in Peter Noble, *Negro in Films*. Ayer Company Publishers, Manchester, 1978.

to consolidated European traditions. However, we cannot ignore the attempts to create, during the 1930s, a black cinema industry even if the investments, as in the case of the Goldberg Brothers, came from white businessmen.

The producer, as we know, can count a lot or nothing in a film. It depends on how much he/she expects to condition it with the power of money. The Goldberg Brothers did not abuse of this. Unfortunately, their films cannot be found easily, like *Broken Strings* (Bernard Ray) co-scripted and starring Clarence Muse, whose character is a violinist. In these productions in which the troupe is mainly African-American (with noteworthy difficulty because, excluding the actors, there does not seem to be many black cinematic technicians) two Westerns with an *all-Negro* cast stand out: *Bronze Buckaroo* (1939, Richard C. Kahn), where light-skinned black Americans interpret Whites, with Herbert Jeffrey as a singing cowboy, and *Harlem on the Prairie* (1937, Jed Buell). Both were shown only in ghetto movie theaters. However it seems that these two films do not disassociate themselves from the stereotypes with which the Blacks are represented in commercial Hollywood cinema, and are still full of eye-rolling specialists and fried chicken, watermelon and pork chop devourers.

Perhaps a certain movie could be more significant (of which I remember only the plot and a few scenes) which portrayed a black vampire – a philosopher-Dracula – lost in his existential problems. And unlike every other vampire, our black Dracula decides to commit suicide (by using the sun's light from the roof of his house) and put an end to the horrors he is destined to face. When he gets to the top (after a never-ending and very difficult climb up) it is dark all around but the first light of dawn begins to shimmer. In the movie theater a few young people shout at his desperate gesture, "Don't do it! No, don't do it!"

Then the years of Sidney Poitier arrive – the black actor who was assigned the most important parts for the creation of a dignified image and portrayal of black people. The road that brings to the *politically correct* begins, with a black doctor who cures a racist white man, with patrols of both black and white policemen, with erotic scenes of mixed couples that do not repeat the old stereotype of the animalesque sexuality attributed to African Americans.

In both popular and successful cinema what became fundamental was the democratic and modern thinking of white screenwriters, directors and producers who supported and created a cinema that wanted to change the attitude of a certain American audience that carried within it, in a rather strong way, stereotypes, prejudices and, as a whole, racist ideology. And though this aspiration was diffused among Afro-American actors, it never took shape in black cinematic or theatrical productions.

Today, however, we can perhaps say that a black cinema has begun. As Donald Bogle writes, "Everything changed with the release of a low-budget independent film entitled *She's Gotta Have It* (1986). Filmed in twelve days in Brooklyn with a cast of unknowns and a budget of $175,000, it was the work of a young African-American director – Spike Lee. The film became a surprising hit."

It is the beginning of a career in which an African-American expresses himself with the forms of his native tongue as a black American. Where he sees the world with his own eyes, with the intelligence and the tics of the ghettos, with a black neo-realistic originality that may be compared to the advent of blues almost one hundred years earlier, of Ma Rainey or Bessie Smith, for its taking a step away from the usual and predictable forms of production (musical and/or cinematic), but which is not naive or folk, like that music was. This comparison is perhaps better with the boppers, between Parker and Monk, but however it may be, this film is the starting point for African American cinema, if and until this definition has meaning.

A Song Is Born
(Howard Hawks, 1948)
Charlie Barnet,
Tommy Dorsey,
Benny Goodman,
Louis Armstrong,
and Lionel Hampton

Rendez-vous de juillet/Rendezvous in July
(Jacques Bécker, 1949)
(Far right) Daniel Gélin

Young Man with a Horn (Michael Curtiz, 1950)
Hoagy Carmichael and Doris Day

The Glenn Miller Story
(Anthony Mann, 1953)
James Stewart, Gene Krupa,
Louis Armstrong, and Woody Herman

The Glenn Miller Story (Anthony Mann, 1953)
Gene Krupa, Louis Armstrong, James Stewart

Pete Kelly's Blues
(Jack Webb, 1955)
Peggy Lee

Opposite page:
The Benny Goodman Story (Valentine Davies, 1955)
Jam session of *Avalon* with Teddy Wilson (piano),
Lionel Hampton (vibes), Benny Goodman (clarinet,
portrayed by Steve Allen), and Gene Krupa (drums)

The Man with the Golden Arm
(Otto Preminger, 1955)
Frank Sinatra

Sweet Smell of Success
(Alexander Mackendrick, 1957)
(On left) Tony Curtis and Burt Lancaster

Ascenseur pour l'échafaud/Frantic
(Louis Malle, 1958)
(Far right) Lino Ventura

St. Louis Blues
(Allen Reisner, 1958)
Eartha Kitt

Anatomy of a Murder
(Otto Preminger, 1959)
James Stewart
and Duke Ellington

SAVING IT TWICE: PRESERVING JAZZ IN DOCUMENTARIES, COMPILATION FILMS, AND SHORT SUBJECTS

Krin Gabbard

Some of the best jazz artists were never filmed under the circumstances that they themselves might have chosen. More often than not they were presented as grotesques and exotics. When we think of Cab Calloway wildly waving his arms and his hair or Fats Waller vigorously exercising his eyebrows and lips, we are recalling the creations of filmmakers for whom such antics made for compelling entertainment. Nevertheless, jazz enthusiasts should be grateful for *any* film of jazz musicians, if only because so little of it exists. Much can be learned from those bits of film that preserve the images of the artists along with their music. Our pleasure in these images can be greatly enhanced when we know where they come from and why there were made.

Documentaries

The jazz documentary was born at the same time that the jazz biopic was in its death throes. In the 1950s, when jazz became known as an art music rather than as America's popular music, it began to seem a worthy subject for documentation on film. On the one hand, jazz became an art with a history worth preserving, especially with the new technologies and ideologies that helped make the documentary cinema a thriving art form in the 1950s. On the other hand, jazz had begun to encourage the same "ethnographic" impulses as other exotic phenomena such as the daily habits of Eskimos in the Arctic Circle or the love lives of Polynesians on the island of Bora Bora. (One of the fathers of the documentary cinema, Robert Flaherty released *Nanook of the North* in 1922 and collaborated with F.W. Murnau on *Tabu* in 1931.) Not surprisingly, some commentators regard Roger Tilton's *Jazz Dance* (1954) as the first jazz documentary. Although the film included footage of jazz musicians Pee Wee Russell, Jimmy McPartland, and Willie "The Lion" Smith, it was more focused on the strange and enchanting antics of Lindy Hoppers at the Central Plaza Dance Hall in New York City.

Jazz purists, however, are likely to regard television features such as *Satchmo the Great* (1957), *The Sound of Jazz* (1957) and *Theater for a Story* (1959), later released as *The Sound of Miles Davis*, as the first jazz documentaries. The first jazz documentaries shown in theaters include *Jazz on a Summer's Day* (1959) and the French film *Django Reinhardt* (1959). Important films built around histories of jazz musicians along with footage of their performances would include *Big Ben* (Netherlands, 1967), *Mingus* (1968), *L'Adventure du jazz* (France, 1970), *Til the Butcher Cuts Him Down* (1971), *Jazz Is Our Religion* (Britain, 1972), *On the Road with Duke Ellington* (1974), *Always for Pleasure* (1978), *Jazz in Exile* (1978), *The Last of the Blue Devils* (1979), *Different Drummer: Elvin Jones* (1979), *Memories of Duke* (1980), *Dizzy Gillespie: A Night in Tunisia* (1980), *Imagine the Sound* (1981), *Ornette: Made in America* (1985), *A Brother with Perfect Timing* (1986), *Celebrating Bird: The Triumph of Charlie Parker* (TV, 1987), *Let's Get Lost* (1988), *Satchmo* (TV, 1989), *Lady Day: The Many Faces of Billie Holiday* (TV, 1991), *A Great Day in Harlem* (1994), and *Charlie Mingus: Triumph of the Underdog* (1998). In recent years, there has been an explosion of intelligently produced documentaries about John Coltrane, Gil Evans, Max Roach, Sidney Bechet, DeeDee Bridgewater, Bill Evans, Sarah Vaughan, and many others. Most were originally made for America's Bravo and PBS networks as well as for French TV's Sept Arte and Ex Nihilo production companies.

Filmmakers who create a documentary about jazz face the same challenges as other documentarians: they must spend many hours filming their subjects in both typical and extraordinary situations and then reduce all of it to a revealing and exciting feature-length film. If the subject is dead, the best archival footage must be found, but the same rules apply. Jazz documentarians have an additional problem, especially after jazz musicians began to think of themselves as artists and developed performance styles with little of the flamboyance typical of more popular musics. To keep it interesting, jazz documentarians are more likely to use unusual camera angles, overlapping images, and quick cuts from the musicians to more animated faces in the audience. Consider, for example, *Jazz on a Summer's Day*, Bert Stern's film about the Newport Jazz Festival of 1958. When Stern's camera is not zeroing in tightly to catch expressions on the faces of performers, it is constantly cutting away to motorboats off the coast of Newport, children playing in parks, and mildly unflattering images of fans scratching and squinting in the sun.

One of the artists filmed in *Jazz on a Summer's Day* was Thelonious Monk, a constant source of fascination for documentary filmmakers, in spite of or perhaps because of his opaque exterior. Director Stern did not even try to penetrate beneath the surface, showing Monk for less than thirty seconds while his camera looked elsewhere during a complete performance of *Blue Monk*. The directors of "The Sound of Jazz," the ground-breaking CBS television program that broadcast live performances of essential jazz artists to a national audience, took a different approach to the problem of Monk by placing an appreciative Count Basie at the other end of Monk's piano. Although he never plays a note while Monk is on the screen, Basie was probably there to domesticate the younger pianist, who was often compared to Basie because of their shared tendency to prefer a few well-chosen notes over more prolix improvisations. Basie's presence made Monk less bizarre by placing him near a beloved figure from the early history of jazz.

Even his death in 1982, Monk was still a puzzle that several filmmakers labored to solve. Matthew Seig's 1991 documentary, *Thelonious Monk: American Composer,* first broadcast on the Bravo cable channel, was keenly focused on placing him within a great tradition, going well beyond an association with Count Basie. Early on the narrator tells us that Monk was inspired by James P. Johnson, who once lived in the same neighborhood as Monk. Duke Ellington and Coleman Hawkins appear in photos with Monk and are named as key influences. Monk's work at the Five Spot with John Coltrane in 1957 shows his effect on the next generation of great jazzmen just as the earlier masters had inspired him. Toward the end of the program, the documentary introduces the group "Sphere," a quartet with two of Monk's former sidemen. The group began its career by recording only tunes by Monk, who died – coincidentally and poignantly – on the group's first day in the recording studio. The torch had been passed.

By contrast, Charlotte Zwerin's 1989 documentary *Straight, No Chaser* is much less interested in placing Monk within a vital tradition of jazz masters than in observing his eccentricities. While the Monk of Seig's 1991 film walks with dignity but is only heard speaking for a few moments, Zwerin records many of Monk's stranger utterances and regularly shows him spinning around in circles for no apparent reason. At best, Zwerin's Monk is a free spirit, too devoted to his music to care about much else. At worst, he is a deeply disturbed individual in dire need of the hospitalization he received on more than one occasion.

In *A Great Day in Harlem* (1994), the documentary about the famous photograph of fifty-seven jazz musicians posing in front of a Harlem brownstone in 1958, director Jean Bach gives us still another Monk. Although the documentary touches on most of the musicians who posed for Art Kane's camera one morning in Harlem, the film devotes a great deal of attention to Monk, portraying him as a trickster figure who could, in the words of saxophonist Johnny Griffin, listen carefully to what the other musicians were saying and then destroy everything they had said with "three or four words." At a climactic moment in *A Great Day in Harlem*, we learn that Monk was late for the photo shoot because he was busy trying on different clothes, eventually choosing a yellow sports jacket in full knowledge that he would stand out in a crowd of people wearing mostly dark colors. To call additional attention to himself in the photo, Monk made sure that he was standing near the two beautiful female pianists, Mary Lou Williams and Marian McPartland.

In their compelling portraits of Thelonious Monk, Jean Bach and Charlotte Zwerin are not especially interested in casting him as one of the great men of jazz. Because documentary cinema has for many years been as marginal as jazz, it has been neglected by many of the more ambitious male filmmakers, leaving a vacuum to be filled by women who are less likely to subscribe to the Great Man Theory of History. Female documentarians may have found it easier to break into a male-dominated industry with low-profile films about relatively obscure artists. Indeed, so many fascinating jazz documentaries have been directed by women that they practically make up a separate genre. A partial list would include *But Then... She's Betty Carter* (Michelle Parkerson, 1980), *Maxwell Street Blues* (Linda Williams, 1980), *Joe Albany: A Jazz Life* (Carole Langer, 1980), *Bix: Ain't None of Them Play Like Him Yet* (Brigit Berman, 1981), *Toshiko Akiyoshi: Jazz Is My Native Language* (Renee Cho, 1983), *Mary Lou Williams: Music on My Mind* (Joanna Burke, 1983), *Ernie Andrews: Blues for Central Avenue* (Lois Shelton, 1986), *Ornette: Made in America* (Shirley Clarke, 1985)*, The International Sweethearts of Rhythm* (Greta Schiller and Andrea Weiss, 1987), *Tiny and Ruby: Hell Divin' Women* (Greta Schiller and Andrea Weiss, 1988), *Listen Up: The Lives of Quincy Jones* (Ellen Weissbrod, 1990), as well as the films by Charlotte Zwerin and Jean Bach.

Regardless of their gender, all jazz documentarians give us their own, highly personal vision of an artist's life and work. Even when the subject is not as inscrutable as Monk, documentary filmmakers tell the story that best fits their own notions of what the artist ought to be, even if it requires them to do much judicious editing. Their films carry great authority, however, because audiences are willing to believe that the documentary camera only reveals the truth. Contemplating the striking differences among the various documentary portraits of an artist such as Monk should help us shed some of these naive notions.

Compilation films

A hybrid genre that offered a few helpings of jazz in the 1930s and '40s consisted of films with words such as "Parade," "Broadcast," "Canteen," and "Sensations" in their titles. These films almost always built slight plots around attractive couples, but the stories were regularly interrupted to feature popular entertainers. The Danish film industry deserves credit for making one of the first of these compilation films, *Krbenhavn, Kalundborg og – ?* (1934), especially because they included some of the best early footage of Louis Armstrong. Filmed in a studio in Sweden in 1933 and re-edited to give the impression that he is performing in front of a live audience, an elegantly dressed Armstrong sings, plays, and even dances in front of the French orchestra with whom he was touring at the time.

Duke Ellington knew how to make the most of his appearance in one of the first of several *Hit Parade* films. Filmed in 1937, the Ellington band performs *I've Got to Be a Rug-Cutter*, complete with a vocal trio drawn from the band's instrumentalists (Harry Carney, Rex Stewart, and Hayes Alvis). Putting down their instruments, the three step forward to accompany the band's regular vocalist, Ivie Anderson. Ellington wrote the tune specifically for the movie, surely knowing that his band would be much more visually dynamic with three singers harmonizing along with Anderson, who practically rushes onto the stage to sing about her need to succeed as a dancing hipster. The body of the film involved the careers of two radio singers, one trying to hide her past as an escaped convict. The other musical numbers in the film were performed by Eddie Duchin's orchestra, and groups known as "Pick and Pat," and "Molasses and January."

The occasional jazz artist turned up alongside comedians, dancers, and classical artists in the films of *The Big Broadcast* cycle (1932, 1936, 1937, 1938), but jazz people became a fixture of the genre when it flourished as a morale-builder during the years of World War II. Many stars were willing to make brief appearances in the canteen and parade films knowing that they were entertaining American boys before and after they went into battle. The plots of many of the films directly involved soldiers and the women they meet at events staged for them. In *Stage Door Canteen* (1943), for example, romance blooms between a soldier and a USO girl while Ethel Waters sings *Quicksand* with Count Basie and Peggy Lee performs *Why Don't You Do Right?* with the Benny Goodman orchestra. Audiences could also see Dorothy Dandridge with Count Basie in *Hit Parade of 1943* (1943), Lena Horne in *Thousands Cheer* (1943), Jimmy Dorsey in *Hollywood Canteen* (1944), and Cab Calloway, Woody Herman, and Dorothy Donegan in *Sensations of 1945* (1944). With the end of the swing era and the high popularity of jazz, the compilation film was more likely to feature rock'n'roll artists in films such as *Rock Around the Clock* (1956), *The Girl Can't Help It* (1956), and *Rock, Pretty Baby* (1956). Still, Count Basie would perform alongside rock groups in the compilation film *Jamboree* (1957) and Lionel Hampton would appear in *Mr. Rock and Roll* (1957), a celebration of Alan Freed and the rock groups he presented on his radio program.

In the 1940s, when the canteens and parades were most successful, the films typically allowed only one African American act into the cast. Filmmakers feared that more than one would lead audiences in the South and elsewhere to boycott the film. The films were even shown to certain audiences with scenes of black performers edited out. A major exception to the rule is *Reveille with Beverly* (1943), thanks to the heroic efforts of Jean Hay, a female disc jockey on whom the film's Beverly is based. Along with Count Basie and Duke Ellington, the film features performances by Bob Crosby and his "Bobcats," the band of Freddie Slack with Ella Mae Morse, and a young Frank Sinatra in one of his first film appearances. Although Ann Miller plays Beverly as an enthusiastic young woman who only wants to cheer up American boys on Army bases by playing their favorite music in the morning (hence the title), Jean Hay was the music supervisor for the film and fought to get the music she wanted. She successfully made the argument that the orchestras of *both* Basie and Ellington ought to be in the film, emphasizing the vastly different types of music they played rather than insisting on two acts with people of color. She also insisted that the bands perform their songs unedited, without cutting away to advance the plot as was too often the case in the various compilation films. Thanks to Ms. Hay's efforts, we now have precious footage of the Basie band playing *One O'Clock Jump* as well as the

Ellington band performing *Take the A Train*, complete with a vocal by Betty Roche and a few of the dance steps with which the unique trumpeter/violinist/vocalist Ray Nance regularly delighted audiences.

Short subjects

The compilation films drew upon a vaudeville tradition that strung together unrelated comedians, dancers, singers, and serious actors in a single evening's entertainment. But because these were Hollywood films, the canteens and parades gave audiences the involving stories and happy endings that were essential to American cinema's success. The industry retained a bit of its vaudeville heritage by putting short films on the bill along with feature films, even if there was no thematic connection. African American artists were making short sound films with experimental technology even before the industry was revolutionized by Al Jolson's singing in the hugely popular *The Jazz Singer*, the first major film with sound. Noble Sissle stood and sang while Eubie Blake played the piano in a short film, *Noble Sissle and Eubie Blake Sing Snappy Songs*, released in 1923. African American subjects were also essential in *After Seben* (1929), with an appearance by Chick Webb and his band, and *Yamekraw* (1930), a tone poem about life in the South with music by James P. Johnson.

Two extraordinary short films from 1929 reveal much about how the film industry conceptualized male and female musicians, especially when they were black. *St. Louis Blues* and *Black and Tan*, both directed by Dudley Murphy, also show that Duke Ellington was already a unique figure among African American performers in the first decade of his career. In her only appearance on film, the blues singer Bessie Smith stars in *St. Louis Blues* as a poor woman totally devoted to a dapper fellow who openly abuses her. At one point, she lies on the floor begging him to come back, even as he takes money from her garter and walks away with another woman. She ends the scene still on the floor, drinking gin and singing the blues. The trope that singers – especially female singers – express their feelings directly through song without intellection completely dominates the film's presentation of Smith's character. At the finale, when she stands at the bar with a stein of beer and sings the title song along with an orchestra and a choir, she is presumably doing nothing more than telling us how she feels about her man and what he has done to her. She just happens to be singing in the forceful and assertive tones we associate with the historic Bessie Smith, who was certainly no one's doormat.

In *Black and Tan*, by contrast, Duke Ellington is a dignified and principled artist. While Bessie Smith does not "play" a blues singer but is entirely contained within the film as a victimized woman, Ellington actually plays himself, a composer and bandleader to whom everyone refers as "Duke." The film begins with Duke at the piano wearing a tie, a vest, and a white shirt, but perhaps because he has immersed himself in the work of composing, he has taken off his coat and loosened his tie. He is clearly meant to resemble a professional man who has come to work dressed in a suit. And unlike the blues singer, who expresses her feelings "naturally" through song, Duke controls every aspect of his music as he teaches his trumpeter, Artie Whetsol, how to play the opening notes of his new composition, *Black and Tan Fantasy*.

Ellington's unique prestige is further in evidence when two illiterate black men arrive to repossess his piano. Played by Edgar Connor and Alec Lovejoy, who also appear in *St. Louis Blues*, the piano movers represent all the minstrel stereotypes that Ellington was already in the process of refuting. *Black and Tan* also features a performance by the beautiful Fredi Washington, who plays a dancer working with Duke's orchestra. Perhaps because she is slim and has fair skin, Washington bears little resemblance to the Bessie Smith of *St. Louis Blues*. Like Duke, she is called by her own name and is in control of her art as a dancer. Later, when Fredi collapses on stage while performing with Duke's band, the man who appears to be running the show orders the musicians to keep on playing even though it is clear that Fredi is seriously ill. At this point, Duke stops his band and walks offstage. No other black actor or musician would be afforded so much dignity in any film, long or short, for a long time to come. Just a few years after he had brought his orchestra from Washington, D.C. to New York, Duke Ellington had established himself as a serious composer and a man of principle. This achievement is all the more remarkable for a man who was black *and* a jazz musician. Thanks to an industry that made a wide range of short, inexpensive films, we have an extraordinary cinematic record of Ellington's early persona. Louis Armstrong was not presented with as much dignity, at least not in his first American appearances. *Rhapsody in Black and Blue* (1932) features the trumpeter in a dream sequence after a hen-pecked black man falls asleep dreaming that he has become "King of Jazzmania" and can order Armstrong and his big band to perform for his pleasure. Armstrong appears in a strange leopard-skin tunic. He is up to his knees in soap bubbles, presumably because the dreamer was mopping the floor before he fell asleep. Armstrong sings *I'll Be Glad When You're Dead, You Rascal You*, and *Shine* with his usual gusto. Unlike the more formally attired Armstrong who would appear the following year in *Krbenhavn, Kalundborg og – ?,* this Armstrong appears content to play the clown. But only when he is singing and gesturing. When Armstrong puts the trumpet to his mouth, we see a musician fully in control of his art, projecting the masculine intensity that would inspire several generations of trumpet players.

As with so much of early jazz on film, we must look beneath the stereotypical, racist images of black musicians to hear and see what jazz artists could nevertheless accomplish. *Pie, Pie, Blackbird* (1932), for example, features Eubie Blake and his orchestra with vocalist Nina Mae McKinney and the extraordinary dancing of the Nicholas Brothers in a nine-minute short that literally connects the blackness of the performers to the child's rhyme about "Four and twenty blackbirds baked in a pie." Roy Eldridge appears at the beginning of his career in the band of Elmer Snowden along with a team of athletic tap dancers in *Smash Your Baggage* (1933), a short that casts all the artists as baggage handlers in a railroad station.

Nevertheless, Duke Ellington continued to stand out as the only jazz musician regularly associated with the art of composing. Like *Black and Tan*, *Symphony in Black* (1935) shows Ellington in his studio, composing at the piano. The film even begins with an elaborately engraved invitation for Ellington to write a "new symphony of Negro Moods." Although Ellington later complained that the final film did not contain the image of African-American life he was trying to promote, he nevertheless succeeded in presenting himself as a serious artist with a mission. The stature of Ellington is all the more remarkable in *Symphony in Black*, in which a young Billie Holiday, appearing on film for the first time, plays the same type of abused woman as the Bessie Smith of *St. Louis Blues*, directly expressing her sufferings in song after her lover rejects her.

Perhaps the most ambitious film in the long history of the jazz short is *Jammin' the Blues* (1944). Before he would go on to produce the series of "Jazz at the Philharmonic" concerts and present jazz artists on his Verve, Clef, and Pablo record labels, Norman Granz worked with the "Life" magazine photographer Gjon Mili to film a group of nattily dressed jazz artists in a carefully staged "jam session." The icon of Lester Young with his pork pie hat and graceful demeanor was permanently inscribed in jazz memory by the opening images of the film: we see two concentric circles in what could be an abstract painting until smoke rises from a cigarette and the circles slowly move up to reveal that it is in fact the top of Young's hat. Eventually the audience sees and hears performances by Harry Edison, Illinois Jacquet, Jo Jones, Barney Kessel, Marlowe Morris, Sidney Catlett, Red Callendar, and John Simmons in a variety of performances, always photographed before a stark cyclorama with no set decorations except an occasional chair. Even when Marie Bryant sings *On the Sunny Side of the Street* and dances the Lindy Hop with Archie Savage, the austere setting for the film provided a striking visual analog for the idea that jazz played by black musicians was a serious art form. The voiceover narration that begins the film even refers to the music as "a midnight symphony."

Very few short films subsequently went as far as *Jammin' the Blues* in presenting jazz as art and in observing musical performances so scrupulously. At the time, the music was seldom taken seriously enough to be given such reverential treatment. And by the time the battle had been won and jazz was widely regarded as art, the victory proved to be a pyrrhic one. Jazz had lost its mass audience and no longer interested filmmakers looking for lucrative subjects to film. Virtually every white swing band had appeared in a short film or a soundie during the 1930s and '40s, and many of the great black jazz artists could be seen in short subjects prior to a feature film. By the 1950s, however, the feature film itself became the main attraction, especially when filmmakers strove to entice audiences away from their television sets. And if there had been more short subjects in movie theaters in the 1950s, they would have featured rock acts rather than jazz performers. The jazz short had served its purpose, and the television documentary, usually funded with corporate money, had become the dominant venue for jazz on film.

Satchmo the Great

Pete Kelly's Blues (Jack Webb, 1955)
Jack Webb and Lee Marvin

THE DECLINE AND FALL OF THE JAZZ BIOPIC

Krin Gabbard

As a genre in the mainstream cinema, biographical films about jazz artists have probably run their course. Although there have been rumors that Leonardo di Caprio is interested in playing Chet Baker and that Jim Carrey has optioned Donald Maggin's biography of Stan Getz, the possibility of these films actually being made is remote. Studio bosses surely know that recordings by jazz artists account for only 3% of all record sales. They also know that large American audiences are not likely to pay to see films about men with substance-abuse problems who play an austere art music. The instructive example here is *Bird*, Clint Eastwood's 1988 film on the life of Charlie Parker. Although the film premiered at high-profile film festivals and was lavishly covered in the jazz press, it only played in theaters for a few weeks and earned back less than a third of its $9 million budget.

The story of how a book about Billy Strayhorn did *not* become a movie is also instructive. David Hajdu's *Lush Life: A Biography of Billy Strayhorn* was a surprise success after its publication in 1996. The book was reviewed enthusiastically on the front page of the "New York Times Book Review" and in many other prestigious venues. It even appeared on a few bestseller lists. A substantial audience was apparently waiting for a story about a charming, gay, black genius who lived and worked in the shadow of the glamorous Duke Ellington in order to protect his privacy. Of course, Strayhorn's story *is* an intriguing one, especially in the capable hands of the accomplished journalist Hajdu. Irwin Winkler, who had produced some of the films of Martin Scorsese, optioned Hajdu's book and commissioned a screenplay from Jay Cocks, best known as the script doctor who saved *Titanic* (1997) as well as the screenwriter for Scorsese's *The Age of Innocence* (1993). Don Cheadle, an extremely versatile actor who has played dangerous sociopaths (*Devil in a Blue Dress*, *Out of Sight*) as well as dignified patriarchs (*Rosewood*), was the first choice for Strayhorn. Denzel Washington, surely the most prominent black leading man of the 1990s, was courted to play Ellington (although Lawrence Fishburn would have brought a more appropriately regal bearing to the role). The pop singer Janet Jackson expressed an interest in playing the part of Strayhorn's great friend, Lena Horne. An inspired choice for the part of Mercer Ellington was Cuba Gooding, Jr.: in films such as *Boyz N the Hood* (1991) and *Jerry Maguire* (1996), Gooding compellingly demonstrates that he can project the kind of pain and frustration that Duke Ellington's natural son felt at being neglected by his father while Strayhorn received most of the father's paternal attentions.

Cocks finished a draft of the script for the Strayhorn biopic, and several important directors were approached. The film was eventually assigned to a young director best known for his work on episodes of television series. The scale of the project was also reduced, and it was eventually conceived as a movie for the HBO cable channel rather than as a theatrical film. Less than two years after Cocks had finished his script, the project was dropped entirely. Although many in the jazz community would have been eager to see *any* film about Strayhorn, it seems unlikely that audiences would have turned out for the story of a gay African American, even if it boasted stars such Washington, Gooding, and Jackson. And by the time the script doctors at a major studio had finished with the project, most of what made Strayhorn fascinating would probably have been replaced with conventional Hollywood melodrama.

But even if the potential audience were much larger and more likely to ensure the success of a biographical film about a jazz musician, the sophisticated, even jaded filmgoers in this audience would probably not welcome a sincere and accurate account of the life of someone like Billy Strayhorn, or for that matter, Duke Ellington, Chet Baker, or Stan Getz. As one wag from the film studies community phrased it in 1994, why is it that Charlie Chaplin gets a terrible biopic and Ed Wood gets a great one? Indeed, *Chaplin* (1992) was directed with high seriousness by Richard Attenborough, whose leaden biopic of Gandhi was sufficiently pretentious to win an Oscar for best picture. Tim Burton's black-and-white *Ed Wood* (1994), by contrast, balanced on the knife edge between satire and straight realism as it chronicled the life of a man often considered to be the director of the worst film ever, *Plan 9 from Outer Space* (1959). For many of the best filmmakers, the bizarre seems to be the favored subject-matter and irony, the preferred tone. How else do we explain the release of high-profile films about Andy Kaufman (*Man on the Moon*, 1999), Bob Crane (*Auto Focus*, 2002), and Chuck Barris (*Confessions of a Dangerous Mind*, 2002)? And how else do we explain the confinement of recent biopics about Napoleon, Catherine the Great, and Victoria and Albert to the A&E television network? In addition, the Biography Channel, Ovation, and the E! network nightly provide documentaries about famous people using archival footage and interviews with acquaintances and scholars. On television and even in an occasional theatrical release, most of the important jazz artists have been given serious documentary treatment, often more than once.

But even if television has made theatrical biopics unnecessary, the absence of major films about Louis Armstrong, Duke Ellington, and Miles Davis – not to mention someone as fascinating as Charlie Mingus – is surprising. A film about Mingus could foreground, on the one hand, the violence to which he often turned in the face of racism and artistic frustration, or on the other hand, the profound pathos in his affair with Sue Mingus, to whom he was married just months before he learned that he had contracted the fatal disease, amyotrophic lateral sclerosis. (Of the two documentaries about the bassist/composer's life, *Mingus* [1968] tends to follow the first path and *Triumph of the Underdog* [1998] the second.) Even a relatively minor figure such as Art Pepper has provided filmmakers with an extraordinary autobiography that could easily be translated into a screenplay. But none of these jazz figures jumped from obscurity to great notoriety and then to early death as did Andy Kaufman and Bob Crane, not to mention Jackson Pollack, the subject of an ambitious biopic in 2000. For Armstrong and Ellington, the lives are too long, and the careers too even. Both had their ups and downs, but there was always steady work and no crash-and-burn endings. Neither Mingus nor Pepper ever blundered into great wealth and then, like Chuck Barris, blundered back into oblivion.

There was a time, however, when a musician only had to be popular to see his or her life made into movie. In 1943, when jazz was America's popular music, and when studios did not spend huge amounts of money in hopes that two or three of their films each year would make even huger amounts of money, Columbia Pictures released a film about the life of Ted Lewis, *Is Everybody Happy?* This may have been the first jazz biopic, although Lewis, the bandleader and raconteur who was extremely popular in the 1920s and '30s and worked with important jazz artists such as Benny Goodman, Fats Waller, and Muggsy Spanier, has long since been written out of jazz history. Like many biopics since, the film relied heavily on the plot of *The Jazz Singer* (1927) to trace the hero's escape from a working-class background, his conflict with a father who disapproved of popular music, his inspirational connection with a mother's love, his affair with a woman outside his original social milieu, and his eventual discovery by a large and adoring audience. *The Jolson Story* (1946) used the same plot to give drama to the life of Al Jolson, who starred in the original *Jazz Singer* and was in fact the model for the film's character Jakie Rabinowitz, who grows up to be the blackface entertainer Jack Robin.

In 1955 *The Benny Goodman Story* was effectively a remake of *The Jazz Singer*, complete with a finale in which the hero is allowed to crossover to a mainstream audience while remaining true to his Jewish heritage. The original *Jazz Singer* had a double ending, with Jack in cantorial robes singing Kol Nidre in the temple to appease the ghost of his cantor father and then with Jack in blackface singing *Mammy* on the stage of the Wintergarden Theater. *The Benny Goodman Story* also ends with Goodman (Steve Allen) in a theater, specifically the famous 1938 Carnegie Hall concert when the clarinetist/bandleader overcame his origins as a poor Jewish boy playing the disreputable music of Negroes and made jazz a concert art for an upscale audience. But the ending of *The Benny Goodman Story* is more economical than its predecessor, with Goodman featuring a stirring Klezmer trumpet solo by Ziggy Elman in the middle of a performance of *And the Angels Sing*, complete with a vocal by the unmistakably gentile Martha Tilton. Goodman did not need to rush to the temple and then back to the stage to show that he could be a thoroughly assimilated popular artist without abandoning his Jewish roots.

In the 1940s and '50s, the white jazz biopic told Americans that their heroes can have it all – love of the public, love of the mother, and in the case of Jews such as Jack Robin, Benny Goodman, and the Jolson of *The Jolson Story*, the love of a beautiful gentile woman. The only price is the hard labor it takes to produce a music that the public can love. Of course, the formula flatters Americans who like to think that they are tolerant and who need to be reassured that they are correct in loving the music that they love. The jazz biopic genre was modified only slightly to tell the story of the African-American composer W.C. Handy in *St. Louis Blues* (1958). As Handy, Nat King Cole overcomes the opposition of his devoutly Christian father and writes songs that delight the American public. Along the way he wins the attentions of an exotic cabaret singer (Eartha Kitt), substituting for the gentile goddess. At the conclusion of *St. Louis Blues*, the hero wears a tuxedo and sings the title song on stage with a symphony orchestra. But he too is true to his own culture, performing the music he learned from black laborers and blues singers. The life of Ricardo Valenzuela, who changed his name to Richie Valens and scored a hit record in 1958 when he put a rock beat to a song from northern Mexico, was given a *Jazz Singer* treatment when it appeared as *La Bamba* (1987). Even the white rapper Eminem chose a script with many resemblances to *The Jazz Singer* when he agreed to star in *8 Mile* (2002), a thinly veiled biopic of his own life.

At least one trope from the white jazz biopic has survived into the twenty-first century. In *8 Mile*, because the white hero performs black music, he must rely on the opinions of African Americans to validate his success. Competing against black performers in front of an almost exclusively African-American audience, Rabbit (Eminem) is reluctant to confront the deeply suspicious spectators but wins them over completely as he triumphs over the black rappers who have disparaged him. A scene in which Blacks wholeheartedly acknowledge the musical superiority of a white artist has been essential to the jazz biopic almost from the beginning. The first *Jazz Singer* banished Blacks from the screens while featuring performances supposedly borrowed from African Americans. But by the 1940s, when jazz increasingly functioned as the popular music most cherished by Whites, and when white musicians continued to be the most popular, it became increasingly difficult to deny that Blacks were the most innovative jazz performers.

Thus, in both *The Glenn Miller Story* (1953) and *The Five Pennies* (1959) (about the pre-modern cornetist Red Nichols), a white musician (James Stewart as Miller, Danny Kaye as Nichols) journeys up to Harlem to hear Louis Armstrong. In both films, the young protagonists drink bootleg liquor from teacups in a speakeasy and begin romantic relationships with the women they will eventually marry. And in both films, Armstrong bestows the imprimatur of jazz excellence on the fledgling musicians. The sexual maturation of young Benny also takes place at a crucial moment in *The Benny Goodman Story*. Immediately after being ridiculed by a young woman for wearing short pants, the boy wanders into a room where the New Orleans trombonist Kid Ory is performing with his band. Benny has never heard jazz before, but because he is Benny Goodman, and because he suddenly needs a musical language to express his feelings after a sexual humiliation, he joins in with Ory's band and plays with all the skill of an accomplished improvisor. Later, when Benny has reached the pinnacle of his success as a bandleader and has begun to romance Alice Hammond (Donna Reed), Kid Ory (played by Ory himself) shows up again, but only long enough to tell Benny that he has "the best band I ever heard anyplace."

A black musician also acknowledges his musical inferiority in *Young Man with a Horn*

(1950), loosely based on the life of Bix Beiderbecke. When the white trumpeter played by Kirk Douglas returns home and plays along with his aging mentor, the black trumpeter Art Hazard (Juano Hernandez) turns to the audience and says, "I taught him how to hold that trumpet he just played for you, but I didn't teach him how to play it – not the way he does." As late as 1999, the trope was still alive in Woody Allen's *Sweet and Lowdown*, a pseudo-documentary set in the 1930s about the fictional white guitarist Emmett Ray (Sean Penn), who idolizes Django Reinhardt. Even though his protagonist's idol is white (or at least a gypsy from Belgium), Allen nevertheless includes a brief scene in which two black musicians tell Ray that he is a terrific musician: "I never heard a guitar sound so good."

A comparable strategy in the white jazz biopic is to show a white musician taking the music of Blacks to new levels, whether to the concert stage at the finale of *The Fabulous Dorseys* (1947), and *The Benny Goodman Story*, or to the World War II military base where Glenn Miller transforms the blues into a morale-building march music. Later in *The Glenn Miller Story*, the men in Miller's band, looking chipper in their freshly-pressed military uniforms, play on without fear even as their English audience ducks at the sound of a falling rocket. Just as the white protagonists who take jazz into ornate concert halls have become the peers of classical musicians, the men in Miller's band have become brave soldiers as well as jazz musicians.

When jazz ceased to be America's popular music in the 1950s, the cycle of white jazz biopics quickly came to an end. (Working with an Italian production company, however, Pupi Avati was able to make an extremely thoughtful biopic, *Bix: An Interpretation of a Legend* [1991]. Avati employed mostly American actors and shot in many of the original locales where Beiderbecke lived and worked.) Films from the 1950s – the biopics of Glenn Miller, Benny Goodman, and Red Nichols – took an elegiac turn, while one of the final films in the genre, *The Gene Krupa Story* (1959), tried to capitalize on the notoriety that surrounded its protagonist after he was arrested on drug charges in 1943 and briefly forced out of the music business. But if the white jazz biopic was dead by 1959, the black jazz biopic was born just one year earlier when Nat King Cole played W.C. Handy in *St. Louis Blues*, even though the film had more in common with the many films about white artists who succeed in life as much as in show business. More commonly, films about black jazz artists were concerned with self-immolation.

The pattern for black jazz biopics was probably established in 1938 when Dorothy

Baker published her novel, *Young Man with a Horn*, shortly after she read Otis Ferguson's essay about Bix Beiderbecke in "The New Republic," also titled "Young Man with a Horn." At the time, little was known about the white cornetist other than that he had made some extraordinary recordings before dying in 1931 at the age of twenty-eight. For Rick Martin, Dorothy Baker's trumpet-playing protagonist, the jazz life is a treacherous one, especially for a Keatsian genius surrounded by philistines. Unable to find the audience he deserves but incapable of giving up his obsessive pursuit of musical perfection, Rick Martin has no alternative but to drink himself to death. Although an early draft of the 1950 film based on the novel ended with Martin dying on skid row after a long bout with failure and alcoholism, the version of the film that was eventually released brought the nurturing spirit, Jo Jordan (Doris Day), to his bedside. The Rick Martin (Kirk Douglas) of *Young Man with a Horn* discovers that there is more to life than jazz and ends up happily married to Jo Jordan.

Films about black jazz artists have historically relied much more on the jazz myths in Dorothy Baker's novel than on those in the film. In 1966 and 1967, two films appeared that, although not exactly biopics, featured self-destructive black jazz artists based closely on real-life models. *Sweet Love, Bitter* (1967), taken from John A. Williams' novel *Night Song*, traced the tragic career of Richie "Eagle" Stokes, a character designed to resemble Charlie Parker. *A Man Called Adam* (1966) ends with the breakdown and death of a trumpeter based on Miles Davis, in spite of the fact that Davis was extremely successful and even drug-free at the time the film appeared. In *Sweet Love, Bitter*, Stokes (Dick Gregory) is a profoundly asocial heroin addict. Playing the alto saxophone (dubbed by Charles McPherson) is the only thing he can do well. In *A Man Called Adam*, the protagonist (Sammy Davis, Jr.) drinks heavily and picks fights with white policemen and black girlfriends. In the most memorable scene, he threatens a powerful booking agent (Peter Lawford) with a broken bottle. The film ends with Adam in a moment of violent despair smashing his trumpet and then collapsing into a dead heap on the bandstand. The endings of these two films contrast sharply with the conclusions of the many white jazz biopics that picture the stars still alive and in their prime. Only *The Glenn Miller Story* ends with the premature death of its hero, but the final image of the smiling, uniformed Miller saying good-bye as he boards the airplane that is about to crash in the English Channel has little in common with the squalid deaths of the surrogates for Charlie Parker and Miles Davis. And one would never confuse the idealized end of Miller with the death of Charlie Parker in *Bird,* when

Eastwood and his screenwriters show Parker recalling the humiliating moment from his youth when a drummer told him to stop playing by throwing a cymbal at him.

Sweet Love, Bitter, *A Man Called Adam*, and *Bird* are built not so much on the lives of the self-destructive jazz geniuses but on the reactions of their white companions. A young schoolteacher (Don Murray) living close to the edge after the death of his wife encounters Richie Stokes in a pawnshop and subsequently protects him from himself as much as from those who would prey on him. In *A Man Called Adam*, much of the action takes place under the eyes of Adam's young white acolyte and trumpet student, Vincent (Frank Sinatra, Jr.). The film ends with Vincent clutching the mouthpiece from Adam's trumpet as if it were a sacred icon. Eastwood's *Bird* has not one but two white characters to help audiences understand the strange behavior of Charlie Parker. The film was widely criticized for relying too heavily on the accounts of Chan Richardson, Parker's fourth wife, and Red Rodney, the white trumpeter with whom he briefly performed in the 1950s. The filmmakers seemed mostly uninterested in what they might have learned from Parker's African-American ex-wives or from the many black musicians who knew him as well as anyone could know a man as complex as Parker. *Bird* suggests that audiences cannot know what to make of Parker (Forest Whitaker), usually photographed in partial darkness by Eastwood's cinematographer Jack N. Green, unless a white person is there to explain. For example, when Parker is institutionalized after a suicide attempt, he confronts an inmate who is playing chess. For reasons that are not immediately clear, Parker continues to provoke the man until they come to blows. Later on, in a scene with a hospital psychiatrist, Chan explains that because Parker has no drugs or alcohol in the institution, he needs to feel *something*, even if it is physical abuse from another person. Perhaps because audiences never see this aspect of Parker's character anywhere else in the film, and perhaps because the filmmakers do not believe that audiences can understand a black man's own explanations for his conduct, they need a coherent explanation from someone who is articulate in a more conventional sense. The filmmakers may also believe that, as much as white audiences may be fascinated by black jazz musicians – with their dark glasses, their jive patter, and their unstable emotional lives – people still prefer to have these images filtered through a more typically Hollywood sensibility.

Placing an articulate white person between black jazz artists and movie audiences was standard Hollywood practice for at least three decades, and in at least one case it seems to have crossed the Atlantic. In the French film *Autour de minuit*/*'Round

Midnight (1986), Dexter Gordon plays Dale Turner, a character based on tenor saxophonist Lester Young and pianist Bud Powell. Both musicians spent a good deal of time in Europe, and both suffered mightily from white racism. Francis Paudras, the commercial artist and jazz devotee who devoted a good deal of his time to looking after Powell, is clearly the model for Francis (François Cluzet) in *Autour de minuit*. At the opening of *Autour de minuit*, Dale Turner is a veteran tenor saxophonist living in Paris, who prefers to drink himself into a stupor when he is not on the bandstand. While most of the people around Turner, including his black female companion Buttercup (Sandra Reaves-Phillips), are interested primarily in taking his money, only Francis understands that the jazz artist is a true genius. In several encounters, Francis tells promoters, fans, and members of his own family (as well as the audience) what is best for Turner. At one point, after Turner has moved in with Francis and his young daughter, we see him flourishing in the comfortable new surroundings, composing at the piano and even cooking for his hosts. When Turner returns to New York and leaves Francis behind, he quickly becomes the prey of exploitative clubowners and drug dealers and dies soon afterwards.

Lady Sings the Blues (1972), based on Billie Holiday's autobiography, may be unique among jazz biopics on more than one level. First, it was something of a success, doing well at the box office and spinning off a successful soundtrack LP. It is also the only major film of its genre to tell the story of a woman, and it goes a bit farther than the two American films from the 1960s in endorsing a black nationalist view of the artist's life. Although Sammy Davis, Jr.'s production company was involved with the making of *A Man Called Adam*, and although the African-American Ike Jones was one of the film's producers, the film's boldest racial statement is to portray the black artist as the victim of a Whites-only power structure. *Lady Sings the Blues,* released at the beginning of the blaxploitation era, goes a bit farther in demonizing the Whites who prey upon the heroine. Otherwise, the film has much in common with the other black jazz biopics.

Diana Ross, whose personal popularity was surely responsible for much of this film's success, plays Billie Holiday as a fun-loving waif who overcomes a difficult childhood only to be turned into a heroin addict by one of the musicians in the white swing band with which she performs as a vocalist. Perhaps because the film consistently vilifies the many Whites who surround Billie, *Lady Sings the Blues* uses a black character rather than a white character to explain the protagonist's behavior to the audience.

When Billie seems to be performing successfully as a singer with a heroin habit, it is Louis McKay who knows that she is hooked. Played by Billie Dee Williams, the black actor once known as "the dark Gable," Louis McKay is Billie's savior, the only person who loves her and knows what is right for her. In fact, Louis McKay was not at all the manly saint that Williams plays in *Lady Sings the Blues.* He was, rather, one of many men who took advantage of Billie Holiday, largely because she seemed to be attracted to unreliable types such as McKay. When she died in 1959, Holiday was married to McKay, who became the executor of her estate and kept a close eye on the making of her biopic. Nevertheless, the filmmakers were able to slip him into a slot that seems to be essential to the black jazz biopic.

The Glenn Miller Story provides another illuminating contrast to a film like *Lady Sings the Blues*. In many biopics from the 1940s and '50s, the hero is devoted to producing something extraordinary and unique, whether it is the electric light bulb (*Edison, the Man*, 1940), a military victory (*Sergeant York*, 1941), beautiful paintings (*Lust for Life*, 1956), or an appealing musical sound. In the Glenn Miller biopic, we see him tinkering with various combinations of notes and musical instruments, eventually finding exactly what he is looking for. It is then up to the audience to discover the music. People who came to see *The Glenn Miller Story* because they liked his music could then congratulate themselves on admiring something to which one man devoted so much care and to which many other people, at least first, paid little attention. In *Lady Sings the Blues*, Billie Holiday is not a thoughtful, careful artist who labors at achieving the right sound. Because the film subscribes to stereotypes about Blacks, as well as about women and singers, Billie is purely reactive. Her singing is a direct, unmediated expression of what she is feeling at the moment. So, when she briefly breaks up with McKay, she sings *Tain't Nobody's Business If I Do* in order to express her defiance and independence, and then *Lover Man (Oh, Where Can You Be?)* to express her loneliness and lingering desire.

In the film's most absurd revision of Holiday's singing career, we see her accidentally witnessing a lynching while on tour in the South, as if she had no idea that such a practice existed. When she gets back on the bus, the audience sees the motionless face of the distraught Holiday but hears her voice on the soundtrack singing *Strange Fruit*. We are in effect told that Holiday spontaneously made up the song after seeing a "black body swinging in the southern breeze." In fact, the lyrics to *Strange Fruit* were written by Abel Meerpol, a New York City public school teacher and a Jew of Russian immigrant origin who published music under the name Lewis Allan. Rather than dramatize the moment when Meerpol brought the song to Holiday, who was so moved by the words that she sat down and set it to music, *Lady Sings the Blues* presents the song as still another product of Holiday's emotional state at that particular moment.

If, as the first musical and the first biopic of a musician, the 1927 *Jazz Singer* set the standard for all future jazz biopics, the film stands out as a typically American lesson in how hard work pays off. Anti-semitism is never an issue in the film, just as it is virtually absent from *The Jolson Story*, and *The Benny Goodman Story*. The conflict in *The Jazz Singer* is between father and son, and even that can be resolved before the end. Nothing else holds back the artist. Once he has resolved his family crises, the jazz singer can then reap the rewards of assimilation, popular acclaim, and the unproblematic love of a mother and a gentile sweetheart. The jazz artists in the biopics must all deal with comparable problems, even when the films are not unacknowledged remakes of *The Jazz Singer*. The conflict in *The Fabulous Dorseys* is between two brothers who cannot flourish within the same big band but who can reconcile once they have achieved even greater acclaim with their own individual orchestras. In *The Five Pennies*, the hero renounces music because he was not there to prevent his daughter from contracting polio, but the film climaxes when the child learns to walk again and the father undertakes a comeback. For the black jazz artist, however, the endings are less celebratory. Although *Lady Sings the Blues* ends with Billie performing for adoring fans, her image is superimposed over tabloid headlines publicizing her arrest and premature death. If audiences at the white jazz biopics could feel proud because they appreciate the music of someone so important as to be the subject of a film, audiences at black jazz biopics could feel good about themselves because they love the music of artists who were unjustly persecuted and abused. The black jazz biopics indulge voyeuristic fascination with drug addiction and self-destruction while providing audiences with the uplifting knowledge that they are capable of feeling great compassion for suffering geniuses.

Django Reinhardt (Paul Paviot, 1959)
Django Reinhardt

Les Liaisons dangereuses/Dangereus Liaisons
(Roger Vadim, 1959)
Jeanne Moreau

Odds Against Tomorrow (Robert Wise, 1959)
Harry Belafonte, Ed Begley, Robert Ryan

Shadows (John Cassavetes, 1959)
(Left) John Cassavetes

Shadows
(John Cassavetes, 1959)
Lelia Goldoni and Anthony Ray

The Five Pennies (Melville Shavelson, 1959)
Louis Armostrong (as himself)
and Danny Kaye (as "Red" Nichols)

The Gene Krupa Story (Don Weis, 1959) Unidentified (with clarinet), "Red" Nichols, Eddie Jackson, and Sal Mineo (as Krupa)

Jazz on a Summer's Day (Bert Stern, 1959)
Anita O'Day

Un témoin dans la ville/Witness in the City (TV title)
(Edouard Molinaro, 1959)
Lino Ventura

The Connection (Shirley Clarke, 1961)

Paris Blues (Martin Ritt, 1961)
Paul Newman and Louis Armostrong

Too Late Blues (John Cassavetes, 1961)
John Cassavetes and Stella Stevens

FICTIONAL JAZZMEN

Gilles Mouëllic

Otto Preminger's 1955 *The Man with the Golden Arm* will go down in film history as the first movie to squarely face the problem of drugs. It is no coincidence, however, that with the exception of Hollywood film biographies about the leading white figures in the history of jazz this is the first time in a major American feature film that the star's ambition is to be a jazzman – to make a living playing jazz.
Other films will follow this lead, from *Too Late Blues* (John Cassavetes, 1961) to *Sweet and Lowdown* (Woody Allen, 1999).
The fictional jazzmen of feature films, though not numerous, make up a fascinating portrait gallery. Many great filmmakers from Otto Preminger to John Cassavetes, Martin Scorsese, Francis Ford Coppola, Spike Lee, Woody Allen, and, to a lesser degree, Martin Ritt, have cast a jazzman in the lead role in order to tell the tale of another America. In these directors' movies it is no longer a case – as in *film noir* – of merely showing the underside, with its widespread corruption and violence. Rather it is an attempt to portray normal men and women fighting to preserve their dignity in a sick world. That dignity is shown as deriving from jazz, and the irrepressible drive to play a music that is *free*, without giving into the temptation of drugs, easy money (*Too Late Blues*), showbiz (*New York, New York*, Scorsese, 1977), or the mob (*The Cotton Club*, Coppola, 1984).
Often jazz-lovers themselves, these moviemakers also strive in their own ways to capture a specific period in the evolution of jazz. But in so doing they face a serious obstacle. All of these movies, with the exception of Spike Lee's 1990 *Mo' Better Blues*, feature white musicians in the starring role. There are many reasons for this and we will return to them in detail later, however they can be summarized in noting that in a Hollywood movie it is difficult if not impossible to give the leading role to a black actor. To give an honest reckoning of the history of this musical genre invented by Blacks therefore is a risky business. Still, many of these movies do manage to portray

with a fair degree of accuracy the daily struggles of black artists, either by having their voices heard without ever showing them (Preminger), by alluding to them repeatedly (Cassavetes), or by showing Blacks and Whites in confrontation – something seen much more frequently since *New York, New York*.

These movies span five decades and the tension between black and white worlds shown in them shifts gradually. From a wholly white viewpoint in *The Man with the Golden Arm* we move to a wholly black one in *Mo' Better Blues*. This shift has occurred gradually, like a slow traveling shot. Black musicians are already visible in certain scenes in *Too Late Blues*, their role throughout the film being that of making viewers feel ill at ease.

In *New York, New York* Jimmy Doyle does make contact with the black jazzmen: they play together on stage at the Harlem Club. But you never enter the black world with him, since every scene is perceived from Doyle's point of view (POV). The sequence in which he smokes a joint with the black musicians is highly symbolic. The camera never goes into the narrow bathroom stalls where the action takes place. Rather, it comes in to search for Doyle, to bring him back to the white man's world.

In Coppola's *The Cotton Club* the border between the two worlds is simultaneously crossed and reaffirmed by showing the reality of segregation and moving continuously from one POV to another, ranging freely from Dixie Dwyer's standpoint to linger on Sandman Williams and the goings-on behind the scenes at the Cotton Club.

With *Mo' Better Blues* you are unquestionably viewing things from the other side: Whites play no more than bit parts.

Jazzmen always play the solitary part, whatever their instrument, and the range of what they play is wide: Frankie Machine is a drummer (*The Man with the Golden Arm*). Ghost is a pianist (*Too Late Blues*). Ram and Eddie are trombone and saxophone players (*Paris Blues*). Jimmy Doyle is a saxophonist (*New York, New York*). Dixie Dwyer is a trumpet-player (*The Cotton Club*) as is Bleek Gilliam (*Mo' Better Blues*), and Emmett Ray is a guitarist (*Sweet and Lowdown*). What unites them is a drive to earn a living from their music and resist the many temptations of the nighttime world: drug dealing, gambling, *femmes fatales*, prohibition, alcohol and sleazy impresarios. Unscrupulous types right out of the *film noir* genre populate jazz movies. Nonetheless the link between jazz and the seminal *noir* movies of the 1930s and '40s is more imaginary than real. In a deserted cabaret a female vocalist's ballad accompanies the solitude of a loner; the silhouette of a sax sculpts the outlines of a vamp; the chords of a symphonic orchestra floating with the nighttime cityscapes swiftly muffle the blaring brasses. That is it, or just about it, and it is not much.

"The convergence of jazz and *film noir* is more myth than historic reality," writes Jean-Louis Comolli. However, as Comolli points out, "That doesn't in any way lessen its importance, since myths are more powerful and less well understood than reality." By giving their movies a *noir* background, Preminger, Coppola, Spike Lee or Woody Allen give their own spin to the myth. You could say the same for Cassavetes and Scorsese, whose characters, seemingly lifted from a thriller by Jacques Tourneur, seem trapped in sinister dead-ends.

Here jazz is more than merely part of the background. It is the goal, a way out. The ambition of the jazzman-hero is to become famous by playing his own music, even though, as Ghost puts it in *Too Late Blues* "That ain't gonna work. You can't touch a rainbow."

Frankie Machine, the man with the golden arm, a morphine addict and croupier in an illegal gambling joint, discovers the drums while trying a new de-tox method. When he gets out of the tank he has only one thing in mind: to master his instrument by listening to black bands playing on the radio and, one day, be a musician himself. For the first time in American movies jazz is neither glam nor colorful ethnic music but rather represents the road to freedom. Frankie tries to get the monkey off his back by inventing a life for himself as a musician – a first and decisive step – with a gig in a big band. He views it as his last chance.

For Ghost (*Too Late Blues*) and Jimmy Doyle (*New York, New York*) the choice between the compromise of mainstream music and the integrity of jazz is much more symbolic. Cassavetes and Scorsese debunk an enduring cliché of the jazz movies of the 1940s and '50s whose archetype is *Young Man with a Horn* (Michael Curtiz, 1950). In it a young white man discovers jazz thanks to several black musicians, one of which becomes his mentor. The disciple soon surpasses his master and imbues jazz with a universal appeal. The message is that while Blacks may excel with the colorful stuff, art remains the realm of Whites.

Cassavetes and Scorsese do not subscribe for a moment to this take: jazz is black music and white musicians no matter how talented cannot but recognize the immense distance that separates them from their black peers. The suffering of a people or nation (to which Whites do not belong) is the essence of black music.

Right from the establishing shots, *Too Late Blues* puts things into focus: black kids drum a beat to the sound of a little white orchestra that comes gradually into view.

Suddenly one of the kids grabs a sax and runs with it, blowing clumsily into the mouthpiece. The white musician tries to get his sax back but the other kids tackle him, pinning him down on a table. This "tension between the black and white spirit," evident once again in the party scene where several black musicians make fun of a singer with limited talents, is an underground theme running throughout *Too Late Blues*. At the end of the movie, after being humiliated in front of the woman he loves, Ghost has become the gigolo of a baroness who has taken on the job of finding him gigs. "If you were Art Tatum... but you're not," she says, before reading a roster of the other great jazzmen she has known. With this Cassavetes is making an obvious allusion to the celebrated Baroness Pannonica de Koenigswarter, a patron of the arts and the eccentric benefactress of Charlie Parker, Charlie Mingus and Thelonious Monk, geniuses with whom Ghost pales in comparison. The real ghosts of *Too Late Blues* are the giants of jazz whom Cassavetes admires. In other words, Ghost is little more than the pathetic ghost of those men who, unlike him, did not choose their destiny, for in the America of the postwar period, when you are black and a jazz musician you are too busy merely trying to survive.

Other ghosts haunt *New York, New York*, the ghosts of the big bands of the 1930s that thrilled the huge dancehalls from coast to coast. Jimmy Doyle is a lost hero, more witness than actor in a changing world. The movie's first scene is a classic swan's song. Young Americans celebrate the end of World War II by doing the swing as the Tommy Dorsey band plays. It is all glitter and glamorous settings, as in an MGM musical. But this dream world does not exist anymore, and it probably only ever existed in the movies. The dancehall scene slowly empties and Jimmy Doyle and his big band wind up playing for a handful of couples, ghosts, too, of days gone by. Doyle's awakening proves painful; he loses his beloved wife, the singer Francine Evans. Doyle wants to live for his music but the music has moved on – to the clubs where black musicians get it on with their jam sessions. At the Harlem Club, where Doyle can finally strut his stuff among fellow top musicians, he is a happy man with a sax. But though he may refuse to bend to the compromises of the white showbiz world he nonetheless does not belong to the world of black jazzmen either.

The world is no musical comedy dreamed by the young Martin Scorsese as he watches films by Vincente Minnelli. *New York, New York* conveys the director's fascination with musicals, accompanied by a bitter awakening, the realization that that fictional movie realm was also a place of tremendous racial exclusion, with Blacks as the number-one victims. In response and far from Hollywood, the Blacks invent the freest and most radical music ever: be-bop.

This meeting of two worlds, with jazz as a possible mediator, seems even less credible to Coppola in the violent, segregated America of the 1920s and '30s. His main aim is to show the Cotton Club, a mythical place in the history of jazz, where Duke Ellington led his band for many years. But the constraints on the production were such that Coppola had to settle instead for a gangster movie starring Richard Gere (Dixie Dwyer). It would be little more than a banal genre film if it were not for the virtuosity of the directing and, above all, the ever-present black music. Tap dance numbers and tunes follow one after another as the ghosts of Duke Ellington, Cab Calloway or the Nicholas Brothers haunt the celebrated stage. As in *Too Late Blues* and *New York, New York*, the world is divided among Whites (Dixie Dwyer, his brother Vincent and Vera Cicero, all in the pocket of the Dutch gang) and Blacks (Sandman Williams, his brother Clay, both Cotton Club dancers, and the wife he loves, the mulatto singer Lila Rose Oliver). Dixie is a jazz trumpet player but he quickly becomes a Central Casting gangster, quitting the music scene with no regrets: the "obligatory" sequences where Coppola has him playing with the black jazzmen leave viewers with no illusions. All the white characters are corrupt and embroiled in violence, iffy money deals and professional compromises. Only the black artists continue to dance, sing, play – and smile. The stage of the Cotton Club is a stronghold where the Blacks take power and resist in the face of this petty spectacle of human vanity. Music is a means of maintaining dignity no matter what humiliations one endures behind the scenes or on the street. The two worlds are irreconcilably distinct: no friendship is possible between Blacks and Whites.

Though Coppola submits without conviction to the conventions of the gangster movie, he makes up for this with frequent music scenes and through them gives movie-goers a glimpse of the film he really wanted to make: the story of Duke Ellington, hero of black music at the moment when it became *the* American music *par excellence*.

As in Coppola's movie, *Mo' Better Blues* centers on a jazz club with a very explicit name: Beneath the Underdog. Spike Lee shuns any reference to the past and situates things in a resolutely contemporary world. Every action plays itself out on stage, in the auditorium or behind the scenes of the Beneath the Underdog: musical or romantic rivalries between Bleek and Shadow, respectively the trumpet and sax players of the same be-bop band; the beating of Giant, the band's impresario and Bleek's childhood friend; then the beating of Bleek himself. The Whites are nothing but leeches: the club's owners exploit the musicians; Giant's debts are the bookmaker's fault; Shadow's white wife barges into the loges before the concert, a no-no. Showing as he does the flipside of the clichés associated with jazzmen, Spike Lee makes Bleek a black saint. Handsome, rich, sporty, smart, talented and hardworking he is the picture of the golden boy surrounded by beautiful women. He is also Spike Lee's militant mouthpiece and freely expresses displeasure at the presence of Whites in the audience at Beneath the Underdog. But as with the two-dimensional character of Bleek, the jazz being played is sanitized by the glamour of the movie, an ideal vehicle for a black identity quest that excludes members of all other ethnic communities. Duke Ellington, Charlie Parker and John Coltrane, whose silhouettes appear in various scenes, are nothing more than bloodless icons of an official jazz history refuted here for all time.

In the end Spike Lee shows himself to be the negative doppelgänger of Martin Ritt who, thirty years earlier, demonstrated the same Manichean dualism. But in Ritt's *Paris Blues* (1961) the question was not exclusion but rather integration. In it Ritt pretends to believe that jazz makes an ideal, color-blind world possible, especially when that world occupies the Hollywood version of Paris underground clubs where a requisitely mixed bunch of listeners come to nod their heads and snap their fingers while grooving in front of delighted black jazz players. The neo-realist angle seems like heavy-handed caricature, as do the characters themselves and the equally unlikely situations they find themselves in. Racial tensions were running high at the time in the United States (the setting is the early 1960s). But in the movie they are reduced to anecdotal incidents in what comes off as a picture-postcard Paris, inhabited by two American musicians. One of them, Ram (Paul Newman), is an exceptionally talented but ill-at-ease composer and trombone player, and the other is his best friend, Eddie (Sidney Poitier), a trumpet player and arranger. Ram, like Ghost, is on the threshold between two worlds, but unlike Ghost, Jimmy Doyle or Emmett Ray he wants to be recognized as a "serious" composer. Perfectly integrated into the world of jazz and admired by the maestro Wild Man Moore (played by Louis Armstrong himself) he nonetheless pays a call on René Bernard, pillar of the classical music world, who advises him to study, in proper order, the rules of composition, harmony, music theory and counterpoint. There is no irony here: Ram in fact stays on in Paris to "learn music." In *Paris Blues* Sidney Poitier and Louis Armstrong are present merely to reinforce the legitimacy of Paul Newman; jazz provides the seductive, colorful background in which everything rings strangely false. Four years earlier Martin Ritt was much more convincing with *Edge of the City* (1957) – a tale about, guess what, the troubled friendship of a black man and a white man, played by Sidney Poitier and… John Cassavetes.

With the notable exception of Bleek, the only black character with a starring role, these fictional jazzmen are complex individuals caught between the white community, whose values they do not share, and their fascination with a black community still victimized by a terrible past. Only Ram appears to renounce jazz to seek recognition in his own milieu.

For Spike Lee, in 1990, accounts are far from being settled, and the symbolic integration of Whites into the world of jazz is not on the cards. In *Mo' Better Blues* he makes no concession about the racial ownership of jazz, thereby reaffirming Coppola's take and underscoring the failures of Ghost and Jimmy Doyle. What he does not wish to see (or cannot recognize) is that times have changed: we are no longer in the Manichean dualist world of the 1930s (in which Blacks are excluded), or the revisionist world of the 1940s (in which Whites supposedly invented jazz).

There is nothing circumstantial about the interest in jazz of Preminger, Cassavetes, Coppola or Scorsese. Each tries to provide movie-going audiences with authentic music, and the Hollywood composers of *Too Late Blues* (David Raksin) or *The Cotton Club* (John Barry) take a backseat. Some of the top West Coast musicians (Shorty Rogers, Shelly Manne, Pete Rugulo, Red Mitchell, Benny Carter) feature on the soundtrack of *The Man with the Golden Arm* and *Too Late Blues*; Duke Ellington's finest pieces accompany *The Cotton Club* and *Paris Blues*, while Ralph Burns' arrangements for *New York, New York*, patterned after Georgie Auld (with Robert de Niro/Jimmy Doyle as stand-ins), exemplify the manner in which the jazz of the early 1940s met the musical challenges of the day. The excellent choice of Georgie Auld, a transitional figure between the swing and be-bop eras, allowed Scorsese to avoid an overt clash between the two successive jazz movements that segued more or less seamlessly.

There is no desire on the part of these moviemakers to selectively sift through or falsify history but rather to look it in the eye and acknowledge, perhaps clumsily at times, that jazz is owed a debt. It is the only musical form to have been invented in America, and its essence is Afro-American. The unease of the white jazz musicians shown in these movies corresponds to the feelings of guilt experienced by the moviemakers themselves.

The characters carry with them this sense of evolving history. Though in part the creations of screenwriters' imaginations, they are all (with the exception of Frankie Machine) inspired by real-life jazz greats.

Several mechanisms are at work here. Emmett Ray and Bleek Gilliam are outspoken in their admiration for their respective role models, Django Reinhardt and John Coltrane. The Williams Brothers, it has been said, brought to life the stars of the Cotton Club who were in reality the Nicholas Brothers; and Coppola shows no hesitation in bringing onto the scene Duke Ellington and Cab Calloway, played flawlessly by stand-ins.

This is absolutely comprehensible: the real ambition of Woody Allen, Spike Lee and Francis Ford Coppola was in fact to make film biographies of, respectively, Sidney Bechet (replaced in the fictional version by Django Reinhardt), John Coltrane (then Miles Davies) and Duke Ellington. All turned out to be abortive projects due to a variety of obstacles including rights, budgets, or screenplays that proved impossible to write (or all three problems combined). The biographical element in *Paris Blues* is embodied in the character of Eddie (Sidney Poitier), an idealized portrait of the many black jazzmen who fled America for Paris to dedicate their lives to music.

As regards Scorsese, he carefully avoided any direct portrayal of real musicians: the fact that Georgie Auld himself plays the sax parts of his fictional doppelgänger Jimmy Doyle is yet another wrinkle in *New York, New York*.

The case of *Too Late Blues* however is more complex. Cassavetes had worked with white West Coast musicians during the filming of the TV series "Staccato." They were the inspiration for the character of Ghost. These were men who sold their talents to Hollywood by playing jazz movie-music, a far cry from the realities of jazz in the late 1950s.

In *Sweet and Lowdown*, the 20th century's last "jazz-film," Woody Allen takes on in his own way the issues of jazz and drugs, jazz and showbiz, jazz and the mob, and the relations between the white and black jazz worlds. Emmett Ray distances himself from the "big issues" of Afro-American music and winds up being a comical figure: illegal substance abuse causes him to lose his memory for four days; his Hollywood ambitions are limited to a walk-on part in a short movie; always armed with a revolver he seems content to shoot rats at the dump and have a few recalcitrant prostitutes working for him. He boasts of his status as "second-best guitarist in the world" after Django Reinhardt, whom he reveres to the point of passing out in the presence of Django's "ghost." The black and white musicians get together late at night and they have jam sessions in a welcoming club. Jazz is a loving embrace for Woody Allen (the first tune played by Emmett is *Parlez-moi d'amour*), and represents a fraternal moment shared with the other musicians, the cabaret audience, and even with moviegoers. Not without irony *Sweet and Lowdown* revisits the relationship of jazz and the movies, with a focus on a specific period in jazz history: the glorious 1930s, when jazz had not yet come to be considered an art. Those just happen to be the magical childhood years of Woody Allen himself. Emmett Ray is the ghost not only of Django Reinhardt but of Woody Allen, who dreams of being a black jazzman in *Zelig* (1983). But these movies are more than just stories about solitary ghosts. Each of these characters long at one and the same time to come into their own, and to belong to a group. Indeed individual freedom is won through group participation. The improvisational part of playing jazz relies on the collaboration of the other musicians. A soloist, after his solo flight, has to rejoin the group and be ready to coordinate with his fellow musicians; the quality of each jam session depends on the ability of the players to step back into line. In this jazz might even be said to embody the mythical values of America itself: the pursuit of individual success and freedom within communitarian bounds. No wonder moviemakers bend over backwards in musical sequences to make moviegoers feel the freedom of improvisation and experience the immense pleasure of musicians playing together in a group. This is about more than just filming the movement of bodies. It is about capturing onscreen the energy transmitted by and between those bodies, and involves allowing the movie to invent itself before the viewers' eyes, like jazz improvisation, in the time it takes for the scene to roll. Beyond the storyline and its characters, what it is really about is letting the music play itself out naturally, at its own pace, and trying to answer the thorny question of how to capture on film that unique human experiment called jazz.

Stormy Weather (Andrew L. Stone, 1943)
Bill Robinson, Lena Horne, Cab Calloway

EPIPHANY AND REVELATION: JAZZ IN FILM

Ermanno Comuzio

Improvisation and much more

A blonde walks slowly on the sidewalks of a big city. Evening. The stores are ablaze with lights and the traffic is steady. Her mind on other things, she continues along, looking around and stopping every now and then, as if she were an outsider to the reality that surrounds her. She remains this way for some time.

If we look at this sequence from *Ascenseur pour l'échafaud* (*Frantic*, 1958, Louis Malle) without audio, what we see is rather banal, monotonous, repetitive – something that seems to have no significance at all. Of course, relating this episode to the context of the film we know that the woman is anxiously awaiting her lover who, after having killed her husband with her complicity, should catch up with her, but instead, he gets stuck in an elevator. The "stroll" in itself is inert. It takes on its rather vital, agonizing and tragic dimension with the music, improvised in front of the movie screen (a circumstance that has in fact made history in the relationship between jazz and cinema) by the great American jazz trumpeter Miles Davis, on tour in France in 1957, and his band composed of four local jazz musicians: Pierre Michelet (double bass), René Urtreger (piano), Barney Wilen (tenor sax) and Kenny Clarke (drums). In addition to the piece that gives life to the film sequence above, Davis and his fellow *jazz cats* improvise nine other numbers, a few of which are very short, while looking at the movie that was projected on the wall of the recording studio (even though the band had, more or less, decided beforehand with the director about their improvisations).

This is only one example of the contribution that jazz can make to cinematic images. *Improvisation* is undoubtedly an important aspect. In fact, a few "purists" believe that it constitutes the very essence of jazz, just like "pure" jazz is identified with American jazz – more precisely, African-American jazz – composed by Blacks. But we know that jazz is something more. Though this does not mean that the element of improvisation is not interesting for a "cinematic" reason as well; in *jazz talk* this is called *Fake*, as in false, simulation, fantasy, imagination, dream. In other words – cinema (*F for Fake*, as Orson Welles is known to have said).

Naturally, we do not intend to define jazz. Many are its vicissitudes and numerous are the aspects and characteristics it has taken on. Let us observe it as it is – the way that we are used to considering and distinguishing it from every other kind of music, even through all the "contamination" and uncertain attributions (precisely with regards to jazz used in films we can speak about "jazzy" atmospheres when dealing with jazz that is anything but "pure").

What is jazz? It is cinema itself that confuses our ideas when the first sound feature entitled *The Jazz Singer* (1927, Alan Crosland) is released, with an Al Jolson "Negro-ized" that has little to do with this kind of music. And Bob Fosse's *All That Jazz* (1979) is anything but about jazz. But at the same time it is once again cinema that attempts, in an imprecise way, to explain to us the meaning of jazz.

This happens, for example, in *A Song Is Born* (1948, Howard Hawks), a film in which jazz is one of the protagonists of the story in so far as it resolves situations. Danny Kaye, editor of a music encyclopedia, records on a tape recorder an entry on the "Birth of Jazz," going from the rhythm of the drums (Zurry Singleton) to the voices, the melody, the Spanish rhythms (Laurindo Almeida on lead guitar), the spirituals (and it is here that the "Golden Gate Quartet" performs, in one of its own arrangements, *Mookin's Bird*, which is a traditional upon which Antonìn Dvorák based the second part of his "From the New World Symphony"), up to true, authentic jazz with the performance of *A Song Was Born*, arranged by Gene De Paul and played, in addition to Zurry Singleton and Laurindo Almeida, by Mel Powell (piano), Lionel Hampton (vibraphone), Tommy Dorsey (trombone), Charlie Barnet (sax), Louis Armstrong (trumpet), Harry Babain (double bass) and others. While all these musicians appear with their names, Benny Goodman (clarinet) pretends to be a haughty "classical music" maestro stuck in for the occasion with these *swingin' cats* ("Benny Goodman? Never heard of him before," he says to his jam session buddies when the name is mentioned).

The first version of *A Song Is Born*, *Ball of Fire*, directed by Hawks as well in 1941, also had something to do with jazz. In a public hang-out the drummer Gene Krupa, after having accompanied Barbara Stanwyck in her song *Drum Boogie,* repeats the same number in an "intimist" version while tapping two matches on a matchbox.

A "new kind of music"

In *High Society* (1956, Charles Walters) it is Bing Crosby's turn to enlighten us about this rhythmical musical genre, presenting the band, guests at his party, composed of Louis Armstrong and his disciples. In a kind of somewhat free and easy "singing his lines," performed with the typical crooner style of this singer-actor, Crosby introduces the number *Now You Have Jazz*, with a school teacher's tone:

I want to show you now
        the size they are (or approximately)
        Jazz music is made.
        When you take some skin...
(at this point the movie camera focuses in on the drummer, Barret Deems)

Jazz now begins.
        Then you take a bass...
(camera focuses in on the double bass player, Arvel Shaw)

Take a bark on the rags...
(Billy Kyle on piano is shown)

Take a blue on a New Orleans boy...
(Armstrong on trumpet)

Ah, you take a stick
        with the lip...
(now we see Edmond Hall, the clarinetist)

Take a bone old phono...
(we see Trummy Young playing his trombone)

Take a spot cool and hot.
        Now you have jazz jazz jazz jazz.

Then Crosby moves on to *Touts ensemble* and while the band is performing he presents the musicians one by one, except Armstrong, who Crosby introduces thusly: "Now listen to this one, who you all know well." Satchmo speaks, specifying that jazz is known around the world – that it is the "King of the People."

In a nightclub, Julie Andrews (*Victor Victoria*, 1982, Blake Edwards) sings *Le Jazz Hot*, a strictly *swing* song in which this "new kind of music" is praised.

How has jazz been used in fiction films? The panorama is immense – a universe. Therefore, it would be better to limit our discussion by excluding for example jazz-films, authentic musicals, biopics, cartoons, though not claiming in any way of being able to cover everything. We will give preference to the "dramaturgical" use of jazz – that is, the cases in which this musical genre is not merely used as background music or is made to be listened to for itself, but is actually part of the events and stories narrated. A discussion, therefore, according to the perspective of cinema, without making any distinction among the different types of jazz or between "authentic" jazz devotees and amateurs. And this written contribution does not aim at being scientifically rigorous.

We all know, in the first place, the clichés of the piercing high notes of the clarinet that from inside nightclubs flood the streets around, the strong beatings from the drums that accompany the screeching of car tires as they race down the avenues, the muffled trumpet of *noir* jazz, the sax that shrouds deceit and loves gone wrong.

An interesting union of sound and images occurs in one of the first talkies made, *Hallelujah!* (1929, King Vidor), and which is not simply an anthology of the various aspects that Afro-American folklore music can take on. In this film, jazz becomes part of the drama (the music is a protagonist that is "necessary" in order for the story to unfold), even if *Hallelujah!* shows those tendencies of compromise and showiness that have always characterized Hollywood productions (in addition to traditional numbers, two new songs written by Irving Berlin were inserted into the film despite the director's opposition).

From the introductory blend of pieces (*Let My People Go*, *Nobody Knows*, *Hallelujah!*) to the finale with *Swanee River*, the entire film is teeming with spirituals and traditionals that carry forth the action: *Swanee River* and the cotton picking (the chorus is actually the "Jazz Jubilee Singers"); the tap-dance, accompanied with the banjo, of children after dinner; the lullabies of the mothers; the song (*Swanee Shuffle*) sung by the girl (the seventeen-year-old Nina Mae McKinney) who infatuates Zeke, the protagonist; *Swing Low, Sweet Chariot* sung by the chorus when someone is killed in a brawl; *Old My Religion* that accompanies the religious services of Zeke who becomes a preacher; *All God's Chillun* during a sermon on redemption, some blues by the mother and the abandoned girlfriend, the chain-gang songs and so on. An agonizing moment of the film occurs when Zeke, who lives with his new girlfriend, returns home tired from work and falls asleep in her arms. She quietly sings *St. Louis Blues*, preparing in the meanwhile for her escape with another man.

Black and *Noir*

An *all-Negro* beginning, therefore. Quite different from the customary portrayal, of long duration, of colored people as inferior and as scene embellishment. At times, however, even in this humiliating condition, black musicians have the upper hand. This is precisely what happens, for example, in *Hellzapoppin'* (1941, Henry C. Potter). The servants of a well-to-do residence – this is all pretend, naturally. In reality, these are top-notch musicians led by Rew Stewart (cornet), Slim Gaillard (guitar) and Slam Stewart (double bass); these last two created the duo "Slim and Slam" – idle around a table upon which there are the instruments that will serve for the white musicians for the party that evening. One makes his way to the piano. Another takes up the double bass. One by one other musicians approach the table and join in, one after the other playing the trumpet, the clarinet, the trombone, the guitar and the drums, pretending that everything is happening by chance. A kind of reversed "Farewell Symphony." And it is with this very *hot* performance and to this devilish rhythm that a group of colored women break out in an acrobatic dance.
With regards to *all-Negro* films, let us recall only "historical" titles such as *Green Pastures* (1937, William Keighley and Marc Connelly), *Cabin in the Sky* (1943, Vincente Minnelli), *Stormy Weather* (1943, Andrew L. Stone), *Carmen Jones* (1954) and *Porgy and Bess* (1959), both by Otto Preminger. But the point is not skin color. Jazz is multicolored, and it demonstrates this in films by putting together both Blacks and Whites.
For example, in *New Orleans* (1947, Arthur Lubin) Louis Armstrong is the leader of a patrol of musicians that abandons Storyville, the infamous *anything goes* section of New Orleans, because of an ordinance issued on November 12th, 1917 by the War Ministry. This exodus will promote the flourishing of jazz in Chicago and in the North (white and black, precisely), but that moment – for its protagonists – is unbearably sad. While walking away they sing and play *Do You Know What It Means*

to Miss New Orleans. This music brings tears to the eyes, and is performed by, in addition to Armstrong, Billie Holiday (in her only movie role, it seems), Woody Herman, Barney Bigard, Kid Ory, Charlie Beal, Red Callender, Zutty Singleton and other *dixieland* exponents.

It is without a doubt that this type of music reigns supreme (or rather, reigned supreme. Now, it is rock'n'roll that rules, even if jazz – often considered a music of the past – is not at all dead) in action and violent films. There is still the *beat* – that greatly rhythmed percussion pounding that vigorously characterizes chase scenes and beatings – and that which we call "syncopation," which is the displacement of beats or accents in a musical passage so strong that they become weak and vice versa. A displacement that is able to create a feeling of unrest and anxiety. In fact, jazz is not the only musical genre that willingly employs this rhythmic "hammering."

Rock and jazz represent two musical dimensions that confront one another in one of the most memorable films on teen angst, *Blackboard Jungle* (1955, Richard Brooks). For another film entitled *Rebel Without a Cause* (1955, Nicholas Ray) the musician Leonard Rosenman used a "learned" and contemporary kind of music, often utilizing dissonance and the uncertainty of the tonalities.

Getting back to *Blackboard Jungle*, this is a story of violence set in an inner-city New York school. The epoch-making opening of the film consists in the explosive *Rock Around the Clock* by "Bill Haley and His Comets," thus marking the official start of r'n'r. Though this is the main kind of music in the story, jazz, too, plays an important role as the "bearer" of "humanistic" values in relation to the apathy and insolence of a few juvenile delinquents. The teacher, an avid collector of rare jazz records (including *At the Jazz Band Ball* and *Jazz Me Blues* by Bix Beiderbecke), lets his class listen to a few pieces, but only fools himself by thinking that jazz music might be able to "soothe the savage beasts." Aware that the teacher cherishes these records, one of the students takes them from their jackets and one by one, sadistically, throws them up in the air or breaks them into pieces while his agonized teacher, too weak to fight back, looks on. Defeated, he leaves the school. This movie, however, does not have any metaphorical meaning; we should not think that this story represents, for example, a clash between two kinds of music and the victory of one over the other.

Cops-and-robbers stories very often use jazz. A few onscreen policemen are immortalized with this music: Peter Gunn adores the sounds of Pete Candioli, Dick Nash, Jimmy Rowles and Shelly Manne. Shaft is immersed in the numbers of Isaac Hayes and Jay Jay Johnson. Inspector Tibbs draws delight from the new notes of Quincy Jones and old tunes by Ray Charles. And it is once again Quincy Jones who leads the actions of the "new centurions" (*The New Centurions*, 1972, Richard Fleischer). Detective Marlowe goes from the melancholic oboe that follows Humphrey Bogart in *The Big Sleep* (1946, Howard Hawks) to the *swing* of (the more muscular) Robert Mitchum in *The Big Sleep* (1978, Michael Winner), to the congenital tiredness of Elliot Gould (*The Long Goodbye*, 1973, Robert Altman) entrusted to the piano that trickles forth "blue notes" of the bar that also acts as this Private Eye's office.

Hot rhythms and flaming pistols

The rhythm of the music is fused with that of the pistons of the Hell's Angels' motorcycles, led by Marlon Brando in *The Wild One* (1953, László Benedek). Here, Shorty Rogers' West Coast band adds excitement to the images, even though the composer of the music is really Leith Stevens (the first to introduce *progressive jazz* in Hollywood). In *Kiss Me Deadly* (1955, Robert Aldrich) gun shots melt together with the jazz rhythms, but melancholic moments of reflection (*I'd Rather Have the Blues* sung by Nat King Cole) are also present. In *The Sweet Smell of Success* (1957, Alexander Mackendrick), the story of a corrupt press agent, the rhythm of the rotary presses is blended with the sounds of Chico Hamilton's quintet. In *In Cold Blood* (1967, Richard Brooks), the story of two killers awaiting their execution, it is the sound of the trap door that opens under them that puts emphasis on the music of Quincy Jones, who in turn takes apart the typical jazz rhythms and turns them into separated, essential elements that are not arranged in a logical fashion but which create the feeling of a lamenting wait.

With regards to death-row prisoners who await their fatal moment, we must also remember *I Want to Live!* (1958, Robert Wise) where the contributions of Gerry Mulligan (sax) define the disordered surroundings in which the protagonist grows up and allude to the unsettling ending that awaits the woman, destined to face the electric chair. One of the important aspects of the film is that Mulligan composed the entire score without giving in to the conventional and usual adaptations that were so in fashion during those years.

Preminger, who gladly makes use of jazz, chooses Duke Ellington for his *Anatomy of a Murder* (1959), with excellent results. The protagonist of the film, a lawyer interpreted by James Stewart, is himself a jazz devotee; he has a discreet collection of records and occasionally "tickles the ivories." His idol, as luck would have it, is Ellington and in a nightclub one evening he gets to play with "Duke." Aside from the subtle elegance of Ellington's musical performance, jazz is often present in both the story and the dialogues of the film. Below is a short dialogue, taken from the movie, between Stewart and Lee Remick, who, while at his house, listens to a few of his records from his collection:

Lee: What a strange kind of lawyer. Listening to music like that.
Jimmy: Why, can't a lawyer love music?
Lee: Yes, but not this kind of music.
Jimmy: Well, I guess I'm a strange kind of lawyer.

With regards to "Duke," it would be impossible here to speak about the countless occasions where movie directors used his music, even many years after the pieces were actually written.
Killers, gangsters, shady characters. Oftentimes jazz is tied to strong feelings – feelings of hate and intolerance. In *Crossfire* (1947, Edward Dmytryk) jazz is present in a homicide scene caused by a veteran (Robert Ryan) who simply cannot tolerate his fellow black soldiers. Kid Ory (trombone) and his band offer the perfect mood to the action. This is also what happens when Ryan falls victim to a brutal beating in *The Set-Up* (1949, Robert Wise) because he refuses to lose a boxing match in order to please a few dishonest betters. Wise is also the director of *Odds Against Tomorrow* (1959), the story of a black singer, a maladjusted veteran and an ex-police officer who organize a bank heist, which ends tragically. The sounds used to emphasize the destiny of these three desperate men belong to John Lewis' *cool* jazz. In the place of the *hot* drum beats and the very high notes of the trumpets, the style is absolutely *cool*, in contrast to the "traditional notion that jazz, in order to be good jazz, has to be sizzling (*hot* was the actual term used back then) and vigorously aggressive."[1] The music of Lewis and his band is instead soft and subdued. They seem to be playing with "detachment and relaxation, almost with reserve, and more for themselves than for the audience."[2] But it is precisely this "softness" that makes the events more unsettling. Unforgettable is the episode where the three men, the night before the crime,

[1] Arrigo Polillo, *Il jazz di oggi*. Ricordi, Milan, 1961, pg. 96.

[2] *Ibidem*, pg. 96.

reflect near a lake, which gradually is overtaken by darkness – each person lost in his own thoughts, harboring unpronounced doubts. This moment is especially sustained by the French horn, the muffled vibraphone and a touch of the harp. The robbery sequence, or rather its preparation, is excellent. The dissonant and tormenting crescendo of the guitar and double bass in the moment of its diapason is abruptly cut short by the clock that strikes six – the hour of the crime.

There is however no need to resort to gruesome solutions in order to discover situations where it is precisely jazz that emphasizes, and oftentimes fuels, the drama that is taking place.

Let us take *The Man with the Golden Arm* (1955, Otto Preminger), for example. Here, Frank Sinatra interprets the role of a born loser, a gambling and drug addict. He is a drummer who is unable to keep up with the pace of the music. The performances of Shelly Manne (arrangements by Shorty Rogers) are incorporated into the score of a non-jazz musician (but quite sensitive to the rhythm), Elmer Bernstein. The results are excellent and very dramatic. Especially moving is the episode where Sinatra, called for an audition, is forced to face the failure of his efforts – the defeat of his attempts at changing his way of life – the impossibility of any redemption. A metaphor of impossible salvation, jazz becomes the figure of perdition in *The Asphalt Jungle* (1950, John Huston), in which the finale shows us a fleeing criminal who loses his freedom in order to listen to some jazz from a jukebox (he is entranced by a teen girl gyrating to the rhythm of the music).

(Provincial) boys with trumpets

Jazz can even become a torture. This is what happens in *The Big Combo* (1955, Joseph Lewis). It is interesting to note that the term *combo* is common to both gangster gangs and jazz big bands. The policeman (interpreted by Cornel Wilde) is captured by some gangsters and in order to torture him their *boss*, Richard Conte, uses one of Shorty Rogers' drum solos broadcast on the radio. He grabs from an accomplice his hearing aid earplugs and inserts them into the ears of the policeman. When the solo arrives, he raises the volume to the maximum, thus causing the policeman spasms of intense pain and agony. The gangster, obviously, is very familiar with the piece and waits for the exact moment of the solo so as to raise the volume and make it explode in the policeman's head.

Jazz as a nightmare, in other words. Let us take *The Naked Lunch* (1991, David Cronenberg). The sax player Ornette Coleman creates sounds that are converging/diverging with respect to the music of the London Philharmonic Orchestra used for the soundtrack (edited by Howard Shore).

Many are the dramas in which jazzmen are the protagonists.

Pete Kelly's Blues (1955, Jack Webb) is the story of a trumpeter, interpreted by the director himself, that rebels against the corrupt goings-on behind concerts. The opening sequence (going to the cemetery for the funeral of the protagonist's old colored teacher) both introduces us to the professional training of the musician and defines the atmosphere of danger and death in which his work takes place. The soundtrack is teeming with interesting performances, from Ella Fitzgerald who sings a piece composed for the occasion by Ray Hendorf (*Pete Kelly's Blues*) to the instrumental numbers of Joe Venuti, Matty Matlock, Eddie Miller, George Van Eps and Nick Fatool.

Another legendary vocalist who sings in a funeral scene, attaining a level of pathos that is almost unbearable, is Mahalia Jackson, who in *Imitation of Life* (1959, Douglas Sirk) sings the *spiritual*, *Trouble of the World*. It is performed during the funeral service of a Negro governess who dies of a broken heart because her daughter, a white child, denied her roots and went off to live by herself. Having arrived too late to make peace with her mother, there is nothing left to do but pay her last respects. It is also thanks to the music that the famous finale of the funeral opens up to a broader and more general meditation on the dramas and contradictions of a country. As writes a scholar of Sirk: "A few frames of the funeral procession through the frosted glass of a store window, the evocative presence of Mahalia Jackson with her touching gospels transforms the final funeral ritual into a dark and solemn epicedium that this director dedicates to America and to cinema."[3]

In *The Rat Race* (1960, Robert Mulligan), which narrates the story of a sax player (Tony Curtis) looking for fortune and glory in New York, the performances by Gerry Mulligan fit in perfectly with the musical score of Elmer Bernstein, the author of very harsh harmonies and rhythms. In the moment immediately after the scene where the sax is stolen, Mulligan's *bluesy* sax solo expresses the protagonist's unrelenting pain. Getting back to films about musicians, *New York, New York* (1977, Martin Scorsese), the story of a sax player of post-World War II tackling both relationship and career problems, is a good opportunity to re-create the atmosphere of the big bands of that

[3] Alberto Castellano, *Douglas Sirk*. La Nuova Italia, "Il castoro cinema" series, Florence, 1988, pg. 90.

age and to recuperate excellent pieces by Duke Ellington, Benny Goodman, Tommy Dorsey, Dizzy Gillespie and many others. The sax performances (Robert De Niro, who took music lessons for three months, is "dubbed" by Georgie Auld) are perhaps not extraordinary (as true jazz devotees sustain) but what remains nonetheless interesting is the dichotomy between the tension of De Niro and the compromises of Liza Minnelli, his onscreen wife. In fact, while De Niro, a restless "purist," wades through the difficulties, Minnelli increasingly wins public favor and recognition by catering to their tastes. "After the shared experience in a big band open to new solicitations and maybe precisely for this reason destined to commercial disaster, the sax player chooses the difficult path, while the singer opts for something decidedly easier: on the one side there are jam sessions, Blacks, combos, while on the other side there is publicity, chart albums, magazines, the musical. In other words, Harlem vs. Broadway – the small, smoke-filled hang-outs vs. majestic theaters."[4]

We already stated that we would not discuss biopics here. But we need to at least mention a "fake" biopic that was inspired by a true jazzman where, among other things, there is once again a funeral. The *Young Man with a Horn* (1950, Michael Curtiz) paraphrases the tormented life of Bix Beiderbecke, the legendary white trumpeter (narrated by Pupi Avati in *Bix*, 1991). Curtiz assures his protagonist, Rick Martin (interpreted by Kirk Douglas), a happy ending, despite the numerous attempts at self-destruction. The music is sensational, even though the trumpet player is "dubbed" by Harry James, whose performance does not faithfully reflect Beiderbecke's dramatic sound. A good moment in the film, though shrugged at by jazz purists, is when the protagonist unleashes his creativity (and therefore evades conventional dance band tunes) and performs with a personal touch *Get Happy*. He is fired right then and there. But the most intense episode is another: Rick Martin, who cannot find inspiration anymore in the routine of the dance bands, takes part in the funeral of his old teacher and, with his cornet, plays *Nobody Knows the Trouble I've Seen*, promising to himself that he will never again betray his teachings. "The genuinely musical aspects are also carried out with discreet precision, if we were to look, for example, at the opposition between the dance bands, characterized by a monotonous rhythm and trite tunes, and the extemporaneous, frenetic, always different and heartfelt jazz."[5]

An interesting detail in the film is that the narrator is Hoagy Carmichael, an authentic musician and one of Beiderbecke's friends in real life.

[4] Guido Michelone, *Il Jazz-film. Rapporti tra cinema e musica afro-americana*. Pendragon, Bologna, 1997, pg. 97.

[5] *Ibidem*, pg. 68.

Old and *New* blues

Jazz contributes in creating particular atmospheres and moods. Blues is already able, with its fixed cadence and agonizing repetitiveness, to carry us through a universe held together by fatality and suffering. *Cantando la pena – la pena se olvida* is a verse by Manuel Machado, referring to that flamenco which, according to some, is related to blues. "Sadness and pain, panic joy and a feeling of frustration: we can say that the entire existential array of human nature exposed to every form of civil and psychological violence has found its poetical and sonorous ritualizing in blues in an agonizing everydayness that gradually evolves into admitting the precariousness of hope in the afterlife and in this world."[6]

Let us begin with a few (fiction) films that already have in their titles the word "Blues." More than one film is entitled *St. Louis Blues*, but leaving aside the documentaries and the biography of William C. Handy, the legendary composer of the piece, let us mention only the movie directed by Raoul Walsh, which is of little importance and of no interest, musically speaking, except for the word "Blues" in the title and for one of Carmichael's songs.

John Cassavetes, a man who really knew his jazz, filmed in 1961 *Too Late Blues*, the story of a young jazz pianist interpreted by the pop singer Bobby Darin. In the film he is not able to make it big in the business. Here the theme, dear to this cinematic genre, of the clash between being faithful to one's own principles as an artist and the compromises that one is forced to make in order to survive is developed.

It must be pointed out that the preceding (and first) film of Cassavetes, *Shadows* (1959), also narrates the story of three jazz musicians. These three brothers are disappointed with their experiences and have given up all hope of avoiding a mediocre existence (the soundtrack, decidedly *free* in style, is entrusted to the double bassist Charlie Mingus, who often improvises, like Cassavetes who on the set would let his actors follow their own instincts).

Instead, *Paris Blues* (1961, Martin Ritt) narrates the hardships of two Americans in Paris – a white trombonist, interpreted by Paul Newman, and a black sax player, interpreted by Sidney Poitier. The first has little talent and sinks into the cheap Parisian nightclub scene, while the second returns to America, set on challenging those bigots who forced him to abandon his country. The story boasts of contributions from Duke Ellington, but there is also a performance by Louis Armstrong (who portrays

[6] Elena Clementelli and Walter Mauro (editors), *Antologia del Blues*. Guanda/Bompiani, Milan, 1977, pg. XIII.

himself in the film) at a jam session in a *cave*. A secondary character in the film, interpreted by Serge Reggiani, is a Gitano guitarist (who alludes to Django Reinhardt). *Mo' Better Blues* (1990, Spike Lee) is the tale of a gifted trumpeter (interpreted by Denzel Washington) who perhaps throws away this talent when he alternates, a bit too often, erotic activities with his music, although a critic affirmed that the film's director "creates embraces that resemble musical performances and trumpet performances that remind one of embraces" (the trumpet as a phallic symbol is quite recurrent). However, the film is successful in its depiction and description of a musician's "work" – rehearsals, contracts, arrangements, concerts, envy among fellow musicians. Soundtrack editor is Bill Lee, father of the director and jazz bassist, composer and arranger who gives preference to Branford Marsalis, Terence Blanchard and Kenny Kirkland, with noteworthy numbers (such as *A Love Supreme* by John Coltrane, a title that alludes to the "supreme love" for jazz).

In *From Here to Eternity* (1953, Fred Zinnemann), *Re-enlistment Blues* (original by James Jones, Fred Karger and Robert Wells) is present at various moments. We first hear the song during the opening credits when it blends in with, and then substitutes, the sound of the marching soldiers, thus revealing right from the start of the movie the melancholic mood that dominates the events in the lives of two unfortunate soldiers interpreted by Frank Sinatra and Montgomery Clift. The second time the song is softly sung in a dormitory by a group of soldiers accompanied by the guitar, while the others keep the beat by quietly tapping their feet on the floor. This is a moment where sadness abounds, even among the rough and tough soldiers. It is present once again and has a dramatic role when Sinatra is stopped in the city – a place where he should not be – by two military policemen and is beaten to death. Here, blues, which functions like a requiem, is also tied to the ill-omened destiny of Clift, the victim's friend, who gets his military service time doubled as punishment (in fact, the title of the number refers to an extension of military service). The tune dies off and gives way to silence with the close-up of the afflicted soldier.

It should be noted that Clift plays the bugle and always carries with him its mouthpiece with which he plays taps at Arlington Cemetery on the day of victory. And it is precisely taps that he plays in the courtyard of the military barracks so as to remember his dead friend. And once again, the same blues tune is in the finale, on Clift killed after a brawl with a violent and malicious officer.

Ragtime

A superb use of blues is made with Handy's *The Long Gone of Johnny Bowling* in *The Defiant Ones* (1958, Stanley Kramer). We hear it three times in the film and always softly sung, without accompaniment, by Sidney Poitier.

The first time is during the opening sequences when Poitier, who interprets a prisoner (who in vain is told to keep quiet by the racist hood, Tony Curtis), is about to be brought to prison. The second time it is used in a consolatory manner when the two, who have escaped but are chained together, are taken by surprise and tied to a pole to await a probable lynching. The third time is in the finale when the fugitives – reconciled after their common vicissitudes – are captured by the sheriff who was on their trail. In this scene Poitier, provokingly staring at the sheriff, begins to softly sing the piece and then gradually raises the tone of his voice as a sign of vindication and pride rather than insolence, as if to say: "You can catch us, but we remain free, inside." Handy's blues is adopted for the occasion by Ernest Gold. With regards to this, we should mention that for the best soundtracks thanks must be given not only to jazz musicians but also to composers of other genres, who though being the main authors of the soundtracks, wisely leave room for freedom, when the need arises, for the inclusion of pure jazz pieces.

A film where traditional blues gives way to "custom-made" blues is in *The Color Purple* (1985, Steven Spielberg). This story is about the cruel fate of a black American girl (in the first decades of the 20th century). Quincy Jones, a musician with a formal training but also a trumpeter and composer for jazz bands like Lionel Hampton's, created original numbers and a work of such skill that his songs cannot be distinguished from traditional pieces. One of these that stands out is *Miss Celie's Blues*, sung by a friend of the protagonist so as to console her (the voice is Tata Vega's). And it is to the unlucky girl that the protective friend sings:

> Sister, you've been on my mind
> Sister, we're two of a kind
> So, sister, I'm keeping my eyes on you…

Continuing with the atmospheres, a "primitive" kind of jazz is used in *Ragtime* (1981, Milos Forman), a fresco of early 20th century America. An important character is the black ragtime pianist (Howard Rollins). Unfortunately, this is not the kind of music that predominates in Randy Newman's score. The black pianist, who is the guest of a group of rich people who are somewhat reluctant in acknowledging his talent, makes a comment that is however interesting: "I read music so well that white folks think I invent it." Since we have mentioned a movie filmed in America by a non-American, we must therefore also cite *Pretty Baby* (1978, Louis Malle) where the colored pianist, interpreted by Antonio Fargas ("dubbed" on the piano by Bob Green), pounds away on his instrument in a New Orleans brothel, which is where the action takes place. The allusion to the legendary Jelly Roll Morton is clear, whose *Buddy Bolden's Blues* is performed, for example. There are also pieces by Scott Joplin, Louis Chauvin, "The Original Dixieland Jazz Band," Mamie Desmond and others. But it was Morton who inspired the film. Malle once said that he had desired, for some time, to make a movie on the beginnings of jazz, interested in Morton who really performed in the brothels of Storyville and who claimed to be the inventor of this music.

The ragtime tunes in *Nickelodeon* (1976, Peter Bogdanovich) are unforgettable. This movie is about the pioneers of silent films. Instead, the music in *The Sting* (1973, George Roy Hill) – taken from the ragtime of Scott Joplin – contains pieces that belong to an era much earlier than the 1930s, that is, the years in which the big "sting" perpetrated by the two buddies Paul Newman and Robert Redford takes place.

The jazz of Mal Waldron evokes a tough, merciless mood in *The Cool World* (1963, Shirley Clarke). For this story of troubled youths Waldron coordinates the performance of the "Jazz-Group" composed of Dizzy Gillespie (trumpet), Yusef Lateef (sax), Arthur Taylor (double bass) and Aaron Bell (drums). There is a dramatic exchange of trumpet and sax that at times oppose each other then blend together into one, as if to express the clash between two worlds – one of "normality" (which the boys in the film barely come in contact with) and the run-down neighborhood where they live.

In *Mickey One* (1965, Arthur Penn) the failures of the protagonist – a nightclub entertainer and victim of depression – are emphasized by the improvisations of Stan Getz (tenor sax). Jazz sets the scene in *The Cotton Club* (1984, Francis Ford Coppola), a film that narrates the story of this historic Harlem hang-out from 1928 to 1935. Instead of using jazz repertories, Coppola entrusts John Barry in the coordination of the noteworthy soundtrack and Bob Wilbur for the arrangements and adaptations, who also plays as a soloist the clarinet and the soprano sax. An endeavor that aims at reviving and recuperating the "philology" of the performances, and at giving, in the same time, a contemporary feel to the pieces played.

The lion's share is given to Duke Ellington, who made it big in this club. Interpreted by a young black actor, we see him perform various pieces, from the *Cotton Club Stomp* to more innovative tunes like *Creole Love Call* and *Mood Indigo*. Various jazz veterans were happily involved in this undertaking, including someone who had indeed performed with Ellington. (Curious note: it seems that Richard Gere, in the role of a trumpeter called Dixie, did not want to be "dubbed" at the horn.)

Smiles after the tears

But jazz is not only violence, drama, pain. To fully discuss and analyze jazz in comedies would require many, many pages. But here, we can proceed by mentioning only the most memorable examples. Consider the well-known tune to *The Pink Panther* (1964, Blake Edwards) composed by Henry Mancini and performed by the talented sax player Tony Coe. The *vieux jeu* jazz (Mancini again) in *The Great Race* (1965, Blake Edwards); the revivalism of *Some Like It Hot* (1959, Billy Wilder) which – presenting the performances of an all-female dance band (though infiltrated by two men) – re-creates ragtime tunes and traditional jazz of the 1920s and '30s with arrangements by Heinie Beau. The tune of *Down by Law* (1986, Jim Jarmush), music composed by John Lurie, will follow this director on his other endeavors. *Thoroughly Modern Millie* (1967, George R. Hill) is the story of a *Roaring Twenties* gal (interpreted by Julie Andrews) who foils the schemes of Chinese gangsters with the help of an eccentric millionaire (Carol Channing). The soundtrack, edited by Elmer Bernstein, is based upon the old and new material of Jimmy van Heusen and Sammy Cahn, Gershwin, Jimmy McHugh, Ray Henderfson and Erno Rapee. The most brilliant number is entitled *Jazz Baby* and is performed by the witty Channing during a party. Dressed in sequins, a short skirt and a tomboy's haircut, the woman describes herself as a child of jazz:

> My daddy was ragtime trombone player,
> My mammy was a ragtime cabaret-er,
> They met one day at a tango tea,
> It was a syncopated wedding
> And then came me...
> I'm a jazz baby...

With her quite unique voice, rough and ironic, Channing continues praising jazz (*That's the only thing I wanna do, so play me a little jazz*) and plays various instruments – from the piano to the trumpet, the banjo, the baritone sax, the vibraphone, played with her feet while dancing.

Songs from other musical genres that have been *jazz-ized* are quite amusing. Let us recall only a few examples, among the infinite quantity. In *Murder at the Vanities* (1934, a "mystery" by Mitchell Leisen) Ellington's musicians, decked out in 18th century costumes, perform Liszt's "Second Hungarian Rhapsody" after having thrown the music sheets into the air. In *Four Daughters* (1938, Michael Curtiz) four girls, the daughters of a music teacher, canonically perform Schubert's *Serenata* (piano, violin, harp, voice) and then rebel against their father's pedantic teachings and replay the piece, *jazz-izing* it. In *Being There* (1979, Hal Ashby), the stroll of the bizarre protagonist along the streets of Washington is accompanied by the jazz version of the theme of the Superman from "Thus Spake Zarathustra" by Richard Strauss, which became famous especially thanks to Kubrick's use of this piece in his *2001: A Space Odyssey* (1968).

We could also cite *The Blues Brothers* (1980, John Landis), even if here we are dealing with jazz-rock (actually, more rock than jazz).

A director who practices jazz even outside movies is Clint Eastwood, fervent pianist. For his films starting from 1985 he has called upon Lennie Niehaus, one-time sax player with Stan Kenton's group and with West Coast bands. Two films directed by Eastwood pertain directly to jazzmen. One is *Honkytonk Man* (1982), the tale of a wandering musician who never abandons his guitar despite the numerous problems (including an illness that ultimately causes his death). The second is *Bird* (1988), a splendid biography of Charlie Parker.

Woody Allen deserves a special category all to himself – the nostalgic clarinetist who in all his films imposes the jazz of his younger years (he grew up listening to the radio station that broadcast "serious" music all day long), but with regards to him and his musical choices much has already been written. A director who, though not a musician, loves all types of music, including jazz, is Martin Scorsese: "I used to live in a crowded neighborhood where you could constantly hear the music that came from the apartments on the other side of the street, from the bars and candy shops. The radio was always turned on, the jukebox played from across the street and in the houses you could hear opera in one room, Benny Goodman in another and rock downstairs."[7]

For example, Scorsese's *The Last Waltz* (1978) is about the final concert of the jazz-rock band, "The Band," and his "film-container" of all musical genres, including jazz, is *Casino* (1995).

[7] Cited in Anton Giulio Mancini, *Angeli selvaggi. Martin Scorsese e Jonathan Demme*. Métis, Chieti, 1995, pg. 75.

Not only America. Jazz Italian-style

And so, without intending it, we have discussed, up to now, American cinema. And European cinema – does it use jazz? Yes, and how! The fact is that this type of music was undoubtedly born and bred in the United States. This holds true a little less for Europe. The Old World, however, was "invaded" by jazz with talented jazzmen and excellent bands. In fact, European cinema at times turns to this type of music.

Let us start with Italian cinema. Jazz is quite sporadic in Italian cinema during Fascism, even though a few pioneers did indeed employ it in perhaps "domesticated" versions in the tradition of the Petralia, Angelini, Semprini, Frustaci bands, present on the radio before in cinema. The Fascist regime attempted to contain the phenomenon by minimizing it, slandering it ("music of savages") or adapting it to local sounds (*St. Louis Blues* became *The Sadness of San Luigi*: Armstrong made an appearance in Turin in 1935). However this may be, a composer like Amedeo Escobar, active, especially, in the cinematic genre during Fascism defined as "telefoni bianchi" (white telephones),[8] but also in adventure films, dramas and comedies, came from the first Italian jazz band – the "Black and White Jazz Band," created in 1921. Alberto Rabagliati, *swing* singer with experience in America, took part in various films. And at times jazz is incorporated into local contexts with much pleasure and enjoyment, like in the 1932 film *La telefonista* (Nunzio Malasomma) where we see Isa Pola being courted by Luigi Cimara, making Sergio Tofano die of jealousy, in a nightclub where an American-type band, with many colored trombone players, performs a catchy Italian tune that has been *jazz-ized* (on the bass drum in a careful ethnic blend there appears the writing "Carlo and His Orchestra"[9]).

More or less authentic jazz must wait for the end of World War II to affirm itself.

[8] This was how the cinematic genre diffused in Italy during Fascism was called and which imitated sophisticated American comedies.

[9] In the original.

And it does this with a vital and disorganized force, especially as a manifestation of a "return to life." It is mostly confined to dance music, to the longing for rhythm ("syncopated music"), diffused by the Hot Clubs that gradually pop up all over Italy and by nightclubs where people want to have fun and forget about the troubles caused by the war.

Neo-realistic cinema – which represents the most valid aspect of Italian cinema during those years – did not know how to make the most of the contribution that jazz music could offer. References to jazz serve, for the most part, in cinema to denote the presence of Americans in a devastated Italy (the *boogie-woogie* was all-purpose). There are few examples of this. We find one at the beginning of *Il bandito* (*The Bandit*, 1946, Alberto Lattuanda), in which Amedeo Nazzari, a veteran returning from Germany, arrives in his city only to find his home and neighborhood in ruins, accompanied by the brilliant rhythm of *A Tisket a Tasket* sung by Ella Fitzgerald. In *Vivere in Pace* (*To Live in Peace*, 1947, Luigi Zampa) it is the horn of a drunken black soldier, hidden by the inhabitants of a small town in the Latium region, that hands him over to the Germans. In another film by Lattuanda (*Senza pietà/Without Pity*, 1948) it is the mix of *All God's Chillun* and *Nobody Knows* that gives wings to the tragic finale where a black military deserter kills himself with his Italian lover, unable to fully realize their love and dream of freedom. Later, Pier Paolo Pasolini makes use of grief-stricken blues (*Sometimes I Feel/Like A Motherless Child*) for the birth of Christ in his *Il Vangelo secondo Matteo* (*The Gospel According to St. Matthew*, 1964), thus suggesting in the moment of joy the tragic ending of a son who would cause, by his death, great pain to his mother.

During the 1950s a series of entertainment films debuts with music by the "Roman New Orleans Jazz Band" and later by Piero Piccioni, Romano Mussolini, Pino Calvi, Piero Umiliani, Armando Trovajoli and other *jazz cats* who offer rather brilliant musical accompaniment, Italian-style. *I soliti ignoti* (*Big Deal*, 1958, Mario Monicelli, music by Umiliani: a film that started the trend), *Crimen* (*… And Suddenly It's Murder!*, 1960, Mario Camerini, music by Calvi) and *Sette uomini d'oro* (*Seven Golden Men*, 1965, Marco Vicario, music by Trovajoli) all had wonderful results.

Humor and comedy even extend into later years. We have, for example, an amusing caricature of black funerals, characterized by slow funeral processions going to the cemetery and fast-paced, joyous returns, in *Escalation* (1968, Roberto Faenza). In the grotesque sequence of the funeral of the protagonist's wife, killed by him so he could inherit her money, Ennio Morricone plays upon the sad procession to the funeral and the joyous return home, which reflects the state of mind of the protagonist who has been happily "freed."

A few "dramatic" results are also noteworthy. Let us take some examples from a few films of Piccioni, the most prolific in this field. In *La spiaggia* (*Riviera*, 1953, Alberto Lattuanda) we have a light jazz that is similar to popular songs – it is the music of the "respectable" people who at the beach on vacation, free of all inhibitions, go wild and try everything under the sun. *Nata di marzo* (1957, Antonio Pietrangeli) has piano jazz that is subdued and melancholic and which defines the protagonist's broken family. And in *Adua e le compagne* (*Adua and Company*, 1960, Pietrangeli) the top-notch performances sound desperate and hateful in the drums, in the low notes of the piano and in the exchange between trumpet and trombone in the moments of defeat. In *I magliari* (*The Magliari*, 1959, Franceso Rosi) jazz acquires precise, harsh and clear-cut significance both when it is onscreen (performed in certain places, listened to at the jukebox, etc.) as well as when it brings to mind a cosmopolitan, modern, international way of life, which is precisely the thing that the small German swindlers would like to have. But this music can also become violent and aggressive like when a boss's vendetta is unleashed because the swindler Totonno (Alberto Sordi) dares to work on his own.

Locals and outsiders under the Tricolor Flag

The guitar and organ mark, at times melancholically then dramatically, the troubles of the very young protagonist in *I dolci inganni* (*Sweet Deceptions*, 1960, Alberto Lattuada), with a *cool* touch in the finale during the girl's return home alone. *Cool* jazz is also present in *La giornata balorda* (*From a Roman Balcony*, 1960, Mauro Bolognini), as well as in other films including *Le Mépris* (*Contempt*, 1963, Jean-Luc Godard), a work that cannot be defined in so far as in the Italian edition the original material was "mutilated," claims the critic Morando Morandini, by the producer Carlo Ponti.

The most interesting, most modern, most "integral" from a musical point of view jazz creation of Piccioni is probably the soundtrack to *Un tentativo sentimentale* (*A Sentimental Attempt*, 1963), a film in which the set designers Pasquale Festa Campanile and Massimo Franciosa debut as directors. For this sad story about a troubled couple (Françoise Prévost and Jean-Marc Bory) the musician composes a subtle plot that, especially in the very beautiful exchange between the piano and the double bass and in the performance of the trumpet (by Nunzio Rotondo), wraps itself around the failures of the characters and their inability to communicate.

Piccioni knows how to obtain good results even with "poorer" means, as is demonstrated in the emotional use of a catchy rhythm (the *let kiss*) in the suicide of the female protagonist in *Io la conoscevo bene* (*I Knew Her Well*, 1966, Antonio Pietrangeli). Other Italian musicians, not necessarily jazzmen, also attain good results. Splendid is *La notte* (*The Night*, 1960, Michelangelo Antonioni) in which Giorgio Gaslini, creator of a jazz hybridized with contemporary concert music and, together with his quartet (consisting of himself on the piano, Alceo Gnatelli on sax, Ettore Univelli on double bass and Eraldo Volonté on drums), illuminates the desolate solitude of a couple, Marcello Mastroianni and Jeanne Moreau. It should be pointed out that the quartet is present "on-screen." The music is not a mere narrative "comment" provided by the classic "invisible band": in fact, the group improvises and plays live during the actual shooting of the film. The performance at the end of the movie is particularly significant and confirms the existential failure of the protagonists, defenseless and desperate after a hopeless night, by a vital jazz that is in contrast to the couple's lifelessness. This performance was recorded right at dawn by the musicians, tired after a night of filming and waiting. If Luchino Visconti nurtures his films with references to classical and opera music, his nephew Eriprando gives preference to jazz. During the filming of *Una storia milanese* (*A Milanese Story*, 1962), the story of a failed love between two young people set in middle-class Milan, Eriprando asks John Lewis if he can use one of his numbers. But since it is not available, this American musician on tour in Milan with the "Modern Jazz Quartet" composes an original soundtrack for the film. However, the members of his band had already returned home, and so Lewis uses the "Milan Quartet" (two American musicians living in Europe, a Belgian, an Italian and a Hungarian gypsy). The music gives the story a *cool* musical dimension – actually, icy, intellectual – which denotes with precision the feelings of the characters.

Even in other instances have Italian directors relied upon foreign jazzmen. Mario Nascimbene, after having "flirted" here and there with jazz, for *La prima notte di quiete* (*The Professor*, 1972, Valerio Zurlini), a tragic tale of an intellectual in crisis, uses the American trumpeter Maynard Ferguson (accompanied by the Italian Gianni Basso, tenor sax). From the exchange of these two instruments, which brings to mind the works of Ellington, a splendid repertory of music is born: "Impetuous, full of tension, painful the phrasing of the trumpet – a phrasing that wanders in the sea and sky of a wintry Rimini, where the film is set," specifies Nascimbene. "The sax is soft and melancholic that instead stresses the desperate search for love and the hopes for happiness."[10]

Bernardo Bertolucci in his *Ultimo tango a Parigi* (*Last Tango in Paris*, 1972) calls upon Leandro "Gato" Barbieri (Ennio Morricone had already used two of his themes for Bertolucci's first film *Prima della rivoluzione/Before the Revolution*, 1964). Barbieri composes and performs for *Last Tango* a soundtrack created with great effort and "contaminated" by other kinds of sounds – from those that are superimposed and indistinct in a modern way to rather romantic pieces by strings. And naturally there is the tango and there is the sax, especially effective in the painful film finale.

[10] Mario Nascimbene, *La prima notte di quiete*. CBS/Sugar Records, Milan, 1972.

Lost and found?

Jazz nurtures all the films of the Italian director Pupi Avati, uncertain in his younger years whether to take up the clarinet or embark upon the career as a director (Lucio Dalla was also a member of Avati's group). Jazz as dream of America by the provincial boys from Italy's Emilia region (*Aiutami a sognare/Help Me Dream*, is the title of one of his films) – a magical world on the other side of the Atlantic – a world depicted on the silver screen, by the musicals and by jazz legends. In his movies (and films for television) jazz is therefore always present. *Cinema!!!!* (1979) is an anthology on jazz with music from Tommy Dorsey, Bing Crosby, Nat King Cole, Louis Armstrong, Frank Sinatra, "Fats" Waller, Benny Goodman and many others. Another movie, *Jazz Band* (1978), narrates the activity of the musical group Avati once belonged to, composed of young boys in the 1950s who, as Avati himself says, possessed no other "reality where they could take refuge, where to pour forth their enthusiasm and hopes than in the world of jazz, Italian-style – actually, Bolognese-style – with a gaze forever fixed on the greats in America."[11]

And in the already cited *Bix* (1991) Avati celebrates a jazzman – the legendary cornet player Bix Beiderbecke – and uses the performances of Lino Patruno (living memory of jazz, cinema devotee and owner of precious jazz film curios) for an interesting operation of reusing original recordings. The arrangements, by the American Bob

[11] Claudio Casarola, *Pupi Avati e la musica*. Degree thesis, University of Parma, academic year 1991-1992.

Wilber, are performed by musicians close to the Chicago tradition (among these there are the cornet player Tom Pletcher, the "voice" of Bix, the sax-clarinettist Bob Wilson and Patruno, who collaborated with the screenplay, on banjo and guitar).

A moment of transition from the old to the new, unfortunately without any follow-up, is the 1980 movie *Oggetti smarriti/Lost and Found*, directed by Giuseppe Bertolucci and produced by his brother Bernardo, who for the music calls upon Enrico Rava (from Trieste) – a veteran trumpeter "imbued" with free jazz and of a vigorous, aggressive and modern personality. In the quite bewildering universe of Milan's central train station the music of Rava penetrates with subtlety and an unsettling effect when the "reproduction" of the real sounds of the station leave room for "reflection." The trumpet and the piano, to which the double bass at times joins in, are the essential instruments of an endeavor that is refined and meditated upon. And it does not matter if we are still dealing with jazz or instead we should speak about music that is informal or polytonal or whatever else. In any case, what occurs in this exchange is that which Marco Borroni calls, in one of his articles in "Cineforum" with regards to cinema and jazz, the "diverging function of the soundtrack," based not so much "on the generic functionality as on the possibility of creating meaning beginning with unique, unexpected and never-before-heard numbers gathered together."[12]

The presence of Rava in a few soundtracks brings us to Battista Lena and Roberto Gatto, editors for soundtracks and representatives of jazz/cinema of the 1980s and '90s. The two (Lena – guitarist and Gatto – drummer) both collaborate with Rava on various projects as well as compose and perform the music for the films of Francesca Archibugi.

The film *Romance* (1986, Massimo Mazzucco, music by Andrea Centazzo) is symptomatic of the new times. The protagonist – a wonderful and elderly Walter Chiari – is a nostalgic of cinema and of jazz: he remembers everything of *Lady Sings the Blues* (1972, Sidney J. Furie), plays the piano and sings good ole American songs, blues and spirituals. At the same time, the musical contribution made by Centazzo fuses this type of music with synthesizers. A new era is truly upon us.

France, Great Britain and "New Waves"

For the other European countries we must limit ourselves to few examples. French directors, like their Italian counterparts, used both home-grown and American jazzmen.

---

[12] Marco Borroni, "Cinema e jazz" in "Cineforum," n. 356, July-August 1996, pg. 43.

Jazz is given preference in the *séries noires* (both in dramas and *noir* comedies) and in the stories of teen angst. In *Rendez-vous de juillet* (*Rendezvous in July*, 1949, Jacques Bécker), for example, the performances of Claude Luter, Rex Stewart and Mezz Mezzrow are present. And *Les Tricheurs* (*The Cheaters*, 1958, Marcel Carné) offers numbers by "Jazz at the Philharmonic" on tour in Paris, with Dizzy Gillespie, Roy Eldridge, Stan Getz, Coleman Hawkins and Oscar Peterson.

The jazz of Jimmy Giuffre, Bob Brookmeyer and Jim Hall (recorded in the United States) plays a dramatic role in *Tant d'amour perdu* (1958, Léo Joannon). The same holds true for the performances of: Art Blakey and "The Jazz Messengers" in *Des femmes disparaissent* (*The Road to Shame*, 1959, Edouard Molinaro) and for Blakey, once again, in the company of others in *Les Liaisons dangereuses* (*Dangerous Liaisons*, 1959, Roger Vadim); Martial Solal in *Léon Morin, prêtre* (*The Forgiven Sinner*, 1961, Jean-Pierre Melville) and (together with Mal Waldron) in *Trois chambres à Manhattan* (*Three Rooms in Manhattan*, 1965, Marcel Carné); Gerry Mulligan in *La Menace* (*The Threat*, 1977, Alain Corneau).

The first film of Jean-Luc Godard, *À bout de souffle* (*Breathless*, 1960), boasts of an original soundtrack by the already-cited pianist and composer Martial Solal, who with his "chamber" jazz provides (after Django Reinhardt) the first original contribution, European-style. Thanks to the music, the story of the thief from Marseilles and his young American friend takes on the feeling of a life thrown away and of a chase towards irreparability (thanks also to the interruptions and cuts made by the director, who even then claimed the right to intervene with the music, which is a material that can be shaped according to one's own needs, or rather, according to cinematographic needs). This is a sign of the "new wave" in French cinema. And not only in French cinema.

Some directors show more predilection towards jazz than others. One of these is Louis Malle, who we discussed earlier with regards to *Ascenseur pour l'èchafaud* and *Pretty Baby*. Among his other films enriched by this musical genre we should mention *Le Souffle au cœur* (*Dearest Heart*, 1971) and *Lacombe Lucien* (1974). The first makes use of the sounds of Sidney Bechet and Charlie Parker, while the second film has the performances of Django Reinhardt and the "Hot Club de France Quintet." Another director is Alain Tavernier, author of a documentary on the aspects of the authentic, original jazz of America's "Deep South" that were still relevant back then, *Mississippi Blues* (1983). Tavernier is also responsible for *Autour de minuit* (*'Round Midnight*, 1986), a movie dedicated to the passion of certain French milieu for jazz. This film narrates the friendship between a young French jazz devotee and an African-American sax player (interpreted by Gordon Dexter while in Paris) who is a gifted musician but quickly heading towards self-destruction because of his drinking problem. It is precisely the admiration and friendship of the Frenchman who saves the musician from total ruin – at least for as long as he remains in France. The jazzman plays be-bop in excellent performances. The numbers (coordinated by Herbie Hancock) are recorded live, and are inspired by Bud Powell and Lester Young, to whom the film is dedicated. All in all, a result not "accompanied" by jazz but "determined" by jazz.

Mention must also be given to British cinema. The most interesting period regarding the relationship between jazz and cinema in Great Britain is perhaps the *free cinema* period, even because the word "free" denotes a particular kind of jazz.

Once liberated from conditioning, the experimenting of new things was undoubtedly the stimuli that fueled, during the period between the end of the 1950s and the beginning of the '60s (the same time of the French New Wave movement), renewal in both cinema (the "young angry youths") and jazz. In fact, an exponent of this music, the sax player John Coltrane, is given the nickname *the young angry man*.

John Addison, composer who loves to flirt with jazz and leader of the "angry" trend, expresses with sharpness the ever-present ambiguity in English films of the period, placing together easy, traditional pieces and really "free" ones, such as in *Look Back in Anger* (1958, Tony Richardson). Here, the protagonist plays the trumpet and participates in jam sessions in nightclubs where the trombone player Chris Barber performs, who is one of the fathers of British jazz during post-World War II; in *The Loneliness of the Long-Distance Runner* (1962), in *A Taste of Honey* (1961) and in *Tom Jones* (1963), all by Richardson, the most intransigent exponent of the movement.

Also noteworthy is a "true" jazzman – Johnny Dankworth – who in England becomes the most celebrated figure of this kind of music. He plays the alto sax and his phrasing, just like the sound of his band, is rather advanced and progressive. Dankworth's music is present in *Saturday Night and Sunday Morning* (1960), *Morgan – A Suitable Case for Treatment* (1966), both movies by Karel Reisz, in *The Servant* (1963) and *The Accident* (1967), both by Joseph Losey. As a rule, in films Dankworth himself plays his instrument, semi-improvising. And especially in *The Servant* he transforms his jazz into something close to the timbres and harmonies of modern "learned" music. Even though at the root there is always jazz – actually, early jazz. In fact, in certain sequences of the movie the music derives from blues and a true, authentic blues sound dominates the night stroll of the "boss," who later becomes servant to his servant, along the streets of London.

But even the "new" British cinema grows old and despite its re-emergence in more recent productions, it is difficult to still find something, in relation to jazz, which picks up this trend once again.

Eastern Europe

Little known, but nonetheless interesting, is the situation in Eastern Europe. Poland is the leading nation with regards to its absorption of jazz. The most important figure is Krzysztof Komeda, who tragically died in 1969. He is brought to the silver screen in 1958 by Roman Polanski and remains this director's musician until his death. Komeda also worked for other directors, collaborating with a cinema that broke with tradition and which was provokingly modern. At the basis of his musical contributions is almost always a kind of jazz that is very brilliant and *free* in its expression, picking up on and making his own the *cool* sounds of Lennie Tristano. We hear this for example in Polanski's films, *Nóz w wodzie* (*Knife in the Water*, 1960), *Repulsion* (1965), *Cul-de-sac* (1966), *Rosemary's Baby* (1968) and in other films such as *Niewinni czarodzieje* (*Innocent Sorcerers*, 1960, Andrzej Wajda), *Mój stary* (*My Old Man*, 1962, Janusz Nasfeter) and *Bariera* (*Barrier*, 1966, Jerzy Skolimowski).

Less interesting is the presence of jazz in the other eastern European cinemas, which however undergo a productive and artistic renewal during the 1960s. And even though Russian cinema has films where youths play their guitars and perform in dancehalls, jazz is rarely and fleetingly present. Instead, in two films jazz is the protagonist. *My iz dzhana* (*Jazzmen*, 1983, Karen Shakhnazarov) narrates the adventures of a student head over heels for jazz and for this reason expelled from a conservatory. The boy, however, does not get discouraged and puts together a quartet, opposed by bureaucrats who claim that jazz is "reactionary." *Taksi-Blyuz* (*Taxi Blues*, 1990, Pavel Lounguine) is the story of a sax player whose musical instrument is sequestered by the taxi driver he does not pay. It illustrates the conflicting relationship between two contrasting types: the artist, on one side, and the petty middle-class person – nostalgic of the regime and worried only about his pay. Seemingly a comedy, the movie is rather bitter and harsh and aside from the contrast of these two differ-

[13] Guido Michelone, *Il Jazz-film. Rapporti tra cinema e musica afro-americana.* Cited above, pg. 121.

ent lifestyles, "in the protagonist's *free* style sounds of the sax there is a cry for help, frustration, the pain and fear of the unknown and for the future."[13]

It should be noted that the theme of the jazz artist opposed by the government authorities of "real Socialism" is present in various Eastern European films.

Things change, but not too much

Finally, let us note, in conclusion to this rhapsodical "toccata," two or three things. The first is revealed to us by an American scholar: "The way in which jazz is used in any film tells us many things about the people that made them. We discover something about their way of life, their feelings, their sense of rhythm and tempo and their ability to narrate, not to mention their cultural attitudes. Considering jazz as a neutral and non-determining element is like turning our backs on the cinematic and dramatic possibilities it has to offer."[14]

[14] Taken from *American Film*, Vol. II, n. 5, March 1978.

In other words, jazz in fiction cinema reveals the soul of the directors. For better or for worse, upon the silver screen it is transformed and becomes a different language. It belongs more to the world of cinema than to the universe of music.

Another consideration derives from references outlined in this discussion. We have given numerous examples, though not a definitive collection. But there are really many movies in which jazz becomes the "key" to interpreting the story. I refer to the moments when we actually *see* jazz, besides hearing it, not so much in that we participate in a performance but that this music becomes an image – it becomes cinema. And yet jazz results particularly consistent with cinematic language. The French scholar François-Bernard Mâche once wrote that "music is very rarely reduced to a simple bearer of meaning; all it has to have is significance, but like the waters in a river rather than like a syllogism."[15] This is an affirmation that adapts itself quite well to jazz and which emphasizes, unintentionally, its adaptability to the flow of the images.

[15] Cited in Jean-Jacques Nattiez, *Musicologie générale et sèmiologie.* Ed. Christian Bourgois, Paris, 1987.

However, it still remains rather strange that the process of renewal of cinema does not rely more on, as one would expect, this musical genre, even if a reason may be the change in tastes and the appearance of new kinds of music (electronic, rock). Today, jazz – long ago were the days where, as Armstrong would say, it was "only good for the feet" – is increasingly considered a "learned" remnant of the past. Leonard Bernstein, great admirer of this music, said the following in 1955: "And so, in a certain sense, jazz has become a kind of chamber music – an evolved and refined art form destined to be listened to, full of the influence of Bartók and Strawinskij and is, therefore, very, very serious."[16]

[16] Leonard Bernstein, *The Joy of Music*. Anchor Publishing, New York, 1994.

In any case, many directors, freed from their bonds to tradition and Hollywood rules, privilege a kind of cinema that welcomes the practice of improvisation and therefore the implementation of jazz should increase and not diminish. It is not even true that jazz must renounce its improvisation, as some sustain, referring to the strict rule of timing, which would coerce musicians to the absolute observance of this. Just as what generally occurs for music in films, these temporal impositions mortify inspiration only in appearance. Fortunately, various are the cases where jazz perfectly adapts itself to the dynamics on the screen; and in the end, even if not obligatory, improvisation or semi-improvisation remains typical of jazz.

Truffaut declared himself contrary to improvisation and other directors uphold that jazz is incompatible with cinema. Lalo Schifrin, Argentinian jazzman who gives preference to this kind of music (even in contaminated form) in his soundtracks, sustains that jazz has been employed too much by cinema.

However it may be, *things change*, as David Mamet affirms in one of his films.

Just like canonical jazz is gradually being replaced by pop music in all of its expressions, passing on to forms that are difficult to define (there are musical expressions that are defined as *non jazz*), and a certain part of present-day film production may actually be called *non cinema*. But these are abstract concepts – theories. What counts, and will continue to count, are the results. Someone once said that jazz is like water under pressure – that it cannot be contained, that it spreads out and constantly transforms itself, overflowing in a thousand directions. Even among images in motion. And jazz is like a water-bearing layer that shows no signs of drying up.

Make Believe Ballroom (Joseph Santley, 1949)
Virginia Welles and Jerome Courtland

A DATE WITH JAZZ: NOTES ON JAZZ AND ANIMATED FILM

Michele Fadda

Let us immediately advance the question, or rather the hypothesis, that at least with respect to cinematic language, the meeting of two dimensions – the visual and the auditive, which seem bound to each another by an almost magnetic attraction – is not always characterized by a smooth and complete integration. This is well-known and specifically involves the relationship between the moving image and music, starting from the advent of talkies. More than seventy years have passed from when Al Jolson first appeared in *The Jazz Singer*. And yet we cannot in any way claim that cinema, over the course of its evolution, has always been able to redeem the soundtrack from its clear and quite shameful position of subordination. Certainly, Eisenstein's contrapuntal intuitions regarding the possibilities offered by sound have been assimilated into various modalities in numerous significant examples. But in the vast corpus of world filmography, this does not prevent something from occurring – that is, in the majority of cases the music does not succeed in leaving behind and going beyond its function as a secondary element or banal filler.

Naturally, we are making generalizations. And seeing that we are doing so, let us dare to affirm the following: that, in theory, this kind of limitation in expression is rarer in animated cinema for a structural reason. Contemporaneous to the advent of the talkie, the art of animation necessarily gravitated towards a dimension that involved its very survival in a "strong" relationship with sound. Here, the music manifests itself in a position that is absolutely not subordinate and the cartoon becomes more than ever a matter of "rhythm." Both the transmutations exhibited by the figures and those rendered explicit in the notes tend to justify each other in a constant exchange between music and iconography amplified to the point where oftentimes we cannot tell which indeed came first – the chicken or the egg. Already starting from the Mickey Mouse of *Plane Crazy* (1928), the effects of sound immediately had a greater impact with respect to "live action" cinema. And in fact, as Scott Curtis so astutely observed, in cartoons it is more difficult to identify the boundary that separates the intradiegetic sound from the extradiegetic one because dynamics can bring about that (in many regards) definitive condition of the audiovisual. And this, not by accident, is called *mickeymousing* – the complete synchronization between images and sounds that constitutes, after all, the very same corpus of "classic" animation.

But which music? Which modality of animation? And which kind of agreement between sound and images? Let us consider the case of jazz – that is, a musical exercise that, at least in theory, for the structure of the organization of each individual number and for its improvised nature, would seem to be in synch with the syncopated progression and with the autonomy and freedom in expression of a medium that, with respect to "live action" cinema, should be self-referential. Besides, if we turn our attention to the production of cartoons during the silent movie era, we realize that the analogy could subsist even without the explicit presence of the music. There exists a sort of interior music in the adventures of Felix the Cat (the character-symbol of the so-called "Jazz Age" and one of the first zoomorphic personifications of the *black character* in cinema) seeing that the very title of a classic by Otto Messmer, *Felix Woos Whoopee* (1928), reminds us how the continuous metamorphoses of the drawings refer to a subjective and dream-like mental state that is completely "in synch" with the *jazz beat* going on in Felix's head.

And yet despite all this, in running through the history of animated cinema in its endless filmography it is not easy to come across titles that refer to the collaboration between cartoons and jazz. There are, nonetheless, examples. But the question that the majority of these films inevitably poses is if a union in expression and intent between the two languages did indeed take place. The fact is that even for cartoons Krin Gabbard's observation regarding cinema (as a whole) holds true: all the aura and the imagery stirred up by listening to African-American music finds itself as being interpreted by and subordinate to the narrative and iconographic framework created by the dominating ideology (obviously white ideology) with effects that in cartoons end up damaging the potential for freedom from pre-established models of Western representation that is specific to both the language of animated cinema and jazz. Norman Klein is correct in emphasizing how the advent of sound in animated cinema marked the beginning of the end of the autonomy in expression of the *graphic narrative* that had reigned supreme in the silent-movie era – those transformations of the ideogram and the graphic characteristics were directed so as to create a world that was out of control and not bound to the laws of representation. In fact, this had characterized not only the films of Messmer but also the series "Out of the Inkwell" by Max and Dave Fleischer. But there is more. It is true that the invention of sound allowed animated cinema, especially during the early 1930s, to absorb the styles (fragmentary, anti-narrative) of an entire precise tradition of popular American entertainment – not only vaudeville but also the world tied to jazz clubs and big bands. However it is also true that with sound the cartoon was inevitably directed towards a canon that, not by accident, would discover its uniting force in the dimension of classical and symphonic music.

This canon is obviously the one espoused by Disney starting from the revolution that was begun by the production, in series, of the "Silly Symphonies." Great animated cinema – who could deny this? But significant also for leading the insubstantiality of the preceding cartoon tradition towards "mass" and "volume" in the description and definition of the characters, in the narrative consequentiality and once and for all within a nature that was fully synchronized and less unpredictable because, as is known, it is sustained by a series of "laws" that guarantee the harmony and wholeness of the "representation." This however comes with a price that involves in particular the autonomy and freedom of the medium because the deviation, imposed precisely by *mickey-mousing*, brought Disney to the well-known *illusion of life* in a perspective that must control all those forces able to suspend the integrity of the representation.

If therefore in *The Whoopee Party* (1932) Mickey Mouse could still appear with his Minnie Mouse in a honky-tonk improvisation of *Running Wild*, already in 1936 in the marvelous *The Band Concert*, Mickey, altered in his appearance (he possesses absolutely no trait that could make him be mistaken for a *jitter*), finds himself successfully conducting an orchestra out of a cyclone with the clear intention of defeating chaos and making his musicians land on the safer "ground" of classical music, perfectly synchronized with the finale of the "William Tell Overture." Even more so (and this is perhaps the example that interests us more) in the famous *Music Land*, this same Land of Symphony finds itself fighting a war with notes against the Land of Jazz with the implicit goal of domesticating the destabilizing force associated with jazz music (even if, not by chance, there is no trace of an authentically "black" presence in this world). And finally, in the false placation with which this cartoon ends, it is declared once and for all the triumph of that model that would consolidate itself in the collective imagery as the cartoon norm.

Now, we know that the "war" begun by Disney has never been completely won and that, fortunately!, there have always existed pockets of resistance even within classic Hollywood cartoons. And yet, in the however unavoidable reign of the full animation imposed on a broad scale by Disney, the parable described by *Music Land* can suggest to us a way of understanding the role taken up by jazz in animated cinema. The point is this: within a dynamics of attraction/repulsion, in the relationship with jazz there exists hypocrisy in recognizing the black component inherent to our culture – the Caliban that is within us that the history of cinema, contrary to Shakespeare's Prospero, always has difficulty in accepting ("this thing of darkness I acknowledge mine" we read in that memorable page of *The Tempest*). In the case of cartoons, the problem therefore becomes that of translating African-American music into an image – of containing it perhaps in an inauthentic iconography or else unleashing a figurative, uncontrolled and metamorphic outpouring. There is in all this both a fear of and impetus towards a force that seems to do away with any pre-established principle of identity and that nurtures itself therefore on the myth that envelopes black music, identified as a totally spontaneous, and therefore irrational, expression. But this attitude always goes from animation (an art practiced exclusively by Whites) to jazz, and not vice versa. It could also happen that black musicians, in following the devilish rhythms of the cartoon characters, recognize in animated cinema those same anarchic and spontaneous qualities also present in their music, thus creating an improvised and fragmentary re-elaboration of standard repertories (which is precisely what happens in the elaboration of the soundtracks of Carl Stalling and Scott Bradley).

But let us examine the case of the jazztoons with Betty Boop directed by the Fleischer Brothers – and not surprisingly the only rivals of Disney during the early 1930s. These cartoons are in fact among the most significant examples of collaboration between animation and African-American music. And yet they fully express the ambivalence of a certain point of view. In cartoons such as the celebrated *Minnie the Moocher, The Old Man on the Mountain*, *Snow White* (all introduced by Cab Calloway's orchestra) or *I'll Be Glad When You're Dead, You Rascal You* (with music by Louis Armstrong) jazz is central and necessarily comes before the images in the cartoons. Each cartoon opens up with a "live" sequence of the band playing, thus suggesting the bond of continuity of the animated part that follows not only with the performance but, more in general, with the dimension of African-American entertainment. This in fact is consubstantial with the surrealist spirit of the Fleischers, incarnating itself in the classic metamorphoses of these shorts, with the voice of Cab Calloway that manifests itself in the unstoppable morphing of the elements or in the dancing of a walrus-ghost that imitates the artist's typical movements and gestures. In any case, what we are dealing with is this: if black music is the primary principle that unleashes the constant transformation of the images, it is also true that jazz music seems to be able to reify itself only in grotesque and mortuary forms, as the absolute opposite of things that are reassuring. The parable of rebelling against her Jewish-American father and family described by Betty Boop in *Minnie the Moocher* does not certainly imitate Al Jolson's story in *The Jazz Singer* because the escape is to another world – to a spooky afterlife – that makes the petite protagonist quickly return to her "Home Sweet Home." The other world Betty flees to is the one that is characteristic of the films of the Fleischers. But it is a universe that is not at all reassuring or infantile and where the not-too-veiled intention of the various personifications of black music is to compromise (even sexually) Betty's integrity. In *I'll Be Glad When You're Dead, You Rascal You* entering into the heart of jazz means entering into the jungle, chased by the head of a savage that is ready to morph itself into the face of the "real" Armstrong. And if these incursions in the land of the "others" remain within an electrifying adventure and not a nightmare, it is only because Blacks are always codified in clown-like dimensions with which artists such as Calloway and even Armstrong himself are identified in a sort of degenerate version of the jazz myth.

A jungle, therefore. This is the privileged meeting ground with African-American music starting from a seminal cartoon such as *The King of Jazz* by Walter Lantz (1930, an animated sequence inserted in a film, bearing the same name, by John Murray Anderson, but used for the crowning of a white artist, Paul Whiteman, as king of the metaphorical "jungle") up to another classic like *Jungle Jive* by Shamus Culhane (1944), one of the most successful examples in the series of the so-called "Swing Symphonies" produced by Lantz. These in fact are the years in which American cinema attempts to transfer onto the silver screen the very fashionable *swing* – a temptation that even Disney gives in to – in cartoons such as *All the Cats Join In* and *After You've Gone* (episodes from *Make Mine Music*, both directed by Jack Kinney). Portrayed here is the music of an artist like Benny Goodman. More in general, in any case, once the metamorphic component that had characterized the cinema of the Fleischers had ceased to exist, the other major studios competing with Disney during the 1930s, '40s and '50s seem to want to crystallize the image of jazz in an amplification of the caricatural component associated with African-American culture. This occurs, for example, in the zoomorphic personifications of the Blacks even within the jungle itself and also in their musical performances that become parodies (like in *Scrub Me Mama with a Boogie Beat* by Lantz, *Tin Pan Alley Cats* by Robert Clampett and later by Friz Freleng in *The Three Little Bops*). Even characters particularly exposed to cartoon derision were added (persons like Fats Waller or Calloway and Armstrong, in films like the already-cited *Tin Pan Alley Cats* or *Clean Pastures* by Freleng).

But it would be incorrect to consider these images of jazz music solely in terms of caricature. Rather, it would be better if we ask ourselves if these same "degenerate" images could not in some way carry with them a message of protest and freedom with respect to those canons of representation that seemed to dominate the cartoons of the age. In fact, no one can deny the anarchic component present in the cartoons created by Warner Bros. or MGM (at least in those directed by someone like Tex Avery) if compared to products from Disney. Even the fact of allowing the presence of, though in caricatural form, Blacks is in itself indicative of the distance that separates these films from the "live action" cinema during those years – a cinema that tended to relegate (or even completely exclude) the figure of the African American to the margins. Cab Calloway, for example, never declared himself as being vexed by the transformations his figure underwent in cartoons – actually he usually showed the Fleischer cartoons in order to promote his concerts. But aside from this, it is Calloway who reminds us how that degraded and degenerate imagery associated with the jungle was not only the product of white ideology but could indeed reveal itself as a gold mine that the African-American artist could use to his/her own advantage. This is exemplified in the parable described in a famous song by Calloway, *Jungle King*, in which inside the "jungle" the "black" monkey is able with the power of his speech to make a fool out of the white lion – the king of the jungle. Not by chance, starting right from this song, a very scrupulous scholar such as Henry Louis Gates was able to identify that figure – the *signifyn' monkey* – that is so very fundamental in defining the identity of African-American culture, where the strength of jazz expresses itself even in a narrative and figurative form. In fact, Franco Minganti observes that the monkey, "forced to accept his physical inferiority compared to the lion, finds in the effects of his language, in the *signifyn'*, the only possibility of surviving in the jungle."

In other words, this representation that would seem to annihilate the "black" component can be used against that same stability of the world white representation imposes. Proof of this can be found in a Warner Bros. jazztoon masterpiece, *Coal Black and de Sebben Dwarfs* (Robert Clampett, 1943). Considered as an example of racist representation and the utmost exploitation of the stereotypes associated with the image of African Americans during World War II, this black remake of *Snow White and the Seven Dwarfs* was, instead, intended by the director to be an explicit tribute to certain black entertainers and to the black community of Los Angeles. The voices of the characters were entrusted to black radio and film actors such as Zoot Watson, Ruby and Vivian Dandridge (who assisted Clampett in writing the gags), and Eddie Beale was to write the music. There exists a clear relationship of the black world with that representation which in theory would seem aimed at exorcising it. In fact, the representation is absolutely similar to the hysteria typical of Clampett's style and in open contrast to the style of Disney. Pure anarchy that is different from (only in the representation and not in the force) the iconoclasm generated by the tales of a strange Uncle Tom in another classic African-American cartoon like *Uncle Tom's Cabaña* by Tex Avery (1947, even if a direct reference to jazz is extraneous to this last work).

Naturally, the matter is quite different if we turn our attention to avant-garde works. Here, the project, not surprisingly related to prevalently abstract figures, is one that not only does not attempt to crystallize the music in the identity of a representation but which in a certain sense involves the complete autonomy of the music from all aura or imagery. From the first experiments of Fischinger in works such as *Studie Nr. 5/Study No. 5* (1927, based on a fox trot in fashion in 1920s Germany) and *Allegretto* (1936), to the geometric representations of Len Lye in animated creations like *Musical Poster Number One* (1940) or the later and more well-known *Tal Farlow* (1958, geometric scratch patterns that accompany Farlow on guitar), then to the cut-up animation or the pictorial elaboration on film of a quite unique and innovative artist such as Harry Smith (*Number 11: Mirror Animations*, which mirrors Thelonious Monk's *Mysterioso*, or *Number 4: Manteca*, in which every brushstroke on the screen should imitate the notes of Dizzy Gillespie), up to arriving at the abstractionism of *Surprise Boogie* by Albert Pierru. In all these examples the avant-garde animation seems to propose itself as the equivalent to the intellectual evolution of popular post-be-bop African-American music, but also as the place for a more authentic relationship between sound and images that is devoid of the pressure imposed by the dominating culture. The best example of this is provided by Norman McLaren in *Begone Dull Care* (1949). This film is certainly a masterpiece and in fact occupies an absolutely central position for the reflection between animated images and music. More than any other individual, McLaren attempted to bring back creativity in the realm of production in order to subtract it in every way from the binds of re-production and repetitiveness. In this way, by following the improvisations of the Oscar Peterson quintet, McLaren rediscovers the most profound analogy between the two languages, thus reinstating a lost autonomy in animation that is unleashed in the typically McLarenesque notion of internal expansion of his universe of figures. This is that *work in progress* that develops itself in the continuous transformations starting from a single plan that cannot be exempt, like jazz, from improvisation and from the rules imposed by "haphazardness." And yet, even in McLaren's perspective we are on the inside of a rather precise mythology associated with jazz music, in the idea of a full autonomy of the black language outside the influence of culture and history which, as we all know well, is not at all possible. And in fact the impression that a film like *Begone Dull Care* creates is that these two worlds that should melt together into a single reality instead run parallel to each another. As has already been written, the union between images and sound is weak with regards to their contents and McLaren and Peterson "are not on the same wavelength nor on a level of relational empathy." Two visions of the world seem distinct as images and music run by. And perhaps the charm of this film lies precisely here – two opposites running after each other that are always on the point of meeting but which never actually do – which is what also happens after all in McLaren's other masterpieces, like the celebrated *Pas de deux* (1968).

However at this point a suspicion is immediate. A "date" between cinema and jazz seems like a non-isolated phenomenon and in certain aspects even inevitable. And yet this relationship that is at times so fruitful and fascinating does not necessarily imply an agreement – a complete understanding and integration between the parts. Rather there exists a dialectical relationship that often appears evident even when African-American music is together with animated cinema to the point where it becomes intentional: like in *Date with Dizzy*, by John Hubley – an emblematic jazztoon that portrays a disagreement between a composer (and not just any old composer but Dizzy Gillespie) and a cartoon director, both unable to come to an agreement on the soundtrack of the film they should create together. And it is certainly indicative that this disagreement is ironically rendered explicit right in one of the most effective examples of the union between jazz and animated film (the work of the animator who perhaps more than anyone else knew how to wed the spirit of black music to his figures). Hubley, very knowledgeable in jazz but also very innovative as a director, experienced first-hand both Hollywood cartoons (first with Disney and then with UPA) and the independent and modernist production of animation. And he seems to realize more than any other person the "semi-autonomous" nature that characterizes both more standardized creations (inevitably exposed to contamination with languages that can put its stability in crisis) and any hypothesis of art that expresses modernity. There is no language that is immune to external influences and both jazz and the animated film must be understood as the meeting points of the meanings. And so, in Hubley's cinema we must always keep in mind the multiplicity and discontinuity of the reference materials. Only to cite one example among the many, in the beautiful *The Tender Game* (1958) the encounter of animation and jazz is therefore above all the manifestation of a feeling two people have when they meet each other – like a tender courting along the lines of Ella Fitzgerald who sings accompanied, once again, by Oscar Peterson. Hubley does not give up on the realistic representations. Rather, and not by accident, he transforms them because his guiding principle is that of a continuous meeting between figures and music and among the figures themselves which, keeping in mind the avant-garde experiences and the more common imagery associated with the cartoon, he does not know how and above all does not wish to stabilize himself in a definitive representation. This notion of the relationship between music and cartoons is also seen in a more recent artist like George Griffin in his *Ko-Ko*, which is an explicit tribute to the great cartoon tradition (Ko-Ko is one of the characters that always follows Betty Boop around) but also to the figure of Charlie Parker, in a reconstruction the modernity of which is not only in recuperating the avant-garde elaboration of forms but especially in recognizing both in animation as well as in jazz the task of working with their own respective destabilizing powers not on the outside but on the inside of the various representations of consumer culture.

In other words, the moral of the story seems clear – the presence of a dialectical relationship does not in any way invalidate the quality of the product. Actually, it is probable that the bounty and greatness of an artistic creation which involves a union between cinema and jazz realizes itself in a perspective of negotiation and not of identity between the two parts. Because here we are not dealing with probing into or identifying specific filmic qualities or the utopia of a presumed purity of African-American music. Once again, we cannot be but in agreement with what Gabbard once wrote: a correct analysis of the phenomenon must always involve the event itself of this encounter which inevitably feels the effects of the "way" in which cinema considers jazz and on the other hand carries with it the signs that jazz inevitably leaves upon the filmic representation, up to suggesting the possibility of another way of considering these things. Only in this perspective of contemporaneous adherence to the "world" and of its protest both the cartoon and jazz can fulfill their most authentic functions and find for a moment the very reasons for their meeting.

BIBLIOGRAPHY

The essay by Scott Curtis referred to here is the fundamental "The Sound of Early Warner Bros. Cartoons" in Rick Altman (editor), *Sound Theory Sound Practice*. Routledge, New York-London, 1992. Regarding the jazz connotations of the Felix the Cat cartoons, please see Donald Crafton, *Before Mickey. The Animated Film 1898-1928*. University of Chicago Press, Chicago, 1993. The observations of Krin Gabbard can be found in *Jammin' at the Margins. Jazz and the American Cinema*. University of Chicago Press, Chicago, 1996. On the evolution of the Hollywood cartoon during the age of talkies and for an analysis of the cinema of the Fleischers and of Clampett's *Coal Black* please see Norman Klein, *Seven Minutes. The Life and Death of the American Animated Cartoon*. Verso, London, 1993. On the topic of "signifyn' monkey" there is Henry Louis Gates, *The Signifying Monkey*. Oxford University Press, Oxford, 1988. While the comment of Franco Minganti was taken from *X Roads. Letteratura, Jazz, Immaginario*. Bacchilega, Imola, 1994. And finally information on Norman McLaren can be found in Alfio Bastianich, *Norman McLaren. Précurseur des Nouvelles Images*. Dreamland, Paris, 1997. The observations on *Begone Dull Care* are of Giannalberto Bandazzi, Alessandra di Luca, Guido Michelone, "Tiens! Quelque chose de neuf! *Begone Dull Care* tra McLaren e Peterson" in Giannalberto Bendazzi, Manuele Cecconcello, Guido Michelone (editors), *Coloriture. Voci, rumori, musiche nel cinema d'animazione*. Pendragon, Bologna, 1995.

DOCUMENTING JAZZ...

Franco Minganti

Live, live, live. Jazz has its own quintessential nature in the live performance, denoting it as an instantaneous art characterized by improvisation. And it is precisely improvisation, as the *jazz discourse* continues, that has been mainly elaborated as a myth-fetish. Cinema and jazz – for some, provokingly, the only original contributions the United States has made to the history of world culture – undoubtedly have parallel histories and noteworthy moments every time they have come across one another. They are art forms that are mostly collective in nature, marked in their development by experiences of fragmentariness that transformed themselves into common practices and by important events in technological evolution.
Starting from the advent of sound the act of filming music performed live has created a series of technical problems that are not to be underestimated – a cinematic image of jazz necessitates a live recording of the sound in order for the end product to be complete and convincing. The *presence* of the actual filming – the scene put into images, the action in the visual field – is amplified by the *presence* of the music to such an extent that dubbing jazz (or rather, adding sound at a later moment) is almost a contradiction in terms, seeing that it compromises the credibility of the music itself and that which we see on the screen. As a consequence, there is no type of fiction that succeeds in doing so. To a good extent, jazz seems to withdraw from the subtle distinctions between the fiction film and the documentary and if there is no performance (music that is actually played) it is truly difficult to be satisfied with something that is reality's likeness.
Certain actors know this all too well, pitilessly caught in the act of the improbability of certain aspects in their interpretations of jazz musicians – but this problem is common to every performance, from popular to classical music, portrayed in cinema. This at times is resolved by calling upon real musicians, maybe even famous ones, to offer extreme close-up shots of their *finger-doubles* at work on the instruments in ad-

dition to providing the musical interpretations that we listen to over the images. Consider certain roles in 1940s and '50s biopics dedicated to illustrious jazzmen and the fact that in order to find instances of an acceptable fusion between jazz and cinema we have to wait for the Dick Gregory of *Sweet Love, Bitter* (Herbert Danska, 1967) – curiously, he was a comedian and not an accomplished actor in his first and only leading part on the silver screen. And then, perhaps, there is the "method" of the Robert De Niro in *New York, New York* (Martin Scorsese, 1977) – but we could notice that, though technically perfect, he was not too attentive to the other musicians when playing. And then of course and above all we have Dexter Gordon, the "real" sax player of *Autour de mimuit/'Round Midnight* (Bertrand Tavernier, 1986).[1]

Something similar to a utopian realization of such a blending between jazz and cinema could already be glimpsed at in a few sequences in movies such as *St. Louis Blues* (Dudley Murphy, 1929), *Hellzapoppin'* (H.C. Potter, 1941) and *Cabin in the Sky* (Vincente Minnelli, 1943). What comes to mind regarding the first film is not only Bessie Smith's performance but the interaction, perhaps still a bit too rigid, of a music that was never too "visible" (but always present in the *soundscape* of the story of betrayed love, blues and booze) with the gospel chorus, the dancing people and the *hoofin'* number. In the second film, special mention to the famous sequence, revealing to us the "natural" Afro-American musicians, with Slim (Gaillard) & Slam (Stewart), Rex Stewart and the "Harlem Congaroo Dancers" interpreting attendants, porters, maids, cooks, waiters who out of the blue improvise a frenetic *happening* made up of jazz and jive, pure energy and sheer fun. In the third, there is Duke Ellington who, putting to use the experience of a few *soundies* filmed during the early 1940s (ancestors of present-day music videos that were made to be shown in special video jukeboxes – a fad that died out a few years later), brings to the big screen an image of Black Music that cancels the ethno-folkloric stereotype. Ellington *as himself* inspires the spontaneous and enthusiastic energy of the dancers who are once again the dynamic and physical reflection of music and its visually explicit alter ego.[2] It is in this sense, I believe, that we could interpret the "utopianism" invoked by Richard Dyer in 1981 and confirmed, on various occasions, by Krin Gabbard in his analyses of the relationships between jazz and American cinema.[3]

Topology of the jazz group. It is most likely Gjon Mili who paved the way with his epoch-making *Jammin' the Blues* (1944). A photographer for "Life" magazine who

---

[1] It is a pity that *Sven Klangs Kvintett/Sven Klang's Combo* (Stellan Olsson, 1976) was not seen that much outside Sweden. This movie is set in 1958 with hard-bop infiltration in popular dance music, and filmed with actors/musicians whose musical sequences – rehearsals, improvisations, dance music – possess a quite rare freshness and effectiveness.

[2] It is not by chance that, together with music, in jazz images there is oftentimes dancing. The dancing is not so much an obvious celebration of audience participation in the music or the iconographic centrality of the African-American body as the quintessence of movement in cinema, but rather dancing is the dynamic equivalent of the immobility of the musicians at work. It is true that over time music gets the upper hand and gradually dancing disappears. And yet jazz would continue maintaining the movement of dancing, of moving the body to the beat of the music, at least as a potential energy ready to unleash itself at any moment. Even be-bop, accused by many as not being danceable music, proposes the anecdotal comment of Dizzy Gillespie who said that the reason why things are undanceable is because we do not know how to dance them.

[3] Krin Gabbard, *Jammin' at the Margins. Jazz and the American Cinema*. University of Chicago Press, Chicago-London, 1996.

with his snapshots contributed to creating an artistic aura around jazz and its interpreters, in the ten minutes of his film goes one step further in this direction: "In austerely presenting the musicians in front of a white cyclorama without set decorations of any kind, the film provided an early visual analog to the evolving idea that jazz was an autonomous art."[4]

[4] *Ibidem*, pg. 110.

Actually, something more could be said: up until that moment cinema had filmed jazz mostly from a frontal view, almost as if the music were played in a theater, or at least with few variations in the types of shots. At the most, there was a dynamics of alternations among the band as a whole, the soloists and the leader. This is how Duke Ellington and his "Cotton Club Orchestra" appeared in *Black and Tan* (Dudley Murphy, 1929) – even with stage curtains. Here the music is almost like a backdrop to the dancers and singers. Things did not go differently in *Symphony in Black. A Rhapsody of Negro Life* (Fred Waller, 1935), with frontal shots for Ellington and his orchestra, then shots from above, with movements that are almost in the style of Busby Berkeley, and finally with fading between the orchestra and "the public." With Warner Bros. & Vitaphone, Artie Shaw had appeared in *Symphony of Swing* (1939) with two sections of the orchestra (saxes and trumpets) first in a single diagonal line, then one section facing the other in a central perspective with Shaw's face superimposed in the middle to dominate the entire shot. Once again in 1943 in the four parts filmed that constitute *Count Basie and His Band*, among imitation palm trees and tents, to a trumpet section placed obliquely and to the drums shot from the front there corresponds the position of the lead pianist seen from the side and for a while even from behind.

Now, in *Jammin' the Blues* the representation of the sound and group hierarchy becomes necessary. The musicians seem gathered around themselves, around a focus point that is the music itself, emphasized by the "network" of glances – among the jazzmen – that weaves the dynamics and the relationship between musicians and instruments, thus greatly involving its relational nature and its dialectical structure and is just one of the many signs of Black Music's *call and response* and *signifyin(g)*. This is a not too implicit anticipation of be-bop, which was so scandalous because its performers often had their backs turned to the audience. In fact, the group seems to play especially for itself, concentrated on listening to one another's sounds, all taken up by their music and art that was not intended for the audience on the other side of the screen. Or rather, a band that is not in the place it is supposed to be in – at the disposition of the "racial" eyes that tolerate the black entertainer at the center of the scene, but for the use and consumption of the white spectator.

The careful directing turns its attention to the faces and the instruments; it would seem like a new philosophy is at work and the network of glances seals the affective dimension of jazz. How else could we interpret the searching eyes of the singer Marie Bryant for the double bassist and then, from far, for Lester Young, or Prez looking at the others, or the smile of Jo Jones at the end? Therefore, we have gone from frontal shots to the movie camera insinuating itself among the instruments, discovering new spaces *inside* the sound. It is as if the third dimension has been discovered and the volumetric reality of jazz becomes tangible to the point where it changes the very same dynamics of the music. *This is a jam session!* an offscreen voice informs us in the opening, among spirals of smoke and the most famous *pork pie hat* in the history of jazz. For the delight of the enthusiast-voyeur, an up-close glance can literally wrap itself around the musicians and instruments.[5] The production of the sounds takes place in extreme close-ups and the body-instrument (or rather the body-instrument interface that gives life to the miracle of musical poíesis) dominates the center with postures and fingering. It is not possible to avoid fetishism, besides fan culture. It is in this way that in the imagery of jazz that virtual archive made up of the structural characteristics of certain instruments is instituted (the phallic inspiration of saxes and trumpets cannot be contested, but even the double basses, guitars and drums with their peculiar shapes makes us wonder). Or of *that* particular instrument played on *that* special occasion by *that* musician with all the accessories – the reeds of the saxes, the skin of the drums, the strings of the guitars – in full show.

But there is more: the profiles of the trumpet, the double bass or the sax played obliquely by Lester Young, and which were skillfully drawn by the photographic eye of Gjon Mili in *Jammin' the Blues*, are the accentuated aestheticism of the iconographic elements of the recent past – the shadows of musicians and dancers, the silhouettes of exotic palm trees, the glowing neon signs of Harlem by night. Probable residues of intentionally caricatural cartoons as well as the silhouettes, the three or four shades of black in Art Deco style inspired by that great Harlem Renaissance artist, Aaron Douglas, that can be found in much early jazz cinema – from *Black and Tan* to "Harlem Rhythm," the fourth part of *Symphony in Black* and from *Hearts in Dixie* (Paul Sloane, 1929) to *Yamekraw* (Murray Roth, 1930) and *The Green Pastures* (William Keighley, 1936).[6]

---

[5] The rotation – filming an object that rotates on its own axis, just as filming it, immobile, by moving around it – seems to be a very important rhetorical aspect in filming. It is the sign of a desire, perhaps romantic, to transfer in some way the three-dimensional quality of reality onto the two-dimensional quality of the image.

[6] If I may, I would like to refer to the paragraph dedicated to cinema and jazz in my "L'influenza di radio, popular music e jazz" in Gian Piero Brunetta (editor), *Storia del cinema mondiale. II. Vol. II*. Einaudi, Turin, 2000 and also to my "Il cinema afroamericano" (*ibidem*).

Epiphany. Along with fetishism, the documentation of jazz through its representation in images has continuously come into close contact with its epiphanic dimension. Many of the legendary moments that made jazz history have been recorded: the audio has been preserved in the ideal sound archive of this music, in balance between the collector's extreme passion and frenetic commercialization. And perhaps strengthened by the proliferation of anecdotal storytelling created by more or less direct, more or less credible and more or less objective accounts. The Parker session of *Lover Man*, the first one of *Strange Fruit* by Billie Holiday, the 27 choruses of Paul Gonsalves' solo at Newport in 1956 with Ellington's orchestra… the list may be endless, but there are no images. Regarding this last example, we only possess the accounts of the people who are leaving at the end of the concert, of the fascinating woman who begins moving to the music and gets up on stage and dances, and of the consequences that that moment may have had on Ellington's musical endeavor and on the entire jazz industry – both untouched by a dangerous descent into unpopularity and recession (in fact, the LP "Ellington at Newport" would sell numerous copies).

If the epiphanic moment is not enough – even because it is not easy to capture, it just happens (who is there is there. And it is not said that the movie or television camera is present in *that* precise moment unless, as is the case more often, the "historic" events are planned ahead by the showbiz suckers for primal events), we can construct and document a substitute romantic paradigm. That is, the *anomie* of the jazz musician, a kind of hero of isolation lost in his genius and in the solipsistic practice of the rehearsal (or rather, of the "eternal solo" perhaps as the background to an impervious setting). For example, Sonny Rollins alone on the Williamsburg Bridge "playing to the river" – this was said in "Jazz" (Ken Burns, 2001), but we have no visible proof. Or perhaps Massimo Urbani alone with his sax on the terrace of his house, in an abandoned industrial hangar or in a deserted Rome – by night – with the Colosseum in the background, in the film *Massimo nella fabbrica abbandonata* (Paolo Colangeli, 2001). Or even, paradoxically, the heroic solitude – at least a bit mad and not strictly musical – of the Charlie Mingus of *Mingus* (Tom Reichman, 1968). But it also comes to my mind, for example, a solo exegete like Steve Lacy who, with his refined and meditative soprano sax, wanders among the "side-scenes" of stone under the sky of the Spasimo Church in Palermo in *Steve Plays Duke* (Daniele Ciprì and Franco Maresco, 1999). All this does nothing but reinforce the idea of the privileged relationship of the jazz listener with the musicians – almost as if we could spy on them and listen in on their privacy in order to catch that fleeting creative moment of their improvised art. If I am not mistaken, it is Nat Hentoff, once again in *Jazz*, who elaborates something similar – *eavesdropping on a private moment* – with regards to Miles Davis.

Television. The endeavor of "documenting jazz" should not greatly change when – historically – television comes into play. Putting jazz into images should be the same, if we exclude the possibility of filming with more than one television camera and giving back *live* that which is already *live*, by means of a directing that functions as the equivalent of an instantaneous editing. And yet Dan Morgenstern, one of the leading and most authoritative American jazz critics, writes that "on the face of it, jazz and television seem made for each other,"[7] seeing that the strong points of television precisely consist in immediacy and the intense feeling of presence. "[Television] is a medium made for events, and every jazz performance is an event [...] The secret is the music's spontaneity, which, when combined with high artistic quality, conveys the feeling of being present at a unique moment of creation."[8]

In the era of live TV – when even recording in Ampex had been available but perhaps it was not routine usage – jazz finds a few magical moments – the kind that allows us to place the phenomena in a historical context with the use of "befores" and "afters." Undoubtedly "The Sound of Jazz" (1957), a CBS television program, is one of these: it opened up new possibilities to the visibility of jazz, to a formidable look inside that music, starting right from the informal aspect of the musicians and from the topology of the performance.

The merits of Robert Herridge, the producer, are countless, especially the fact that the only copy of the program that has survived (due to the archival negligence of CBS) is his. "The Sound of Jazz" is a rather particular documentary or perhaps it is simply a top-notch TV program that was able, by means of a good dose of luck, to document well an entire phenomenon to the point where it captured a spirit that extended well beyond the event that was filmed in that precise moment. The search for "honesty" on the part of the producer – Nat Hentoff, jazz critic asked to collaborate with the project, recalls the usual caveat of Herridge: *Keep it pure!*[9] – seems consubstantial with the planned session to the point where it does not pass unobserved by the television audience, perhaps casually sitting in front of the tube on a December afternoon in 1957. Hentoff himself remembers the letter of a woman spectator fascinated by the program because it was so rare on TV to have the opportunity "to see real people do-

---

[7] Dan Morgenstern, "Jazz and Television: A Historical Survey" in *Jazz on Television*. Museum of Broadcasting, New York, 1985, pg. 8.

[8] *Ibidem*.

[9] Nat Hentoff, "'The Sound of Jazz': Sunday afternoon, 5-6 p.m., December 8th, 1957" in *Jazz on Television*. Cited above, pg. 40.

ing something that really matters to them."[10] The feeling of reality of the jam session is strengthened by the decision to show the music right where it is being created – in a television studio. No set design or staging (those horrible television – and cinema – jazz joints that poked fun at *caves* and clubs in Beat Generationesque settings). Actually, even the (re)productive machine of TV shows stays onscreen – the television cameras (with the very visible CBS logo), the cameramen, the studio assistants and the few others present. And no need is felt for a filter audience in the studio for the applause that differentiates the times and rituals of the public performance and is an easy identification for the audience at home.

The artists are dressed normally, and it seems as though the era of uniforms – the tuxedos and bow-ties that make these musicians look like black waiters in fancy restaurants or those who know "where their place is" – has come to a close. Except for the totally dignified icon of the super-elegant Ellington at the head of his orchestra, the extraordinary fluidity of the music is now restored and reinforced even through the refusal of rigidity in parts and uniforms. The improvisational nature of jazz played here is amplified by the contribution of the cameramen who are asked by the producer to "improvise" the shots – or rather, to look for never-before-seen cuts. In fact, it would be Jack Smight (a future cinema director of merit) who would see to the instantaneous editing from up in the director's booth.

Jazz, as sustained by many, is a music that is able to speak for itself and thus the script and the presentations are cut to the minimum – just the names of the performers. "Very briefly, because music, we feel, should be listened to and not talked about," says an offscreen voice on "The Sound of Miles Davis," the second endeavor by Herridge, as producer, for CBS. On May 31st, 1959 Studio 61 at CBS in New York hosts Miles Davis and the Gil Evans orchestra: "theater for a story," the one narrated in his own way, with music, by Davis, especially in *So What* with the sextet in which we also see John Coltrane. Decidedly, these television programs and jazz no longer need those "aesthetic" devices – the silhouettes, the set design – which had marked the history of its representation in images. The jazz performance, the musicians and the instruments are the show – an absolute, simple and spontaneous show.

Naturally, worrying about certifying the authenticity of the performance, jazz put into images faces certain physiological limits as well. For example, there is the rigidity of the musicians, conditioned by the shape of their instruments (pianists and drummers forced to sit down "at their stations") or by acoustic and technological necessities (sax

[10] *Ibidem*.

players and trumpeters "fixed" in front of the microphone at the moment of the solo and very careful so as to direct their respective instruments to attain the best sound possible). Even the setting of the performance and the logistics of the shot risk adding limits seeing that the presence of an audience almost always conditions those who film a concert. It comes to mind, for example, the static nature of the images of *Charlie Mingus Sextet* (1964), a television documentary of a concert held in Oslo, hosted in an elegant concert hall before an extremely composed Norwegian audience. With microphoned instruments that liberate mobility onto the stage and with the advent of the shoulder camera and the steadycam, jazz loses the rigidity of its first performances and can display itself with greater freedom of movement. And it was this same freedom that Robert Herridge had given great impulse to by attentively capturing the dynamics of the performance and the postures of the musicians.

The settings. The imagery of jazz that has grown over time is useful in documenting it but also in increasing the possibilities of understanding a music that is oftentimes considered difficult and complex. Along with the recording of the live performances (absolutely crucial) often the images that contextualize it and render it culturally comprehensible and up-to-date have been provided.

If we consider the music that is played, on one side we most certainly have the jazz club and the recording studio. The first is the temple consecrated to the ritual of the concert, of the jam session, of the coming in contact with the audience – the sign of a biography that is both personal and social at the same time. The second is the place of the mysteries of jazz record production – the smithy of the gods. At times it is profaned by the absolutely indiscreet eye of the movie camera, like in a few exquisite and "stolen" images of Thelonious Monk in the recording studio which ended up in *Thelonious Monk. Straight, No Chaser* (Charlotte Zwerin, 1989).

On the other side there is the festival and the one at Newport undoubtedly paved the way for future events (but every single festival – be it big or small, American or European or Japanese, young or old – has its own autonomy and originality). The documentation of these is destined to become, in addition to an archive, a sort of indelible time capsule able to preserve the freshness of live music and, *in any case*, a piece of jazz history.

For example, *Jazz on a Summer's Day* (Bert Stern, 1959) does not document only the 1958 edition of the then young Newport Festival, but also is able to capture the spirit of an America at the close of a decade – powerful, relaxed, in search of inspiration, perhaps hedonistic and longing to abandon itself to the pleasant pursuit of that intriguing music. Offering us images of Newport that are equally distributed among the setting, musicians and spectators, and at the same time pointing the camera lens on precise, original and innovative types of shots, Stern documents the mood and atmosphere of the Festival where even the audience becomes part of the show. The reflections off the water from the port perfectly sustain the sounds of Jimmy Giuffre's sax, Bob Brookmeyer's trombone and Jim Hall's guitar, which we hear before we see them connected to the images of the musicians on the stage – a very tight shot that melts together faces, bodies, the gilding of the instruments. Stern, photographer at work in his only film, chooses fluidity, liquidity and abstraction to wed sounds and images, just like the solo of Monk in *Blue Monk* reminds us of the glittering ocean and the fluttering of Sonny Stitt's sax are impressed upon the veers of the contestants in the America's Cup. To this Stern adds a few brief glances upon the stage "in between performances" (which are sweet and penetrating at the same time, even if we have not yet arrived at a backstage documentary "philosophy") when the musicians are involved in tuning up and sound checks, when the fans mingle with the musicians and when we see the picnic-like atmosphere that characterizes this Festival.

Here we are in the realm of what the French call *documentaire à commentaire* – the creation of the image by means of the editing that is supported by the comment of the offscreen voice (here, at times, excessively naive and self-complacent). *Cinéma direct* has not yet taken hold (with the live filming of the sound) of the various Leacocks, Maysleses, Pennebakers who would surely have done justice to the documentation of live music and of its behind-the-scenes rituals. Other images of Monk come to mind – those that, originally filmed in 1968 by Michael and Christian Blackwood, ended up in *Thelonious Monk. Straight, No Chaser* and these are the more "private" ones, always in a *direct cinema* style, and filmed in the dressing and hotel rooms of the tours of this pianist and composer.

Instead if we consider the musicians, as artists and as human beings, other settings that the jazz documentary explores come to mind, especially those of memory. Let us take, for example, a recent classic *A Great Day in Harlem* (Jean Bach, 1994): through the memories of the protagonists, the documentary recuperates the story, actually the collection of stories, behind a famous, if not historic, photo of Art Kane for "Esquire." On a regular day back in 1958 a large number of jazzmen from the New

York area were photographed with a brownstone located on 125th Street in Harlem. That image and the documentary that narrates its genesis capture an affective sphere that only jazz can offer – a network of relationships that this snapshot places before the recesses of the protagonists' memories. The relationship between black/white and color – between filmed sequences and the editing of sequences of photographic images – certainly invokes nostalgia, but there remain very few doubts on the humanity of those involved, on the friendship and reciprocal respect among jazzmen, on the dynamics of a musical culture that is truly collective.

Jazz for the new millennium. In addition to the enormous quantity of films that portray and document jazz performances all over the world – generally in color, often simple and not particularly elaborate – and the video compilations dedicated to individual artists, there still is the desire to offer jazz to the spectators not only as a musical performance, but as a moment of reflection on the music and its protagonists. It is precisely this look inside on the alternating of black/white and color and the logic of the interview of today (color) so as to comment on the past, on yesterday (black/white), that appears as being the direction in which today's jazz documentation is headed. This ranges from the affectionate tribute, biographical in structure and perhaps with new and noteworthy considerations by critics like in *Charlie Mingus: Triumph of the Underdog* (Don McGlynn, 1998), to the quasi-presumption of offering a narration of the entire history of jazz like in the already-cited "Jazz" by Burns (a super-production that appears to have drained all the energy from the *jazz discourse*, all its pros and cons, to dedicate to the image of the music).
Despite the well-known scarcity of jazz on film (proverbial are the very few images available of Charlie Parker or Lester Young or Art Tatum), there is however much interesting visual material out there. Often, unfortunately, issues involving copyright (and the relating costs) cut short the possibility of using precisely those sequences that would serve to exemplify certain discussions.
With regards to the possibility of documenting jazz on television channels in the Western world in the best way possible, seeing the quality of much jazz in circulation today, the "raw materials" would certainly not be missing. But the world of commercial television, obsessively on the lookout for shares and sponsors, does not think it necessary to create room for jazz, which is forced to very limited appearances that are poorly planned and (too often) poorly realized from a technical point of view. Perhaps these

are entrusted to a director who is not familiar with neither the music nor the musicians, and unfortunately the consequences for the music itself are disastrous. In other words, we cannot but complain about the lack of technical crews like the one at CBS led by Herridge or the one on the (too short-lived) broadcast of Steve Allen, *Jazz Scene U.S.A.* (1962), where jazz had finally found a satisfactory visual style close to the energy and spontaneity of the music: shots, zooms and fading captured the physical side and immediacy of the musical creation, as well as the spirit of the music, by means of the expressions of the musicians (or rather, all those non-verbal moments that nonetheless draw emphasis on the interpretation and style, on intuitive communication, on signals among musicians to lead the music in the desired direction).

Today on the jazz documentary scene the real risk may however be that of solely sponsoring the pedagogy of the past – of reinstating a vaguely museum-like uniformity, of being pleased with the neo-orthodoxy of "jazz as 'America's classical music'," [11] and abandoning the vivacity of a music that is in continuous transformation and the stimuli for in-depth historical-aesthetic analyses of the reasons and motives for such transformations.

In other words, jazz may even fall to ruin, which is precisely what Thelonious Monk once affirmed, but it is probable that there will always be someone who is willing to film it and document its events.

[11] Scott DeVeaux, "Constructing the Jazz Tradition" in Robert G. O'Meally (editor), *The Jazz Cadence of American Culture*. Columbia University Press, New York, 1998, pg. 505.

Una storia milanese/A Milanese Story (Eriprando Visconti, 1962)

The Cool World (Shirley Clarke, 1963)

A Man Called Adam
(Leo Penn, 1966)
(Top) Frank Sinatra Jr.,
Ossie Davis.
(Bottom) Sammy Davis Jr.,
Cicely Tyson,
Louis Armstrong

Sweet Love, Bitter
(Herbert Danska, 1966)
Dick Gregory

Lady Sings the Blues (Sidney J. Furie, 1972)
Diana Ross (as Billie Holiday)

Sven Klangs Kvintett/ Sven Klang's Combo (Stellan Olsson, 1976)

New York, New York (Martin Scorsese, 1977)
Robert De Niro and Liza Minnelli

Passing Through (Larry Clark, 1977)

Mississippi Blues (Bertrand Tavernier, 1983)

The Cotton Club
(Francis Ford Coppola, 1984)
Richard Gere, Diane Lane,
James Remar

Autour de minuit/'Round Midnight
(Bertrand Tavernier, 1986)
Dexter Gordon

Bird
(Clint Eastwood, 1988)
(Right) Forest Whitaker (as Charlie Parker)

Interviews

CONSTITUTION, BASEBALL, AND JAZZ
INTERVIEW WITH KEN BURNS

Antonio Monda

AM: How did your big project on jazz begin?

KB: I made five films on American history at the beginning of my professional life, and each one was about critical events in the history of this country. When I was doing a nine-part series on the Civil War, I knew I would follow it with a lighter, smaller project on baseball, which had been a love of mine since I was very young. While working on baseball, I began to see that American history was too often focused on wars, generals and leaders and not on the institutions or cultural phenomena upon which the society was built. For example, the cultural and revolutionary importance of Jackie Robinson. As I was working on baseball, and using jazz to make the central critical episodes of the 1920s, '30s, '40s, and '50s come alive, I interviewed a great essayist called Gerald Early. He told me that in two thousand years American civilization would be known for three things: the Constitution, baseball and jazz. These are the three most beautiful things that America ever created.

The way I interpret it is that the genius of America is improvisation: if you think about the Constitution, four pieces of paper written at the end of the 18th century, it is able to deal with the most complicated problems that we have at the beginning of the 21st century. Baseball is a stick and ball game that every culture has some variation of, but in America it has been transformed into a ballet with infinite chess-like combinations. And, at the heart of the only art form that America has invented, there is the idea that I do have to play the notes on the page in the European tradition, but, I can play the idea, and together with what you feel, we could create something that anyone can dream of, which is, to create art. I can tell you that I soon realized that the films I was making were a trilogy.

AM: How different was the directorial approach on jazz, compared with baseball and the Civil War?

KB: Jazz was the most complicated and difficult, and therefore the most satisfying. The style is, in a sense, similar: the commentary of experts, the first person voices reading from historical records read by the finest actors that we have, a kind of energetic exploring camera that moves the landscape of still photos, some live modern cinematography, and the collection of newsreel footage. Nevertheless, my subject was something traditionally used as background music. Generally, music is brought in at the end, amplifying emotions that the directors already hope are there. And I was beginning with music that was not only the background, but the middle-ground, the foreground and in those films which dissect an individual tune it is like hyper-ground, as in *Star Wars* when all of a sudden everything moves into the next speed. When you hear John Hendricks dealing with the old tune *Grove and High*, you realize the possibilities in space and time for a new relationship to narrative. I think that from a directorial point of view that was my challenge and struggle to tell that new way of thinking and creating.

AM: Do you think that the language of jazz influenced the language of movies or vice versa?

KB: When I talk about Louis Armstrong and his importance in music, I am talking about the importance that Albert Einstein had in physics, the Wright Brothers in travel, Freud in medicine, Picasso in painting and so on. Jazz and cinema are perfect expressions of modernism, and are parallel. So it is not really about what influenced the other, it is about being the perfect expression of the 20th century, and looking to break out of all forms: the stasis of a photograph and a painting, the limitation of a musical form that had several centuries. Jazz enters a world where several ideas and interpretations of art and existence were bankrupt, and it perfectly mirrors the idea of failure and, at the same time, of revolution of the language. Jazz and cinema give an ecstatic sense that none of the failing interpretations could render. They are blood brothers of a modernist sensibility.

AM: Tell me something about the films on jazz that you like.

KB: Frankly, I don't like them. There has always been an attempt to make a film about jazz that was in the cinematic sense of what jazz is. This to me is a redundant exercise and generally cancels each other out. While in fact where one finds jazz in movies is in the exhalation of breath from the horses in the cold morning in Kurosawa's *Kumonosu jo* [*Throne of Blood*], which is not a literal but a completely emotional and ecstatic translation of Shakespeare's *Macbeth*. You find jazz in the exploding sweat of Jake La Motta's defeat in Scorsese's *Raging Bull*. You can find jazz in a car chase of a B-movie, and of course you can find jazz in the soundtrack of many films. But I prefer to suggest the purely emotional feeling that comes from movies, or music that is able to transform you and me. I personally like *Bird* as a movie, but it is not jazz. Instead, I see Shakespeare's lines, and the best interpretation of his art in that pure idea of Kurosawa. That's jazz for me.

AM: Tell me something about its relationship with other forms of language and art…

KB: I describe jazz and the blues like underground aquifer, and it is easy to see a relationship with expressions such as Impressionism and Dadaism. It is suggestive to think for example that Jackson Pollock was listening to Charlie Parker, but more than seeing who was first, and who influenced whom, I am interested in underlying that the muse that tormented Pollock is the muse that is not unfamiliar with whatever did inspire Charlie Parker.

AM: Who do you think is the most cinematic among jazz artists?

KB: There are several answers to this question. One might consider the lives of Charlie Parker or Billie Holiday because the arch is so tragic. Or even John Coltrane. One might take Miles Davis through the length or variety of chapters. But the one who is most important to me is Louis Armstrong. Because he is a saint. In jazz everyone disagrees: it is part of its freedom. But no one disagrees on Armstrong: he is a gift from God. While I was preparing the film, I met a medium to whom I spoke about the disagreements of all the consultants except with regard to Armstrong, defined by everyone as "an angel." Her reply was merely: "the biggest wings I have ever seen." He is *the* subject of jazz. He is the man who took jazz from ensemble music and transformed it into soloist art, inventing, for the lack of better words, modern time, or swing, playing behind or ahead of the notes. When Duke Ellington listened to him playing with the Fletcher Anderson orchestra at the Roseland Ballroom he said, "I want him playing every instrument." Coleman Hawkins was almost ready to quit, because he felt that he had listened to God. And in addition to that, he transformed singing, and I am not talking only about scatting. Once they asked a guy leaving for a trip what he took to survive, and he said a toothbrush and a picture of Armstrong. Just looking at him makes you feel happy. All these artists, and in particular Armstrong, touched our hearts in a spiritual way. It is a religious experience that deals with our daily lives and hopes.

AM: Can you point out a use of soundtracks that you believe is particularly effective?

KB: I want to repeat that I believe that music is not something that you add at the end. Most of the times I see that music has been put to jazz something up, to make it faster, or cool. I treat music as an organic thing, and I found great examples of soundtracks especially in documentaries. Once again the use of jazz is not jazz. I find the B-movies of the '50s often have a sense of jazz, because they are B-movies, then the atmosphere becomes important, and at the end are more honest in their relationship with jazz.

AM: Who is the unsung hero of jazz?

KB: Sidney Bechet, for the singularity of his vision in expressing his personality and his art. Jazz is about how you are as much as how good you are. He was larger than life. But also Clifford Brown, for the tragedy of a life cut short. I love the clarity and beauty of the playing, and the generosity of the human being. He was always ready to help a younger player, and he died in a car accident because he decided to play a night on which he wasn't scheduled just to replace a friend.

AM: Particularly in jazz there is a lot of the mystique of the damned hero.

KB: Sure, but it was definitively not the use of heroin that made Charlie Parker's music good, but it was something else in a man who was bedeviled by this addiction. And I think that Clifford Brown came and showed that it hadn't anything to do with drug use, with lifestyle. His only addiction was chess. The sources of great jazz have come from sons of privilege, such as Duke Ellington, and sons of poverty, like Louis Armstrong, or even more like Benny Goodman, a starving child from the Jewish ghetto in Chicago, who literally didn't have anything to eat.

CINEMA & JAZZ: VERY CLOSE, VERY FAR
INTERVIEW WITH ALAIN CORNEAU

Baptiste Piégay

BP: Was there a connection between your discovery of jazz and the movies?

AC: My father was a jazz lover before World War II, so it was the music I grew up listening to at home. Dad was a disciple of Hugues Panassié and had stopped at Charlie Parker but he was lucky enough to get into Duke Ellington's first concert in Paris. I caught my father's contagious passion like a virus.
As an adolescent I had my moment of rebellion and got into Parker and then, when I was in high school, Miles Davis. Their music has been with me all my life – it's with me today.
Like others of my generation I was fortunate enough to live in a time when jazz was open to all kinds of music exploding on the scene – what's inaccurately called "world music." Mostly it came from India and Asia, but there was also a rediscovery of the baroque going on. It felt to me like there was an obvious relationship between these musical forms. Today they're all mainstream and vibrant though of them jazz might be considered a little less so…
Jazz was the music that shaped me and taught me to appreciate other kinds of music, but I still feel a special closeness to what goes by the pretentious name of "Afro-American" music. I think there are basically two kinds of people who like listening to music: those who feel the swing, and those who don't. Movies came along for me about the same time the early Miles was making me groove, with Coltrane on the rise – I'm talking about the height of the Blue Note period.
That's when I started to pay a little more attention to how I watched films. In my mind the relationship between jazz and film didn't develop overnight – I had to play an active part myself to understand it. I'd been a musician for a while, and I'd gotten to know the American military bases near where I lived. Each had a club where it was mostly Afro-American music being played. I got drafted to play the drums. There was always a movie theater on base too. I wondered for a while which way I was going to break – into the movies or music. I wound up getting into the movies because, I thought, perhaps mistakenly, that that kind of music wasn't entirely for me, that I wasn't good enough for it. I told myself that there was plenty of scope in cinema for me to work with music.
After finishing at IDHEC, where I did a thesis on "Jazz and Cinema," I wrote to the magazine "Cahiers du Jazz." Then I spent several months in New York, where free jazz and other shall we say "musical adventures" were in full swing. I tried to make a movie with Daniel Berger about that scene, but it didn't work out. So I moved back to Paris and got into film directing as an assistant.
By getting into the business I realized that, beyond the soundtrack, there were lots of working similarities between making movies and playing music. Music and film both start with themes, on some pretty profound topics, and in the end the outcome is ambiguous, it toys with the emotions. It's all about rhythm, sequences, and leitmotiv, and montage is very much like playing music. I've come around to being happy about making movies, as if I were playing music.

BP: Has your background as both a drummer and a music theorist helped you as a moviemaker?

AC: I'd like to think so… Let me answer that first as a movie-lover. I'm as much a movie-lover as a moviemaker – I enjoy going to the movies as much as I do making them… I learned early on that I was very sensitive to the fact that there are films with swing – that have it – and others that don't. I might very well dislike the subject or screenplay of a movie or at least its "message," yet like the way the film is made. It's a question of form, rhythm, feeling. I picked up this approach from music, from having played and listened to a lot of it. The process as a moviemaker is more mysterious. It starts with the writing, unconsciously, whether it's an original screenplay or an adaptation, and where you go from one line to the next already indicates the direction you're going to take. Being on stage, working with a film crew, is a lot more cumbersome than playing music. Sometimes I get nostalgic about those moments that fill you with hope, when everything goes right, when things just take off and fly. It happens once in a while, usually thanks to the actors. Sometimes it's like a rush, or like hypnotic slow motion, like music.

It's during montage, though, that the relationship becomes identical. There are sequences where things start to swing, with long shots and close-ups, cut-tos and so forth, that are just like in music. I've only dared to make one movie about music, not about jazz but French baroque music, *Tous les matins du monde* [*All the Mornings of the World*]. While I was making it I really got down to the nitty-gritty. I felt that in what's labeled "baroque music" you find you're going after more or less the same sounds, the same things soloists are looking for to play, the same rejection of the vibrato and of sentimentalism, just like in a lot of jazz or Indian music. I really came to understand the osmosis between movie directing and music. All this comes from a lot of listening to and playing music.

BP: Say "jazz" and a lot of clichés spring to mind for most people: smoky clubs, nighttime, drugs...

AC: First of all you've got to remember that the histories of jazz and cinema are almost like identical twins. They were born more or less at the same time and were able to mature thanks to the development of technologies such as the motion picture camera, celluloid film, and so forth, as far as the movies go. For jazz, it was the advent of recording technology. Without records could jazz have taken off? Could a jazz musician who didn't cut records survive – on the local scene, sure, but beyond that? There's a dependency here on technology that doesn't exist in other art forms. When it comes to stereotypes you've got to watch out. You're talking about a very French take on things: the French were very good because they realized early on the importance of jazz, something the Americans didn't. But they also tried to pigeonhole things and came up with some pretty rigid stereotypes. Instead of talking about jazz, you're better off talking about Afro-American music: I listened to as much blues and gospel as jazz. There was a time, back in the 1960s and '70s, when Rollins was playing calypso, and jazz-lovers were up in arms about it, but it was great stuff... Those stereotypes exist because there's a romantic vision of jazz that fits a lot of people's expectations, and it's plain inaccurate. I like Eastwood's *Bird*, it's a very fine movie, but it puts across a romantic-desperate-suicidal image that I think is far removed from the reality of Parker's life, though that doesn't make the movie any less beautiful. Parker didn't die because he was suicidal or neurasthenic but because, in the first place, he was black, and also because he was a kind of ogre who exploded like a plane in mid-flight. He wouldn't eat one hamburger, he'd eat ten of them. There's a scene in the movie with Parker, where he's playing beautifully and facing a kind of screaming, blaring sax player who seems to be nerving him up. But that's totally wrong, they're playing the same way... Miles Davis listened to R&B... Jazz has had a very violent, powerful, prolific but short life.

It was born as a working-class baby, in the cotton fields, churches and whorehouses, it's fundamentally a mixed race, vulgar, impure, in the finest sense of the term. Then, after Parker, jazz fell under the influence of the western European intellectuals of the twelve-tone and Pierre Boulez schools, who ran it into the ground. Luckily other forms of Afro-American music have retained their vibrancy... There are still some great jazz musicians but I can't help thinking that they're fighting a rear-guard action, and that means they're losing a lot of listeners. We're a long way from "The Jazz Messengers," not to mention Bechet, who were the rock'n'roll of today, meaning everyone listened to them but at the same time they were rebels. Today jazz is lousy, to Americans "it's poison" in the movies. The backlash has been very powerful.

BP: Two of your movies, *Tous les matins du monde* and *Le Nouveau monde* [*The New World*], raise the question of how to capture music on film...

AC: Well, I was going to have to deal with that question at some point in my career. *Tous les matins du monde* isn't a movie about music. But music is the heart of the movie. It was something I had to make, I'd been obsessed with it for years and couldn't find the key. Pascal Quignard and Jordi Savall helped me find that key. I girded myself with a really harsh esthetic take – I had a lot of deep-seated preconceptions about the esthetics, in order to break into that world from the outside. *Le Nouveau monde* was very different, a pseudo-biography, a tale of reciprocal influences, of a personal initiation into a universe full of contradictions. It was about showing how the American influence on France at the time caused a culture shock, whose effects are still felt today. American domination – which we didn't feel as such – offered us this subversive music – jazz – and we certainly felt that American influence, but at the same time there was opposition to it. This to-and-fro motion still exists.

BP: Based on your experience as a moviegoer and moviemaker, how should one go about making jazz and the movies meet?

AC: It's complicated because there's no such tradition, though there are a few music movies. There's never been a broad movement or genre, just a handful of specific movies, each very different from the other. To start, there's the problem of racism in Hollywood, which has always chosen to use ersatz, to sanitize. When you look at the history of musical comedy, and this never ceases to amaze me, it's clear: you see people tap-dancing and there isn't a black face on the screen, there's no black music. In Gene Kelly and Fred Astaire's day there were some great black tap-dancers. Similarly you never see the real Duke Ellington or Count Basie, you see phonies... In *The Cotton Club* you do see black dancers and musicians but that's way late in the game, it's a nostalgia movie. Luckily period movies that caught some incredible dancers live have been rediscovered.

That's part of the answer. There's another part, a deeper part that draws on the mix of voices, the expressions – a kind of scrambling. Something came to me, a contradiction to be worked out: doing an improvised jazz soundtrack for a narrative shock movie, as if someone were talking in the soundtrack but the images showed something else. It's a real problem that stems from the isolated nature of the voice of the soloist against the regular background rhythm. Jazz is not music made for accompanying movies, even though there have been a few successes with it: Charlie Mingus managed to work with John Cassavetes, Miles Davis with Louis Malle, Jimmy Smith with Pierre Granier-Deferre in *La Métamorphose des cloportes* [*Cloportes*]. It's always isolated cases, though. I only tried it once, with Gerry Mulligan, but there wasn't much improvisation and only during silent, non-speaking scenes, when the music transcribed what was going on in the character's mind. Jazz expression is too much like speaking.

BP: When you use jazz in a soundtrack does it impart something in particular to a character or a storyline?

AC: Jazz is too powerful to be background music, unless you're talking about piano bar stuff. It's too direct for comfort. It runs away and won't be told how to behave. Directors get panicky, they can't figure out how to restrain it, muffle it. It can't vehicle action per se, unless it's a gag routine. Trying to pin down improvisation to moving images isn't that easy. Jazz is very close, but at the same time very far, from cinema. It's very photogenic on celluloid and looks great. The best photos of musicians are of jazz musicians. Tavernier pulled it off with *Autour de minuit* [*'Round Midnight*] where you really see the jazz onscreen, like in Eastwood's *Bird*. I think you have to deal with jazz in the movies on a case-by-case basis – there is no single theory.

BP: There are several key jazz movies in the history of the cinema: *Shadows* (Cassavetes), *Odds Against Tomorrow* (Robert Wise), *Bird* (Eastwood), *The Cotton Club* (Coppola), *Ascenseur pour l'échafaud* [*Frantic*] (Louis Malle), *Anatomy of a Murder* (Preminger)... Which of these resonate for you?

AC: All of them! Among those that I like best from my days there are two extremes: *Anatomy of a Murder*, because of Duke's classicism, which was at the height of its powers at the time, and expressed the same point of view as Preminger on the ills of civilization. At the other end of the spectrum was *Shadows*, which is imbued with urban paranoia and was made at a time when Cassavetes was totally explosive and getting into the dismantling of the storyline and improvisation, and that made the movie very close to jazz. Mingus' music – he said he was lower than a hound dog – was in sync with the anger of the film. Those two dialectically opposed movies were both very successful in assimilating jazz.

BP: Cassavetes' following film, *Too Late Blues*, uses West Coast jazz and features only Whites...

AC: I don't want to put Cassavetes in the same box as everyone else but that's not surprising: in American movies when someone picks up a trumpet it's almost always a white man. There's a movie where Red Nichols and Louis Armstrong are playing together and Armstrong stops to listen to Nichols... You just have to hang your head... It's a tale of ordinary racism...

Recently there was *Ali* by Michael Mann who really talks about the times he describes, and tells the truth, and he also happens to really swing... He's come a little late in the game but better late than never...

The movie about Billie Holiday wasn't great. You see her winding up at Carnegie Hall, a white man's opera house and it's supposed to be the pinnacle of success for her – I just shake my head... That's a long way from the truth about Billie...

Speaking of which, you've got to wonder to what extent jazz can be the subject of feature fiction. A good example is Clint Eastwood's first movie, *Play Misty for Me*, which centers on the story of Errol Garner (Misty)... It's not only a very successful movie – you also get to see the Monterey Jazz Festival, featuring Cannonball Adderley. Eastwood surrounded himself with great people, like Lennie Nielhaus, who really knew about music. Eastwood is one of the few mainstream Whites who loves and understands black music. In *Série noire* all you had was popular music and I really enjoyed doing the montage. Duke Ellington's *Moonlight Fiesta* was playing in the mind of the character of Patrick Dewaere, for the old-fashioned, fuddy-duddy side, the palm trees, the white tux, that were obviously in total contrast with the image of the movie. In places like that jazz can create a fictional world and bring across the darkness of a character. I do think you can make movies about the lives of great musicians. Take Thelonious Monk, for example – the greatest jazz movie is *Straight, No Chaser*. Could you top that in a feature film? It's really Monk, judging by what little I knew of him personally, and by what little is known of him. You see him as a full-blown mystery, there's no bluffing, and the choice of the music is amazingly astute.

Should a movie be made about Django Reinhardt? I think so, but I wouldn't dare to make it, he's too much the gypsy, so better leave it to Tony Gatlif. Speaking of Django, Louis Malle made excellent use of him in his movie on Collaborationism, even if it was a bit decorative and nostalgic. Django actually played in only one movie, with Jean Richard, where you see him in a train compartment… It's really complicated to film musicians in a feature. There's something mysterious about them, something that's burning within them, and their life beyond music just isn't very interesting.

I hung out a little with Coltrane, an extraordinary personality, but in a hollowed-out way. He didn't talk much and didn't seem to have much to say. All he thought about was playing music. He wouldn't have had it in him to talk shop. These musicians don't express themselves in musical terms, and not much in terms of character, either, and that's what's so hard to film.

BP: One of the problems of jazz and the movies lies is fact that it's free-floating music so capturing it on film is an almost impossible challenge…

AC: Absolutely. This might sound shocking but I think it's sort of like a bullfight.

I'm a real aficionado and I think you can just about capture *la corrida* documentary-style but not in a feature film. It's like jazz, there's a blind spot. It's impossible to turn it into a feature. You can use a bullfight to explain why you can't make a feature out of jazz: you can show an actor but you can't film that moment when he's face to face with the bull, because the bull can do what he pleases and you can't make the scene conform to what you want. Handling and directing become impossible.

It's the same, equally inexplicable magic with jazz: the swing in jazz and the tempo in a bullfight, that extremely slow motion moment when the bull passes by. It's as if time were suspended, and you don't know the where or the why.

BP: Do you think the deep-rooted relationship with jazz that Clint Eastwood and Woody Allen have pays off in their movies?

AC: Yes, it certainly does. With Allen I think it fits his moral sense. He's thoroughly into the modern world, he's thoroughly tortured and jazz is a comfort to him, it allows him to live in the past, in a kind of eternal childhood that helps him get through daily life and the process of ageing.

Eastwood's case is different. He isn't wedded to jazz. When he uses it it's because he needs it as an unspoiled wellhead he can't do without, so he doesn't feel totally lost in the United States. He could've wound up a totally stupid, B-rate Hollywood type – something he's never been – and I think jazz was a reality check for him and helped him to find those underlying truths that he needs to keep himself going and continue to make movies freely. I think that hanging out with jazz musicians has helped him lead his double-life. He's both an actor who makes a lot of money and a moviemaker who does what he pleases.

He produced a really beautiful movie, *The Last of the Blue Devils*, about the survivors of Count Basie's band, and he chipped in to help complete the movie on Monk. You can only be extremely thankful to him for that. The difference between Allen and Eastwood is Eastwood inspires people to write scores for him and develops over time. Nielhaus has written some great music for him.

BP: I've noticed that free jazz is never used for soundtracks…

AC: Portal made a few… Once in a while you get a waft of it to go with a chaotic scene but otherwise it's pleonastic… I experienced free jazz full force… I played with Ayler on American military bases – he was a real peasant, a hayseed and a total mystery… I don't get that music… It's not just incompatible with the movies: I don't know what it is compatible with. We're living in a fascinating age, with a major culture shock going on, where the various avant-gardes of the '70s to '90s found a point of convergence: free jazz. Like dodecaphonic music, it crashed and burned. Today everything is being re-evaluated: free jazz, abstract painting, the nouveau-roman type novel… I have no idea who free jazz is directed at: not at black audiences, I don't think it was ever conceived for them. It's no coincidence that just when R&B was at its height electric blues was being born again in Chicago…

As far as the black community in America is concerned, there were LeRoi Jones, Sun Ra, Sheep… It was highly politicized. We're talking about the post-Black Panthers period, after Malcolm X. These were guys I was very fond of. None of them was in Harlem – they were down on the Lower East Side. There was a feeling that some kind of search for identity was going on, but at the same time there was a loss. Rap had already come onto the scene in the form of slam, which came from church preachers, then it disappeared and was reborn ten years later as rap. It's a tough mix to handle. Has free jazz left behind a musical genetic heritage? Yes, there is one, but it's hard to follow, it's very mixed up in what I hear these days. Let's say some cell matter is still alive and being used. I think we've come to the same question Schoënberg asked himself at the end of his life: "dodecaphonic music is possibly a way forward but certainly not the only way forward." Can you really play music that is totally arhythmic and atonal? That's an overall question and I don't have the answer but I think the answer is "no." I haven't found a response anywhere in the world…

We were all very sure of ourselves back in the '70s. We listened to Xénakis, Boulez, Stockhausen. We thought it was the future and it turned out to be a dead end…

Jazz and black identity are closely tied. For example in *Sweet and Lowdown* the black musicians are there to make the white guy look good… In *Le Nouveau monde* the character of the pianist, a white guy, asks himself several times whether he's legit playing jazz, which he associates with Afro-American culture.

It's a kind of American cultural knee-jerk. I was brought up with a contrary view, maybe an overly harsh one. Even if it is incorrect to claim that only Afro-Americans can play jazz, you're pushed toward that view as a reaction. Happily nowadays you've got Prince, who sells lots of records. The battle goes on, there's progress. There's still this notion in America that to be acceptable jazz has to be "orderly and civilized."

With Eastwood, who has the best intentions in the world, there are still traces of this approach: he needs to see Parker in a certain light in order to understand him, while in fact it's absolutely impossible to understand Parker through his life, and that's what's wonderful about it. If I wanted to "understand" him then I'd follow Eastwood's path. You can ask yourself the same things about gospel: can people from the Western world, with their culture, understand gospel and what goes on in churches? The Westerner is going to think it's only about making money, sure, but that doesn't exclude the mystical aspect, and you get to the end of the thought and don't know what to add. That's why I love all kinds of music, because they are irreducible. Reducible music is dead music. No doubt that's what killed free jazz: it reached the limits of conceptual art, which was a flash in the pan. No doubt it had to do that but I don't think the expression "conceptual art" is a contradiction.

The energy, the scream of free jazz remains but it's not enough.

BP: As a moviemaker you've encountered many jazzmen: Michel Portal and Cliffton Chénier in *France, société anonyme* [*French Anonymity Society*], Gerry Mulligan in *La Menace* [*The Threat*], or the Ron Carter-Buster Williams duo, with Philippe Sarde, in *Le Choix des armes* [*Choice of Arms*]… And there's Duke Ellington's *Moonlight Fiesta* in *Série noire* or the musicians filmed live in *Le Nouveau monde*… In each case what were your intentions?

AC: I have no pre-established cinematic rulebook. I try to create a new form for each screenplay. The same thing applies to music. Chénier seemed ideally cast for a really weird movie, a kind of puppet theater. With the magic he possessed at the time, the way he would swing with the accordion and sing in French, all that seemed exactly what I needed, and he brought along with him an ironic commentary.

With *La Menace*, where I said nothing about the characters, I wanted the movie to be like a Fritz Lang maze, something purely mechanical, and I needed a fantasy element that would express what was going on in the minds of the characters. At first I wanted Mulligan to play the baritone sax solo, later on he worked with arrangements. I wanted Montand's character to carry Mulligan's music along. I chose Mulligan for his baritone sound, for the beauty of it, which clashed with the movie's rough 'n' ready feel. I needed a sentimental overture because to my mind Gerry Mulligan *is* a sentimental musician. In *Le Choix des armes* I was thinking of Ravel and Ron Carter. Sarde proposed doing both at the same time… and we wound up with the Carter-Buster Williams combo. Sarde had them accompanied by the London Symphony Orchestra. I have some great memories of recording that music in London. The orchestra was stunned by what Carter was doing with the bass piccolo, it was incredible.

There was a break, in keeping with the movie's image, in which I wanted to show the break in a certain tradition associated with French *noir* cinema, a break between the movies of Jean Gabin and Lino Ventura, and those of Gérard Depardieu, with a kind of clash of forms, represented by the clash of the two kinds of music, which actually worked well together. There was some improvisation with the bass during the chase and shooting scenes.

BP: Jazz is often associated with crime novels in moviegoers' minds…

AC: That's not entirely wrong. For me the great thing about crime stories is this search for identity, in the dark. Even if it is a cliché, jazz does possess that nocturnal prowling quality, where an isolated character feels his way along. Crime story settings look a lot like the scenes where jazz was played once upon a time: darkness, alleyways, potentially clandestine encounters, the feeling of being on the edge, to know the truth and fly in the face of everyone else… Also, crime stories have to have that swing. An art film or a melodrama or a psychological drama might or might not swing but a crime story has to swing, or forget it.

BP: Do you think that matching jazz and symphonic music might be a way to get people to listen to jazz in a movie? For example Philippe Sarde and Eddie Sauter worked with Stan Getz…

AC: Yes, absolutely. Getz had already done it himself in *Focus*, which he recorded with the arranger Eddie Sauter in 1961, four years before they worked together on the music for Arthur Penn's

Mickey One. Contrary to what music-lovers think, jazz musicians adore working with those big orchestras. I don't think it's a bastardization, you can arrange matches, just as you can find meeting points between Western and Eastern music, or a soloist and a symphonic orchestra. It's an approach that has been explored, even by Hollywood.

BP: Let's talk about *Le Nouveau monde*, a movie that tackles the question of filming music, and at the same time is a homage to jazz and the discovery of jazz.

AC: I think we're all made up of many influences and the worst thing is to deny them. I had to declare that this influence – of America and jazz – was decisive for me, and that it hadn't gotten in the way of my life. It was even more than an influence: it was total fascination. I wanted to show it, to bring it to life onscreen embodied by jazz. It's a movie made after the fact, later, and I'm still surprised to see how few movies have been made about those days. Maybe not everyone lived through things like that at the time, but the American bases were everywhere. I'm sure the last nail of American influence was driven home back then. The war was just over and there was a taboo about what had happened. The arrival of the Americans was a breath of fresh air for youngsters. The Americans really did give us something. Compared to them we were in a Third-World situation, we were poor and hungry. Finding those Blue Note records in the base commissary seemed like something extraordinary.

BP: The movie shows jazz as being associated with coming of age.

AC: I don't believe in the purity of the individual. We're all a mixed bag and full of contradictions. When the initiation process continues throughout your life and not just during your adolescence the strongest influences ram right into each other and are assimilated later on, and that's what makes up the particularity of an individual. There was no reason to hide what came crashing down on me when I was eight years old. Everyone forgets that the Americans left after '48 and it was the Marshall Plan. US GO HOME was written everywhere. The Communist Party must have gotten about 25 percent of the votes and Stalin was a threat. For me it wasn't a question of whether they were right or wrong to be protecting us, but to get on base and enter a world that seemed a better world. We fraternized a lot with the Afro-Americans and segregation on base was still very much a reality. We were deeply touched by something we came to understand later on: the American black soldiers felt that with us things were different, they didn't have the same problems with racism that they had in the United States and in the army. You've got to put their arrival here in context. Priests still went around wearing robes, ladies dressed in black, and there were still horse-drawn carriages around. To be eleven years old and see these three black guys roll up in a Buick, smoking hash, was really something – something was definitely going on there…

The character of Gandolfini exemplifies this: he has respect for black musicians but doesn't see them as human beings…
He sees them as clowns, entertainers… They're there to dance and play music but that's it.

BP: In your opinion what does the future hold for jazz and the movies?

AC: If you're talking strictly about jazz it will be a chaotic scene. If you're talking about Afro-American music in the wider sense then plenty might happen. R&B and gospel have great potential. The fate of jazz in the movies will depend a great deal on the personal relationships of moviemakers to jazz. Some musicians like Sarde have tried to make a push toward jazz but nowadays most are leaning toward Tibet or Corsica…

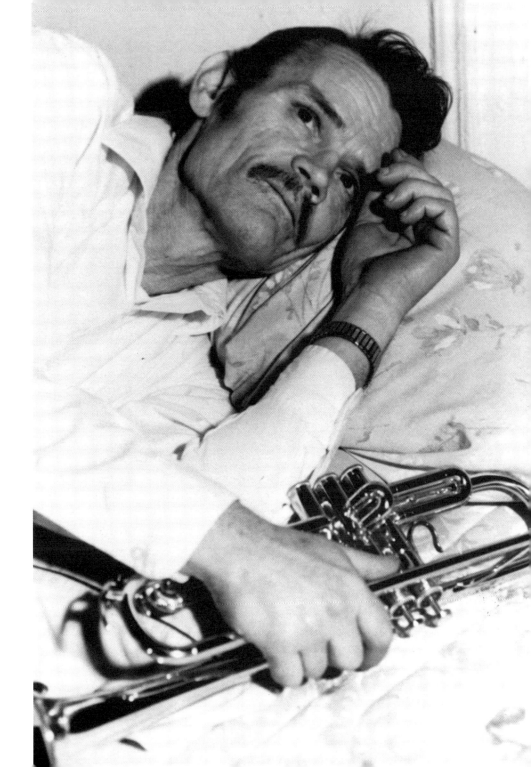

Let's Get Lost
(Bruce Weber, 1988)
Chet Baker

Autour de minuit/'Round Midnight
(Bertrand Tavernier, 1986)
Dexter Gordon

NO BIOPICS, PLEASE
INTERVIEW WITH BERTRAND TAVERNIER

Baptiste Piégay

BP: Do you see a relationship between your first experiences with jazz and their impact on the way you make films?

BT: Absolutely. It may have been a reaction, possibly an unconscious one, to my father. His taste ran to literature, all kinds of literature, from crime novels to Balzac and René Char, and classical music. It was a way to distinguish myself from someone who was enormously cultivated, a way to assert myself. Very early on, as soon as I could, I became a regular moviegoer – I was in boarding school. I started buying jazz records when I was 13 or 14 years old, and giving myself music appreciation lessons.

BP: What are your earliest memories of jazz?

BT: Oh, I recall very clearly: it was Don Byas – I'd bought a 45 of his – and an LP of Roy Eldridge, with Oscar Peterson at the organ, produced by Norman Granz. There was also that mythical, famous "The Jazz Guild" record series, with the great jazz standards, that came free if you bought a Tépaz record player, and it featured Charlie Parker. The other big revelation was Ellington, one of the first, if not the very first jazz musician I saw in concert.

BP: So jazz and movies were closely tied to the assertion of your personality...

BT: Yes. I started reading about jazz and like everyone else at the time read Hugues Panassié and Boris Vian. Panassié was very useful when it came to recommending reliably excellent records but I never agreed with him when it came to the ones he eliminated. I learned early on that when people gang up on an artist they're often misguided, whether that meant being against Benny Goodman or be-bop, it showed they were narrow-minded. But the advice they gave on Armstrong, Bechet or Ellington was very useful. Panassié was always more influential, then Vian came along and corrected certain misconceptions of his, and helped open other doors for me, which I had been opening spontaneously anyway. Once I went to listen to Miles Davis in concert at the Salle Gaveau as part of the Jeunesses Musicales de France youth music series (I was a member of this association). Miles turned his back on the audience. He played a bunch of pieces from *Ascenseur pour l'échafaud* [*Frantic*].

BP: When you started out as a filmmaker how much did jazz count in your work?

BT: Jazz had unconsciously taught me freedom of narration and improvisation. I think I figured out very quickly that the relationship between film directing and the screenplay didn't at all coincide with the usual stereotyped metaphors, whereby the screenwriter was the composer and the movie director was the director of the orchestra – or if you prefer the architect and the guy who builds the house he designed. The relationship could be more accurately represented by a jazz musician and a theme he's playing that he might not necessarily have composed himself. He can respect it faithfully or not but in the end the interpretation will be his own. I found out that in America teachers of screenwriting courses used the theater as the reference and taught that a screenplay had to be put together in acts. I didn't see the cinema as coming from the stage. For me film was musical. Jazz taught me harmony and counterpoint. Contrary to what the press was saying at the time the raw material was very largely written material because all the musicians of that generation had done advanced studies in music and then had chosen to take a leap into the void. When you're filming a scene that isn't scripted and cut to the millimeter you can experience similar feelings.

BP: In fact jazz makes its influence felt equally during the screenwriting, filming and editing...

BT: Absolutely. I've often had references to jazz, including in my directions to actors. In the movie directing it wasn't necessarily a reference that I physically communicated to people; I thought a lot of Ellington, or Gerry Mulligan when he played counterpoint, the mix of timbres that just shouldn't have been able to come out at once but did.

When it comes to giving directions to an actor, take the example of Isabelle Huppert. I told her the velvety smoothness of her acting reminded me of Johnny Hodges in *Le Juge et l'assassin* [*The Judge and the Assassin*].

BP: What are your feelings as a moviegoer about films explicitly about jazz, like *Shadows* or *Anatomy of a Murder*?

BT: *Shadows* made a big impression on me. It picked up on the language of jazz in another way. I adored the interplay of nighttime images and Mingus' music. *Anatomy of a Murder* satisfied the kind of cravings you have when you listen to a record: to see jazz musicians write movie music.

It had to be a moviemaker who wasn't from Hollywood to have that idea. One can never thank Preminger enough for having cast Ellington. It seemed crazy that no one had thought of it before, except for appearing like a backdrop in some movies, where he provided a kind of musical intermission, at times pleasant, lively and successful but never anything that took advantage of his musical genius. He was recorded like a music hall star, like Armstrong and a few other musicians. You've got to say that American movies for a long time didn't know how to exploit Ellington's talents. That said it isn't clear that they'd all have been able to write movie music. Still I think it would have been possible to make use of the talents of Billie Holiday or Ellington, and Armstrong, too.

BP: There's also the example of Robert Wise's *Odds Against Tomorrow*...

BT: Certainly, there were directors way back in the 1940s and '50s who made use of jazz musicians either to play roles or do variations on the theme of a tune the studio held the rights to. Once in a while, especially in the movies of the 'Thirties, you'd hear some jazz and could recognize the musician playing it. I believe it's *Mood Indigo* playing in *Dark Corner*. When you'd hear jazz playing it was often associated with the atmosphere of a speakeasy, or sin... Frequently when you stepped into a den of depravity it was to a jazz beat. Until the early 1950s no one tried to use jazz as it really was. Often American directors' contracts specified that they had no input into the music for the soundtrack. They delivered the finished film and the studio took care of that. Everything depended on the relationship they had with the studio or the producer.

Often, once the film was finished, most of them didn't even come in to hear the music being recorded. In Howard Hawks' biography you read about how he only came in once after the print was finished. Many studio musicians came from Europe, like Steiner, Korngold, Rozsá, and they weren't necessarily into jazz. Their culture was inherited from Mahler, Brückner...

When there is a jazz tune it's often written by someone else.

Things changed progressively when people like Wise, who had a different kind of educational background, with a degree of freedom built-in, managed to bring in something else, for instance John Lewis in *Odds Against Tomorrow*, or Mulligan in *I Want to Live!*. Those two choices were held up at the time as proof of Wise's genius.

BP: In the collective imagination jazz often evokes clichés and stereotypes – nighttime, dicey spots and so on. What are the challenges involved in filming jazz or integrating it into the soundtrack?

BT: To film it you've got to tackle those clichés. That said, those clichés often contain a degree of truth. Some people criticized *Autour de minuit* [*'Round Midnight*] saying it was a cliché to show an alcoholic musician. Unfortunately, having dealt with a lot of situations of that kind I realized that that cliché wasn't necessarily a cliché at all. When you're filming musicians I think you've got to record live, which is what I did in *Autour de minuit*, but nine times out of ten you have actors mimicking musicians. I think you can only be faithful to jazz if you take the same risks as the musicians who play it when they play it, meaning they might not be at the top of their form. Wayne Shorter really liked that approach. He thought that, by taking on those risks in the filming the movie was made the way jazzmen actually play. I was lucky enough to have great guys behind the cameras, especially the second cameraman, Yves Angelo, who was himself a classical pianist and who felt his way around and played it by ear, so to speak, sensing when a solo was about to begin. He always felt what was coming at the right time.

I think you've really got to love jazz to film it and when you do the clichés are no longer an issue.

As far as handling the music goes, it's just as complicated. Some movies are really dated because of the way they use jazz, some crime movies in particular, where music was typed, like in TV serials. Several talented composers like Lalo Schifrin or Quincy Jones know how to adapt the jazz genre for TV. I'm thinking of *Un témoin dans la ville* [*Witness in the City*, Edouard Molinaro] where the way jazz is used doesn't do the film any favors.

I'd go so far as to say that it dates it. Louis Malle made admirable use of Miles Davis, insisting that he improvise, and the result is extraordinarily immediate.

Among the high points there's also Martial Solal's music for *À bout de souffle* [*Breathless*].

BP: To return to the question of live recordings, there's another approach, the one developed by Clint Eastwood in *Bird*. He films Forest Whitaker playing Charlie Parker but it's not Whitaker playing Parker's music. Do you think this is a dead end?

BT: Not necessarily. Anyway, I think that whatever approach he'd used, Eastwood would have caught flak from certain purists. And in any case having a musician play the way Parker played would've been idiotic, because he would've fallen way short of Parker. All the more so since Eastwood had chosen to do the biography of a musician whose sound was so recognizable.

As far as his choice to clean up the soundtrack I'll refrain from commenting. He was often unjustly attacked. He was fully cognizant that certain people are allergic to jazz, because of the recording conditions involved, and you might find that regrettable, proof of a lack of imagination but, having had to face that problem, he tried to fight those prejudices by re-recording the musical scenes, with musicians who made an effort to be very respectful. He was walking a tightrope. Maybe if the technology had allowed him to pick up the music better he wouldn't have had to do it. It's not necessarily something I would've done myself but in any case it didn't affect the emotion I felt when I watched the movie.

Personally I didn't want to do the biography of a famous person because you know you're going to catch that kind of flak. I'd add that you don't make movies like that for a handful of jazz lovers; you try to reach out to moviegoers who've never been fans. My movie wasn't just about jazz but rather about the creative process. Some American critics saw in it a continuation of *Un dimanche à la campagne* [*A Sunday in the Country*], which addressed the exact same issue: a painter who's run out of inspiration and is stuck on the same subject. In *Autour de minuit*, the story was about a guy who, by endlessly searching, winds up about to croak.

Some jazz critics have a "museum guard" side to them – something jazz musicians detest and rail against. Miles Davis was always virulent about this attitude – people who set out to decide what's jazz and what isn't.

When someone pointed out to Victor Hugo that a certain expression he'd used was not French he'd say, "from now on it is." It was up to him to decide what it was.

Ever since I've been a jazz-lover I've seen plenty of jazz musicians condemned under the pretext that what they play isn't jazz. Ten or fifteen years later their records would be rehabilitated. I remember the extremely negative criticism the duo recording of Armstrong and Ella Fitzgerald got, and even some records by Ellington… I do not find that "museum guard" side in people like Alain Gerber, Jacques Réda, Francis Marmande or Michel Contat, who write remarkably well.

BP: To go back to what you were saying about the work of Yves Angelo, how do you set about capturing on film something as elusive as improvised live music?

BT: You try to be clever, to be ready with multiple cameras and not have them start running at exactly the same instant, according to the shot, so that there's always one that's rolling, and be ready for anything. I gave cues and prompts to the place-numbers I'd set up during rehearsals. I couldn't be behind camera number two so I put my trust in Angelo. We filmed the way you bring airplanes in to land on the deck of an aircraft carrier…

Between takes there could be six or seven minutes, but Shorter at one point did three reprises of the chorus, which wasn't planned.

We also worked on the settings and the acoustics. Herbie Hancock had checked the sets with some very precise demands in mind. Alexandre Trauner (the set decorator) made it clear to him that he'd worked on the first French sound movie and that he was fully cognizant of sound-related problems… When Herbie tried the piano he said, "If all jazz clubs could have this sound it would be fantastic."

You also have to work with good people. I got a very helpful hand from Henri Renaud.

It's important to communicate clearly with the musicians. You've got to understand them to be able to film them right. You've got to listen to musicians, be one of them. The best compliment I got came from Michael Powell, who told me he'd understood what jazz was all about by watching the movie, and not just because of the screenplay, but because of the way the movie was directed – the framing and angles.

In Venice Dexter Gordon told me, "Bertrand you managed to make a be-bop ballad and ballads are the hardest things to play."

BP: Do you think that the use of jazz in an original soundtrack contributes to the building of the storyline or the fleshing-out of a character?

BT: Jazz has unquestionably contributed something there. Some images are intimately linked with certain jazz passages. Jazz also helped modernize movie music. It has also been a great weapon in the fight against racism. Jazz musicians have done as much as a lot of politicians to get access to civil rights. It could've had even more of an influence if Hollywood had been less mean-spirited and had used jazz musicians as more than just the musicians in jam sessions. I think Jimmy Rowles played the piano for the theme music for *The Pink Panther*, and a lot of others earned a living playing music for cartoon soundtracks. No one thought of exploiting Billy Holiday's acting talents but she would've been great working with Joseph Losey or John Berry.

The lives of the jazz greats could've inspired some extraordinary films: Armstrong's tough start, Ellington's relationship with the agents who wanted him…

BP: So do you think jazz can be the subject of feature film?

BT: Easily. I demonstrated that in *Autour de minuit*. Scorsese also showed it in a way in *New York, New York*, or Eastwood. Those are very powerful, varied stories. I think that in terms of the storyline there was more to be gotten out of Ellington's story than what was achieved in Coppola's *The Cotton Club*. When you read Ellington's biography you realize there were some fantastic scenes there, especially when it comes to fighting for royalties. Jazz is all tied up with the struggle to survive. A lot of jazz musicians flirted with illegality for a variety of reasons, first of all because it wasn't necessarily considered respectable music, and furthermore because the conditions they worked under led them off the straight-and-narrow and, finally, there were all the problems with alcohol, drugs and the mob to deal with. So with that kind of backdrop there are plenty of stories to tell…
There are obstacles and among them was the fact that for a long time it was hard to film Blacks and Whites together. I think that in the famous short movie *Jammin' the Blues* the white and black musicians are filmed separately. Dexter Gordon used to say that by having black musicians play in his orchestra at Carnegie Hall, Benny Goodman was as important as Martin Luther King. Dexter had enormous respect for Goodman and Billy Eckstine, and for Lionel Hampton for his hard-working quality.

BP: I get the impression that Eastwood responded in two ways to the issue of how to make jazz part of a feature: with *Bird*, and with *Play Misty for Me*, his first movie, whose storyline is built around Erroll Garner.

BT: That movie proves early on that for him jazz isn't just music to accompany a film. Jazz really is part of the dramatic art. Eastwood is among the moviemakers working today who really know jazz well. Even though Scorsese is more inclined toward pop music he does use jazz and you even get a riff of it in *Gangs of New York* by Othar Turner, who shows up in *Mississippi Blues*…

BP: Jazz's relationship with the movies is closely tied to documentaries. I'm thinking specifically of *Straight, No Chaser*, about Thelonius Monk, or *Let's Get Lost*, about Chet Baker. There's a kind of reluctance to use the feature film format…

BT: Just as in the world of singing and music hall performance, where there are a lot of documentaries, and few features like *A Star Is Born*. Very often, in features the temptation is to limit oneself to the "biopic." I had an idea for a feature involving Ellington but the biography bored me, it's a genre that doesn't excite me, so I opted to invent a story.
But for the Americans biography seems like the only way to approach jazz, because there will be a famous name that will guarantee a certain amount of publicity and pull in a certain number of fans.
Even when you meet those conditions it isn't a cakewalk: jazz has never been recognized mainstream music. Right now it's easier to make a movie using Eminem's name, with *8 Mile*, than to tell the story of Monk. On top of that, there's something paradoxical about jazz: the most dramatically exciting thing might not necessarily lead to a big box-office seller. What's interesting is to draw inspiration from the lives of musicians who went through hard times, who had trouble making it, or who died young, and that's not necessarily going to sell well. If you look at the lives of musicians whose experiences are in opposition to that image you find Dizzy Gillespie or Sonny Rollins, but do their lives, even when transposed fictionally, have enough going on to make a good movie? Is there a story? It's striking that guys like Chet Baker or Charlie Parker inspired lots of writing while Dizzy, who perhaps discovered as many things as Parker, and who always lived a happy life, hasn't inspired as much.
There is a romanticizing of jazz that may well be somewhat reductive.

BP: One thing about the use of jazz in the movies stands out: the absence of free jazz. It seems like a blind spot, something that's almost never used…

BT: But you don't hear contemporary music either… First of all, I hate that expression, free jazz… It makes me want to run away to avoid using it. It suggests somehow that Coltrane, Mingus, Parker, Bud Powell were not "free"… I don't know anything freer than the music they played.
I don't know what the reason is for the absence of free jazz. But you can't necessarily put Schoënberg or Boulez into all movie music either. Some kinds of music overwhelm the images, while others make a better match. Maybe it's a kind of music that has to be listened to, and listened to from start to finish.

BP: It has often been said that jazz is tied to the assertion of black identity. I get the impression that one can better understand *Autour de minuit* by watching *Mississippi Blues* – a voyage through the Deep South to the roots of blues that affirms black identity through music.

BT: Yes, *Mississippi Blues* is a voyage among other things, not just through rural blues but also down the road of gospel, which also lies at the wellspring of jazz. In its final version the film was also a study of racial problems. There was a scene set at the university in Oxford, Mississippi where they are celebrating the twentieth anniversary of the admission of the first black student. The complete version of the movie shows the relationship of blues to the race situation. There's no question that blues is part of black people's roots, even though the current generation is ignoring that fact and distancing itself from it while heading over to musicians, many of them white who have assimilated the blues, like Eric Clapton or Bruce Springsteen. That particular identity is no longer claimed, even though a few years back Spike Lee made it his battle-horse. Nowadays it's as if instead of claiming that heritage black people want to show that they had their own version of modernity. It's true that blues and jazz are part of their roots but, having said that, if you talked to Dexter Gordon about it on the set of *Autour de minuit* he was very careful to say that he was never one of those cotton pickers and pointed out that he'd studied music, like Miles Davis. He didn't lay claim to that musical heritage – he said he'd mixed it with others.

Here's a paradox for you: the great jazz music was rejected by Blacks; Parker was defended by European Whites and the critics both black and white; but he wasn't necessarily popular with black people who instead of him preferred the big dance bands that were much more syrupy. Jazz was a music that cemented the identity of black people but wasn't necessarily claimed as its own by those same black people.

BP: Two things strike me about the character of Francis in *Autour de minuit*: his love for the cinema and his almost compulsive need to capture with a camera what he sees and experiences.

BT: It was a way to include myself in the movie. I wanted to do a portrait of a jazz-lover, a music-lover, with all the obsessive, destructive qualities that that might have.

It's not a tale of a spotless white knight that rides in to save someone who's lost. It's a story about two lost souls who help each other through mutual admiration. There's a wonderful line in Victor Hugo that goes, "There is in admiration something indescribably comforting." The admiration that the character of François Cluzet has for Dale Turner comforts him, keeps him alive, but even if it gives him a reason to live it doesn't make him capable of taking care of his daughter or the wife who left him. I wanted to show the extraordinarily positive and the negative powers of admiration.

BP: Francis is a satellite of Dale Turner's character…

BT: He exists so that the character of Dale can go on living: without him, Dale would doubtless have disappeared earlier on. At the same time, he cuts himself off from the people who were closest to him. That was very important to me, it was a way to insert something very personal: the passions I've had for certain people, for the cinema, have sometimes had painful consequences and led to misunderstandings with people close to me.

I didn't just want to tell the story of a savior but of someone blinded and made egoistical by admiration. I wanted to show the paradox of egoism that affects those who want to save the world.

BP: Where did the idea come from to create a character that's a cross between Dexter Gordon, Lester Young and Bud Powell?

BT: From the absolute refusal of doing a biography. I wanted to invent a fictional character and break away from established models. It was always going to be a musician and not an actor in the role. As soon as I saw Gordon the idea of breaking with models took hold of me. Gordon insisted that, "I'm not Powell, and I'll never be him, I'm closer to Lester Young. I can understand some of the emotions Bud feels but I will never be him."

That worked out well because I didn't want to get trapped in a biographical register, I wanted to grasp certain feelings and have the freedom to color them as I chose. I didn't want to have the order of those emotions dictated to me by reality, and that created some tensions with Francis Paudras, who Dexter couldn't stand seeing on set… Paudras thought it was a plot against Bud Powell. One day Gordon arrived on set really sick – he'd been drinking heavily the night before – and he was incapable of playing *Celia*. Francis imagined there was a plot: Dexter, who was jealous of Powell, therefore didn't want to record *Celia*… it was total paranoia. He and I also had a run-in because I'd noticed that in the credits *Fair Weather* was noted as having been written by Kenny Dorham, which is how it's registered with the Library of Congress in Washington. After investigating this, several musicians confirmed to me that Kenny Dorham had never stolen credit for a composition in his life, but Francis was persuaded that it was Powell's composition.

Anyway I could not have put in anything other than what was registered at the Library of Congress in Washington! On top of that anyone could have sued and won.

BP: What got you interested in the relationship between Paudras and Powell?

BT: The opportunity to construct a relationship between people who help each other. To Paudras' mind he'd carried Powell in his arms, but I wanted to add some complexity. At a certain point it's Dale Turner who's going to help him. For months we had trouble writing about these musicians, guys who are extremely laconic, who only spoke to one another when they played, and left the rest to be inferred. What was needed was a musician who didn't play jazz, someone to catalyze these emotions and make the current of feelings more approachable, someone from the outside who would break into this world.

BP: How did you come to work with Herbie Hancock on the movie's original score?

BT: Originally I wanted Carla Bley but Warner Brothers imposed Herbie and we worked together in complete agreement. We chose all the music together, and the musicians, too. Dexter intervened several times.

When we started working together I got really scared because Herbie was always late. I took him myself to his chanting sessions with a Buddhist sect, where they chanted the same phrase for an hour until they went into a trance. He did this chanting with Wayne Shorter, and could not have been more serene. When I took him home I'd get the feeling there were bees buzzing around…

Once we started filming not a single problem arose. He was absolutely exquisite, though sometimes I wished he had been a little more forceful, but I don't think it's in his nature, he didn't want any conflict. When we worked on the arrangements, Ron Carter was very present; when he was composing, Hancock didn't take into account the minute-by-minute timing so Ron found the way to wind up the numbers, which is what made me want to work with him again on *La Passion Béatrice* [*Beatrice*].

I had a disagreement with him about the ending. He wanted at all costs to co-sign a number with Stevie Wonder. I would've liked the finale bolder; he plays it with Astor Piazzolla…

BP: Could the finale be taken as a homage not only to Dale but to jazz itself?

BT: I didn't want the movie to be seen as a homage to *a* musician, I wanted to close with the names of other musicians, I wanted to go beyond a homage to the lead character, unlike *A Star Is Born*, and through that reaffirm the generosity of jazz.

Some Like It Hot
(Billy Wilder, 1959)
Tony Curtis, Jack Lemmon,
Marilyn Monroe

St. Louis Blues (Allen Reisner, 1958)
(Right) Nat "King" Cole

ALEPH: WHERE ALL MUSIC MEETS
INTERVIEW WITH LALO SCHIFRIN

Bill Krohn

Jazz and cinema

LS: Jazz and cinema were born at the same time. The Lumière Brothers had their first public screening in 1895, and that same year things were happening in New Orleans. So I have been able to embrace the two arts of my era together. Not out of snobbery – just because I liked them!
When I was first composing music for films, I didn't like the idea of jazz scoring too much – I felt that jazz in cinema had too often been associated with drugs and prostitution. But in *Bullitt*, for example, Peter Yates did something I had never seen before: Jacqueline Bisset and Steve McQueen spend the evening together at a cafe, and you know by the end of the scene that they are lovers, even though nothing is said. You know because Yates had a live jazz combo playing which they are listening to, and he could cut from her face to the music to his face, and so on. I later re-recorded the music in the studio because there was audible camera noise.
Anyway, that gave me the idea that I could do a jazz score for this movie, because the character is an aficionado – he's cool. And musical ideas started to come to me. But I liked doing it that way, because this time, jazz is associated with the GOOD guy!

BK: It's like the scene in *The Cincinnati Kid* where you know by watching McQueen listen to the blues singer that he's thinking about going to see Tuesday Weld.

LS: Exactly, although that was recorded live in New Orleans – I didn't have anything to do with it. But afterward, it gave me ideas for the score. Eventually I ended up writing the title song with Ray Charles, and it was a big hit.

BK: Did you write the music for *Chilly Winds* at the beginning of *Pretty Maids All in a Row*?

LS: Yes. Mike Burt did the lyrics. *On the Ground* from *Cool Hand Luke* became a hit, too – but my biggest hits were the two songs in *Kelly's Heroes*.

In any case, I began to see that the rhythms of jazz – and its unpredictability – went well with film narrative.

Jazz and classical music

LS: I had classical training in Argentina, and then, through the French Embassy, I applied for and was awarded a scholarship to study music in Paris. This was still under Peron, and you had to go to the police to get your passport – the Special Section, whose specialty was torturing people. I was really worried about going, so I enlisted the help of a friend; he said, "If you aren't back after two hours, we'll do something." I thought, "Two hours!!"
When I went there, I could actually here the tango being played in the basement – that's how they covered the screams. I got through it by appealing to the policeman's chauvinism, describing what a great honor it would be for Argentina to have me accept the scholarship. In *Tango*, the film I did last year with Carlos Saura, I used those memories in the section called "Repression." It's the most powerful piece of music I ever wrote.

BK: In your liner notes for your first "Marquis de Sade" album you observed that one link between 18th century music and jazz, which you were marrying in that album, was improvisation.

LS: In the 18th century and long before, all the way back to the Middle Ages, improvisation was part of the classical music tradition – improvised song, beginning with the troubadours, but also instrumental improvisation. When I was in Paris I used to go to mass every Sunday to hear Olivier Messiant improvise. My friends thought I was crazy going to mass! More recently I did a series of CDs called "Jazz Meets the Symphony," which are like jam sessions I imagined taking place in a big club at the intersection of two streets, one of which is in Vienna, the other in New York. On the fourth CD of the series I have a piece called *The Miraculous Monk*, in reference to Bartok's "The Miraculous Mandarin" and Thelonious Monk – because Monk was the American Bartok, and didn't know it!

The record company my wife and I founded to release some of my music that isn't out on CD is called "Aleph" in honor of Jorge Luis Borges. I knew him – I attended his lectures when I was a student in Buenos Aires. The Aleph in his story is the place where all points meet, and my music is like that, with respect to jazz and classical forms. My interest in that musical tradition went past the 18th century to the Romantics, the French Impressionists, Webern, Berg, Schoenberg, Stockausen, Berio…

Music and cinema

BK: Speaking of musical modernism, listening to the credit sequence of *The Beguiled* last night I realized it was *musique concrete*.

LS: The car chase in *Bullitt* was *musique concrete* – that's why I didn't have any music over it. I built the tension until just before the chase starts and then told Peter Yates to let it play without music, because the sound of the two cars is already a form of music. And it was important for the audience to be able to hear the difference between the two cars to follow the sequence.

BK: There's also no music over the long chase sequence in *Dirty Harry* – the sound of breathing as Harry gets more and more tired would be spoiled by scoring.
When you did something like *The Beguiled* credit music for Don Siegel, with whom you did six films, was that something you worked out together?

LS: Completely. That's why he always insisted I be there when the film was mixed.
A film is the modern equivalent of an opera. In real opera, the artist is the musician; in film, the artist is the director, and the music has to fit the director's vision.

BK: Siegel told me he was a mandolin player.

LS: Yes, I had forgotten that. He wasn't a musician by any means, but he was able to communicate his ideas to me. We were very good friends. I miss him.
In the case of *The Beguiled* the film started off with sepia photos, with the sounds of war overlaid by strong percussion…

BK: And when it comes to your credit, the explosions overwhelm the percussion. After the image goes to color you continue with a big romantic cue over the scene where Eastwood is found in the woods by the little girl.

LS: Not romantic – erotic.

BK: There were many more cues in that film than you might usually have had for, say, an action film. Was it because it was a psychological story?

LS: Yes. It's a very complex story, and we needed a variety of music to convey what is going on inside the characters. It's one of the best scores I ever did, and I think Don's best film.

BK: To take a memorable action sequence, the scene in *Telefon* where Charles Bronson kills Donald Pleasence before he starts World War III… It takes place in a bar where the police are watching, so Bronson has to be careful. You had a mechanical player piano going all through the scene, punctuated by the rattle of a caged snake that gets loose at the end. Again, was the sound design – as it would be called today – something you and Siegel worked out together?

LS: Yes. And I composed the music for the player piano – it isn't just an old piano roll you're hearing. It was recorded for the film by a musician playing a prepared piano.

BK: I wondered about source music watching your 1960s and '70s work again. For example, in the scene where Angie Dickinson seduces her student in *Pretty Maids All in a Row* she puts on a jazz record, and that becomes the soundtrack for the scene.

LS: I composed that music and recorded it for the scene.

BK: Let's take another example I love in *Dirty Harry*, although the audience might not even realize they're listening to a *tour de force*: Harry and his new partner are driving along a street at night past endless strip joints and honky-tonks, and you hear the different sounds and musical fragments drifting out of the joints they pass, while a discontinuous saxophone line binds the sequence together… a less mannered version of what Henry Mancini and Orson Welles did at the beginning of *Touch of Evil*.

LS: Don wanted to have a montage of street noises and music coming from the places they drove past, so I composed every piece of music you hear. In those days we did everything ourselves.

BK: You scored the first film of the director who changed all that with *American Graffiti*, George Lucas.

LS: That was after I worked with him. For *THX-1138*, which is about an Orwellian world, I composed an oppressive score, but because that oppressive future society wears a friendly, smiling mask, I also composed – deliberately – the worst music I ever wrote. They have this silly *Muzak* playing everywhere all the time, so I had to imagine what the *Muzak* of the future would be and compose that as source music in counterpoint to the oppressive score.

BK: Another example of something you do – in your first film directed by Clint Eastwood, *Sudden Impact*, Sondra Locke is spying on a pair of lovers at the beginning, preparing to shoot the man. You have her music – suspense music, kind of eerie – going simultaneously with a jazz instrumental playing on the radio, counterpointing the simultaneous music-lines the way the action is counterpointed by inter-cutting.

LS: I believe in counterpoint between the visual and the musical. In medieval counterpoint there were three lines: the *canta firma* was the main line, then you had the high notes and the bass line. The high notes were sung by *castrati*, and it was a harsh, aggressive sound – in your face, like the images of the film. The *canta firma* is the story, and the bass is the music.

BK: Or rather, an aesthetic whole you envision as being composed of sound effects, source music (like the music on the radio in that scene) and underscoring...

LS: ... and dialogue. In my own compositions I have worked a lot with orchestra and voice, so I know how to score a sequence where there's conversation without covering the dialogue. Sometimes I'll say to the director, "Why would you want music here? It's just two characters talking." And he'll say, "Yes, but one actor didn't give me the performance I wanted, so you'll have to make up for it with the music." I say, "Ok," and once I have scored the scene, the problem of music and dialogue doesn't have to be solved in the mix – I plan for it.

BK: Getting back to your work with Don Siegel, I love the credit sequence of *Charley Varrick*: beautiful pastoral images of a small town somewhere in the Southwest beginning its day...

LS: ... followed by the most violent bank robbery ever filmed up to that point. Don said he didn't want the audience to know what was coming, so I wrote a peaceful, pastoral cue that condensed a lot of Americana in just a few minutes for the credits.

BK: It's a gorgeous little composition in its own right, starting off with a few bars of an Indian flute over shots of the desert at sunrise, then a gospel-inflected piano riff as the town comes to life, followed by the entrance of the jazz flute, strings, horns and finally electric guitar backed by a disco ensemble, all in about two minutes!

At the end of the film, when Walter Matthau is meticulously implementing his plan to get rid of his partner and throw the Mafia off his trail, you must have felt like you were back on "Mission: Impossible." It's mostly silent images of this elaborate plot being carried out, and you need the music to hold the audience, just as you did every week on the TV show.

LS: It is "Mission: Impossible," with one difference. At the beginning of the TV show you were always told what the mission was. In *Charley Varrick*, you don't know – he trusts no one and tells no one what he's doing. So I needed a lot of "thinking" music for Matthau's scenes.

On "Mission: Impossible" I had a specific theme for the mission. Bruce Geller, the show's creator, wanted a different theme for each member of the team, but I said, "No. They're a team carrying out a single aim, so we need one theme for that."

You know, I'm writing my autobiography. And thinking back to that show I realize what an incredible thing it was that CBS, a liberal network, let Geller make Castro the villain in the pilot. Geller had been at the Rand Corporation, and I think he was knowledgeable about Cold War intelligence operations.

BK: The inevitable question: What was your inspiration for the "Mission: Impossible" theme?

LS: Panic. I had a very short deadline to come up with credit music for the pilot.

BK: Any comments on the very different treatments accorded your theme by Danny Elfman and Hans Zimmer in the *Mission: Impossible* movies?

LS: They were respectful. And I'm pleased that those movies built a bridge that connected a new generation to my theme.

Let me tell you a story about Don Siegel and the *Charley Varrick* credit sequence. While we were recording that cue I decided to play a joke on Don, who was in the booth, so he couldn't hear what I was saying to the orchestra. I told them that the first time we played it, I wanted them to go crazy when they got to Don's credit at the end: dissonance, scales, wailing horns... shoot the works. So they did, and when Don's cue came up, it was total pandemonium. Then we played it the way it was supposed to be, and he came out of the booth: "You almost gave me a heart attack!" he said.

BK: Not that different from what happens when your credit comes up on *The Beguiled*...

LS: That's right. But Don was not one to let anyone put anything over on him. So when we were mixing – I told you he always wanted me at the mix – and had gotten up to the fourth reel, he said, "Don't come in till eleven tomorrow. The sound effects on reel four aren't working – we have to fiddle with them, and you don't need to be there for that part."

So at eleven I came in, and from the mixing studio where they were working I heard the sound of my pastoral Americana music from the start of reel one. I said, "What the hell… We finished reel one. Why are they playing that?" As I went down one flight of stairs after another, the music got louder, and it was unmistakably the music for the credit sequence.

So finally I burst through the door, and up on the screen was the most God-awful pornographic montage I've ever seen, involving actual bestiality, women having sex with animals – I have no idea where they found that footage. And playing over it was my little pastoral Americana composition for the start of *Charley Varrick*. And you know the amazing part? It worked!

Let's Get Lost
(Bruce Weber, 1988)
Chet Baker

Straight, No Chaser (Charlotte Zwerin, 1989)
Thelonious Monk, Howard McGhee,
Roy Eldridge, and Teddy Hill (1948)

The Hot Spot (Dennis Hopper, 1990)
Don Johnson

Mo' Better Blues (Spike Lee, 1990)
Denzel Washington and Joie Lee

Mo' Better Blues (Spike Lee, 1990)
Joie Lee

Taksi-Blyuz/Taxi Blues (Pavel Lounguine, 1990)
Pyotr Mamonov

Bix (Pupi Avati, 1991)

Le Nouveau monde/The New World
(Alain Corneau, 1995)

Kansas City (Robert Altman, 1996)

Sweet and Lowdown
(Woody Allen, 1999)
Sean Penn
(as Emmett Ray)

Sweet and Lowdown
(Woody Allen, 1999)
Sean Penn
(as Emmett Ray)

Calle 54 (Fernando Trueba, 2000)
Gato Barbieri

Appendices

CINEMA AND JAZZ: CHRONOLOGY

Gilles Mouëllic and Michele Fadda

Notice

This select, subjective chronology includes short reviews of more than 200 movies with widely varying relationships to jazz. Features and animated movies account for the bulk of the reviews for obvious reasons: an entire book would not be long enough to list the countless times jazz concerts have been taped, primarily for television.

The use of jazz in movies has evolved greatly over the decades. While an appearance in a short movie or a cartoon by Louis Armstrong or Duke Ellington might have sufficed to capture audiences' attention in the 1930s, the decade that followed took a more decisive step toward integrating jazz into American moviemaking. At the time, several movies were made that featured a more or less accurate vision of the history of jazz. They were followed by typically Hollywood-style film biographies of the white jazz greats. A new focus was the rising generation of brassy-sounding composers who grew out of Duke Ellington's big band. Of note among them were: Elmer Bernstein, Lalo Schifrin and Quincy Jones, who set a new standard for crime genre or "cop movie" music. That standard was modeled on Otto Preminger's 1955 *The Man with the Golden Arm*.

In the '50s and '60s jazz gained acceptance worldwide and inspired moviemakers as diverse as Louis Malle, Jerry Lewis, John Cassavetes, Johan van der Keuken, Shirley Clarke, Melvin van Peebles, Bernardo Bertolucci, and, later, Francis Ford Coppola, Martin Scorsese, Spike Lee, Woody Allen and Clint Eastwood. The goal of the following selection is to highlight the wealth and diversity of jazz in the movies.

1920s

Full-Length Features and Short Films

The Jazz Singer
(Alan Crosland, USA, 1927)
If this is jazz then any Broadway music is jazz; Irving Berlin's numbers don't really swing. At least the word "jazz" has entered movie history with the film's title.

Black and Tan
(Dudley Murphy, USA, 1929) SM*
The world's top orchestra, the Cotton Club dancers, Dudley Murphy's bold renditions and Duke's tears: simply marvelous.

Hallelujah!
(King Vidor, USA, 1929)
Astoundingly beautiful music, black voices, moving choruses and dancing bodies. The first talkie masterpiece.

St. Louis Blues
(Dudley Murphy, USA, 1929) SM
1929 again, a great year: Bessie Smith, abandoned by her man, sings her heart out in a more than lifelike honky-tonk, with the James P. Johnson orchestra.

* SM = short movie

Cartoons/Animated Films

Studie Nr. 5/Study No. 5
(Oskar Fischinger, Germany, 1927)
The first example of abstract graphic art in a jazz movie. Based on a kind of fox trot composed by Jolindo Guerrero, very popular at the time in Germany.

Felix Woos Whoopee
(Otto Messmer, USA, 1928)
After having spent the evening at the Whoopee Club, a drunken Felix the Cat wanders along the streets of the city at night, chased by strange apparitions. This is a silent cartoon, but the morphing images allude to the jazz beat inside Felix's head. A Messmer classic.

1930s

Full-Length Features and Short Films

Check and Double Check
(Melville Brown, USA, 1930)
Among the earliest appearances of Duke Ellington's orchestra, which plays *Three Little Words* and *Old Man Blues*.

The King of Jazz
(John Murray Anderson, USA, 1930)
Hollywood invents "its" jazz, called soon after "symphonic jazz." A testimonial to the endearing Paul Whiteman, with Eddie Lang and Joe Venuti.

The Big Broadcast
(Frank Tuttle, USA, 1932)
Light-hearted comedy with fine music by the Mills Brothers (*Tiger Rag*), Cab Calloway (*Minnie the Moocher*) and Benny Carter (*Hot Toddy*).

Rhapsody in Black and Blue
(Aubrey Scotto, USA, 1932) SM
Short musical, with Louis Armstrong in ludicrous postures. Forget the picture; listen to the voice and trumpet.

Belle of the Nineties
(Leo McCarey, USA, 1934)
Worth viewing for Duke Ellington doing "Sensation House," and its accompanying songs by Mae West.

Murder at the Vanities
(Mitchell Leisen, USA, 1934)
Duke Ellington's prestigious orchestra plays *Ebony Rhapsody* in a great musical number.

Symphony in Black
(Fred Waller, USA, 1935) SM
Short movie in which Duke Ellington's orchestra and Billie Holiday's voice shine bright.

Pennies from Heaven
(Norman Z. McLeod, USA, 1936)
A nice number by Armstrong in a club, with Teddy Bruckner and a walk-on by Lionel Hampton.

Swing Time
(George Stevens, USA, 1936)
Fred Astaire in black face doing "Bojangles of Harlem" in a moving homage to the inventor of tap-dancing: Bill Robinson.

The Green Pastures
(William Keighley, Marc Connelly, USA, 1936)
A far cry from the extraordinary *Hallelujah!*, spirituals revised and corrected by Hollywood follow in rapid succession in this "black" revisitation of the Old Testament.

Artists & Models
(Raoul Walsh, USA, 1937)
Louis Armstrong scares away gangsters with his trumpet's supernatural powers. One of the many stereotyped Satchmo movie appearances.

Shall We Dance
(Mark Sandrich, USA, 1937)
Fred Astaire does "Slap that Bass," an extraordinary duo tap-dance number partnered with… the engines of an ocean liner. The black mechanics practically swinging from tree to tree quickly appear then disappear from the sequence.

Every Day's a Holiday
(Edward Sutherland, USA, 1937)
Mae West reportedly demanded Armstrong be cast; he plays a street-sweeper with an astonishing gift for music. Edifying.

Hollywood Hotel
(Busby Berkeley, USA, 1938)
Benny Goodman's orchestra in a Busby Berkeley musical. Several big band numbers but also *I've Got a Heartful of Music* in a quartet with Goodman, Gene Krupa, Teddy Wilson and Lionel Hampton.

Going Places
(Ray Enright, USA, 1938)
Armstrong again, this time as a stable boy in charge of a horse named Jeepers Creepers who won't win unless Satchmo plays his horn!

Alexander's Ragtime Band
(Henry King, USA, 1938)
Irving Berlin's songs, Alfred Newman's music: jazz according to Hollywood, a far cry from the big bands that had America dancing.

Cartoons/Animated Films

The King of Jazz
(Walter Lantz, USA, 1930)
In the forest, Paul Whiteman is crowned the king of jazz. Famous also for being the first sound cartoon in color, it was the introductory sequence to the movie by Anderson mentioned above. Carl Laemmle personally commissioned Lantz to do the job.

I'll Be Glad When You're Dead, You Rascal You
(Max and Dave Fleischer, USA, 1932)
Louis Armstrong, the singing cannibal, pursues Betty Boop.

Minnie the Moocher
(Max and Dave Fleischer, USA, 1932)
Betty Boop again, with Cab Calloway's orchestra (*Minnie the Moocher* and *Tiger Rag*).

Dinah
(Max and Dave Fleischer, USA, 1933)
One of many jazz cartoons by the Fleischer Brothers, this one with the Mills Brothers.

The Old Man of the Mountain
(Max and Dave Fleischer, USA, 1933)
Cab Calloway, cartoon hero, at Betty Boop's side.

I Heard
(Max and Dave Fleischer, USA, 1933)
Another minor Fleischer classic with Betty Boop. Music by Don Redman.

Snow White
(Max and Dave Fleischer, USA, 1933)
Betty Boop and Ko-Ko the Clown in this *Snow White* remake with Cab Calloway singing *St. James Infirmary Blues*. One of the most important cartoons made by the Fleischers.

Music Land
(Wilfred Jackson, USA, 1935)
Among the best-known Disney "Silly Symphony" pictures: the Isle of Symphony and the Isle of Jazz battle with classical music and jazz as weapons.

I Love to Singa
(Tex Avery, USA, 1936)
Parody of *The Jazz Singer* in one of the first cartoons directed by Avery for Warner.

Allegretto
(Oskar Fischinger, USA, 1936)
Abstract angles to the jazz rhythms of Ralph Rainger's *Radio Dynamics*. The movie was to have been a sequence of Paramount's *Big Broadcast*, but Fischinger, who'd worked in color, refused to include his work in a B&W film.

Woodland Café
(Wilfred Jackson, USA, 1937)
This Disney cartoon caricatures the Ellington and Cab Calloway orchestras. Ward Kimball, who later founded the "Firehouse Five Plus Two" Dixieland jazz band, was one of the animators.

Clean Pastures
(Friz Freleng, USA, 1937)
A Warner Brothers jazz cartoon that parodies *Green Pastures*. Saint Peter, worried by the low turnout at his nightclub Par-o-dice, gets a hand from angels Cab Calloway, Louis Armstrong and Fats Waller, who descend from heaven.

Swing Wedding
(Hugh Harman, USA, 1937)
Among the last cartoons of the "Happy Harmonies" series, with Louis Armstrong, Bill Robinson, Cab Calloway and Fats Waller as ridiculous frogs. Deplorable clichés, great music.

1940s

Full-Length Features and Short Films

Strike Up the Band
(Busby Berkeley, USA, 1940)
Mickey Rooney as a jazz drummer (with Lee Young as stand-in) who dreams of joining Paul Whiteman's orchestra.

Hellzapoppin'
(H.C. Potter, USA, 1941)
Very fine jazz sequence with Rex Stewart, Slim Gaillard, Slam Stewart and "The Lindy Hoppers."

Birth of the Blues
(Victor Schertzinger, USA, 1941)
Whites invented jazz, all jazz. Someone had to try getting away with it. Here it is.

Syncopation
(William Dieterle, USA, 1942)
The same questionable story of tracing the history of jazz with an almost totally white group of musicians: Benny Goodman, Joe Venuti, Gene Krupa, Harry James…

Hit Parade of 1943
(Albert S. Rogell, USA, 1943)
Musical comedy with several pieces by Count Basie leading his orchestra (Buck Clayton, Freddie Green, Jo Jones…)

Reveille with Beverly
(Charles Barton, USA, 1943)
An ambitious disc jockey at a radio station, with Duke Ellington, Count Basie, Bob Crosby, Frank Sinatra…

Cabin in the Sky
(Vincente Minnelli, USA, 1943)
Very Minnelli, a spicy evocation of the Deep South's black community with, among others, Lena Horne, Louis Armstrong and Duke Ellington playing a magnificent *Goin' Up*.

Stormy Weather
(Andrew L. Stone, USA, 1943)
Black artists are highlighted in this typically Hollywood production, but Bill Robinson, Cab Calloway, Lena Horne and "The Nicholas Brothers" do the most beautiful tap-dance number in movie history.

Jammin' the Blues
(Gjon Mili, USA, 1944) SM
The warmth of blues, the beauty of jazz captured in a few sumptuous minutes filmed by the great Robert Burks, Hitchcock's future sidekick. If there were only one left…

Le Vampire
(Jean Painlevé, France, 1945) SM
Documentary on vampires, to the accompaniment of Duke Ellington's *Black and Tan Fantasy*. An unlikely yet magnificent match. André Bazin is right to title his article "Beauté du hasard" [The Beauty of Chance Encounters].

Assassins d'eau douce
(Jean Painlevé, France, 1947) SM
Painlevé once again brings in Ellington and the evocative powers of jazz to accompany his short tales of submarines (*White Heat* and *Stompy Jones*).

The Fabulous Dorseys
(Alfred E. Green, USA, 1947)
Jimmy and Tommy Dorsey in one of the first movie biographies featuring white jazz. Many others will follow.

New Orleans
(Arthur Lubin, USA, 1947)
All the Hollywood jazz movie clichés of the period are here. It's saved, as often happens, by Louis Armstrong's appearances and, what's much rarer, by Billie Holiday. Lots of exasperation for a few minutes of joy.

Yoidore Tenshi/Drunken Angel
(Akira Kurosawa, Japan, 1948)
Kurosawa's first major movie, with an un-

forgettable cabaret scene: possibly a rendition of Cab Calloway's *Hi-De-Hi-De-Ho* played by a great Japanese jazz orchestra with a highly colorful singer.

A Song Is Born
(Howard Hawks, USA, 1948)
Historians of "serious" music discover a passion for jazz. A "scientifique" take that's highly questionable, with Lionel Hampton and Louis Armstrong.

Rendez-vous de juillet/Rendezvous in July
(Jacques Bécker, France, 1949)
A future ethnologist and filmmaker (Jean Rouch isn't far off) dreams of Africa in the immediate postwar period, as youths rediscover freedom (and jazz) in the cellar clubs of Saint-Germain-des-Prés in Paris. With a magnificent walk-on by Rex Stewart.

Cartoons/Animated Films

Boogie-Doodle
(Norman McLaren, Canada, 1940)
One of McLaren's first experiments for the National Film Board of Canada. Music by Albert Ammons.

Musical Poster Number One
(Len Lye, UK, 1940)
Abstract figures set to music composed by members of various English jazz ensembles. This was the opener to English WW II propaganda shows.

Scrub Me Mama with a Boogie Beat
(Walter Lantz, USA, 1941)
A wild boogie-woogie stirs the inhabitants of Lazy Town from their idleness. One of Walter Lantz's best jazztoons.

Coal Black and de Sebben Dwarfs
(Robert Clampett, USA, 1943)
Famous Warner Brothers cartoon, an Afro-American variation on the theme of *Snow White*. Originally condemned as racist. In fact Clampett's anarchistic spirit shines through in sync with the "black music," the exact opposite of Disney-type sentimentality.

Tin Pan Alley Cats
(Robert Clampett, USA, 1943)
Another minor Warner classic cartoon. Cats Waller leaves the Salvation Army and is enticed off the straight-and-narrow by the music of the Kit Kat Club. With the notes of a trumpet solo Cats goes into ecstasy and comes to his senses in another world where madness reigns.

Cow Cow Boogie
(Alex Lovy, USA, 1943)
A "Swing Symphonies" cartoon produced by Lantz, to the rhythm of the piano tunes by Meade Lux Lewis.

Jungle Jive
(Shamus Culhane, USA, 1944)
One of the best cartoons in the "Swing Symphonies" series produced by Walter Lantz. The sea washes up a bunch of musical instruments on an island beach. But it's Bob Zurke's piano playing that takes the lead.

The Pied Piper of Basin Street
(Shamus Culhane, USA, 1945)
Remake of the celebrated fairy tale: another well-known "Swing Symphony" produced by Walter Lantz and directed by Shamus Culhane, set to the music of the trombone player Jack Teagarden.

Sliphorn King of Polaroo
(Dick Lundy, USA, 1945)
The adventures of a trombone player on the island of Polaroo. Jack Teagarden's trombone solos on the theme of the song that lends its name to this cartoon. Produced by Walter Lantz.

Jasper in a Jam
(George Pal, USA, 1946)
Objects in a hockshop come to life to the rhythms of Charlie Barnett's music and the voice of Peggy Lee. The best of Pal's puppetoons.

All the Cats Join In
(Jack Kinney, USA, 1946)
An episode of *Make Mine Music*, a full-length Walt Disney animated film. A group of adolescents run amok as a jukebox plays a song by Benny Goodman's orchestra.

After You've Gone
(Jack Kinney, USA, 1946)
Another *Make Mine Music* episode. Instruments take on human characteristics to the music of the Benny Goodman quartet in an almost surreal register.

Uncle Tom's Cabaña
(Tex Avery, USA, 1947)
Through the voice of the biggest tall-tale Uncle Tom in the history of film, the improvisations of African-American storytelling amplify the anarchy of the images up to extreme consequences. Undoubtedly one of the greatest masterpieces by this Hollywood animation legend.

Date with Duke
(George Pal, USA, 1947)
Duke Ellington turns perfume bottles into virtual instruments to create his "Perfume Suite." One of Pal's best-known puppetoons.

Number 4: Manteca
(Harry Smith, USA, 1947)
Animation achieved by hand painting directly on the celluloid film: every stroke corresponds to a note in Dizzy Gillespie's *Manteca*. One of the painter-animator-alchemist's first jazz collaborations, later discovered by the New American Cinema.

Bumble Boogie
(Jack Kinney, USA, 1948)
An episode of *Melody Time*, produced by Disney. Jack Fina's piano plays a swing vari-

ation on a theme by Rimsky Korsakov, accompanying the adventures of a bee in a Salvador Dalì-like, surreal landscape.

Begone Dull Care
(Norman McLaren, Canada, 1949)
The great McLaren draws inspiration from the Oscar Peterson trio. Seven minutes of bliss.

1950s

Full-Length Features and Short Films

Young Man with a Horn
(Michael Curtiz, USA, 1950)
Romanticized biography of Bix Beiderbecke, played by Kirk Douglas, with Harry James as stand-in, and Hoagie Carmichael as the omniscient narrator. Black folklore and white art.

The Strip
(László Kardos, USA, 1951)
Mickey Rooney as a jazz drummer, with Louis Armstrong's numbers and, among others, Earl Hines, Barney Bigard and Cozy Cole.

The Glenn Miller Story
(Anthony Mann, USA, 1953)
James Stewart in the role of the ideal, tolerant trombone player and orchestra leader. With a jam session directed by Louis Armstrong. The most watchable (of the many) 1950s white biopics.

The Band Wagon
(Vincente Minnelli, USA, 1953)
A gem, with a ballet soberly titled "Jazz," an ironic, arm's length revisitation of the relationship between jazz and black movies. Fred Astaire in private goes wild for Cyd Charisse's legs.

Private Hell 36
(Don Siegel, USA, 1954)
Highly conventional crime story with a score by Leith Stevens and all the big West Coasters.

The Benny Goodman Story
(Valentine Davies, USA, 1955)
Highly sentimental biopic of the master of the swing clarinette. En route you bump into Teddy Wilson, Stan Getz and Lionel Hampton, among others.

The Man with the Golden Arm
(Otto Preminger, USA, 1955)
Frank Sinatra as a junkie saved by his passion for jazz (!). Music by Elmer Bernstein, with the Shorty Rogers orchestra, and a very brassy, trend-setting sound.

Pete Kelly's Blues
(Jack Webb, USA, 1955)
Cop movie filmed in color, set during Prohibition, with a big-hearted hero who leads a small jazz band. A sumptuous black funeral scene, a clarinettist played by Lee Marvin, and a whorehouse run by… Ella Fitzgerald.

High Society
(Charles Walters, USA, 1956)
Remake as a musical comedy of *The Philadelphia Story*, worth seeing for the handful of Armstrong pieces.

The Wild Party
(Harry Horner, USA, 1956)
Somber scene in a cabaret filled with vicious layabouts, including a failed pianist. The house orchestra is none other than that of the great Buddy DeFranco, heavily featured.

Sweet Smell of Success
(Alexander Mackendrick, USA, 1957)
Noir movie meets jazz, with a backdrop of corruption and unscrupulous ambition in the big-time newspaper world. Tony Curtis and Burt Lancaster move through big-city hell, among jazz clubs, with Elmer Bernstein's nervy music.

Sait-on jamais?/No Sun in Venice
(Roger Vadim, France, 1957)
John Lewis and "The Modern Jazz Quartet"'s highly sophisticated music, with Milt Jackson's "watery" vibes, in the freezing, time-warp atmosphere of wintry Venice. As surprising as it is successful.

Ascenseur pour l'échafaud/Frantic
(Louis Malle, France, 1958)
Miles Davis flanked by Barney Wilen, René Urtreger, Kenny Clarke and Pierre Michelot, playing to Jeanne Moreau's nighttime dalliances. Allowing Miles to express Jeanne's emotions and desperation through music was the best idea ever in the movies.

I Want to Live!
(Robert Wise, USA, 1958)
Johnny Mandel's first movie score, taut and lean. In collaboration with Gerry Mulligan, Art Farmer, Bud Shank, Frank Rosolino, Pete Jolly and Red Mitchell.

Moi, un noir/I, a Negro
(Jean Rouch, France, 1958)
"I wanted to make movies the way Armstrong played the trumpet" (Jean Rouch, "Jazz Magazine," April 2001). A major influence on Jean-Luc Godard, who wrote two great pieces on it for "Cahiers du Cinéma." Just prior to *À bout de souffle*.

Les Tricheurs/The Cheaters
(Marcel Carné, France, 1958)
Jazz was in fashion, as proven by the dream line-up of musicians (Dizzy Gillespie, Coleman Hawkins, Stan Getz, Ray Brown…) pressed into service by one of the many avatars of the youth culture raging at the time.

St. Louis Blues
(Allen Reisner, USA, 1958)
Another romanticized biography about William Christopher Handy this time, a famous music publisher dubiously proclaimed the "inventor of the blues," who'd just died

in 1958. Saved by the elegant voice of the great Nat King Cole.

Django Reinhardt
(Paul Paviot, France, 1959)
A moving evocation of Django's life and career. A must-see also for the commentary by Chris Marker.

Deux hommes dans Manhattan/ Two Men in Manhattan
(Jean-Pierre Melville, France, 1959)
Homage to American movie world set in nighttime Manhattan, where you meet jazz songstresses and lost-soul musicians. With a chase scene set to music by the Martial Solal orchestra. America reinvented by the movies and jazz.

Imitation of Life
(Douglas Sirk, USA, 1959)
Annie, the black sheep, is laid to rest, accompanied by the sublime Mahalia Jackson singing *Trouble of the World*. Earth-shaking.

Un témoin dans la ville/Witness in the City (TV title)
(Edouard Molinaro, France, 1959)
Fashionable French cop film, with an excellent score by Barney Wilen, with Kenny Clarke, Kenny Dorham, Duke Jordan and Paul Rovère.

Anatomy of a Murder
(Otto Preminger, USA, 1959)
The first real Hollywood movie score composed by a jazzman: Duke Ellington, at last. A major success with, for the history books, a moving duo by James Stewart and Duke himself.

Some Like It Hot
(Billy Wilder, USA, 1959)
The stuff is hot, very hot, a lot hotter in fact than real jazz. But with Marilyn Monroe on board even hardcore jazz-lovers are willing to make an exception. Nobody is perfect...

Odds Against Tomorrow
(Robert Wise, USA, 1959)
A very dark, *noir* thriller about racism, with Harry Belafonte and Robert Ryan, both driven by hatred. John Lewis' perfect score is a latter-day reinvention of the myth of "black music for dark *noir* films."

The Gene Krupa Story
(Don Weis, USA, 1959)
An oddity dedicated to the famous drummer, played by Sal Mineo. For fans only.

Jazz on a Summer's Day
(Bert Stern, USA, 1959)
Documentary on the Newport Jazz Festival, with lively camera work by a filmmaker who asks himself the only pertinent question: *how* do you film music?

Les Liaisons dangereuses/ Dangereus Liaisons
(Roger Vadim, France, 1959)
Worthwhile for the music by Thelonious Monk and Duke Jordan, with Barney Wilen and Art Blakey and "The Jazz Messengers."

The Five Pennies
(Melville Shavelson, USA, 1959)
Romanticized biography of the cornet and trumpet player Red Nichols, played by Danny Kaye.

Shadows
(John Cassavetes, USA, 1959)
A watershed: Charlie Mingus and Shafi Hadi on the soundtrack improvising with actors; montage done to a jazz beat. The model for all jazz films.

Staccato
(Various directors, including John Cassavetes for five episodes, USA, 1959)
Cult TV series, with Cassavetes as jazz pianist-detective, surrounded by the best of the so-called West Coast jazz musicians.

Cartoons/Animated Films

Gumbasia
(Art Clokey, USA, 1953)
The best-known example of clay-animation set to jazz.

Dixieland Droopy
(Tex Avery, USA, 1954)
Droopy the Dog plays a Dixieland record over and over again, ruining the neighbors' peace and quiet. A minor work compared to Avery's great cartoons for MGM.

Number 11: Mirror Animations
(Harry Smith, USA, 1956)
Collage and cut-up animation techniques on the theme of Thelonious Monk's *Mysterioso*.

The Three Little Bops
(Friz Freleng, USA, 1957)
The fable of the Three Little Pigs rescripted as a short Warner Brothers animated movie, with music by the Shorty Rogers trio. The three little pigs' houses are nightclubs, knocked down by the wolf's trombone slide.

Surprise Boogie
(Albert Pierru, France, 1957)
Abstract graphic inventions and a jazzy beat in this most famous work by Pierru, French master of animation and follower of McLaren.

Adventures of an*
(John and Faith Hubley, USA, 1957)
The visual discovery of the world by a child, symbolized by an asterisk. This celebrated jazz cartoon by the Hubleys features music by Benny Carter's big band and a solo by Lionel Hampton.

Harlem Wednesday
(John and Faith Hubley, USA, 1958)
Harlem as represented by the animated pictorial works of Gregorio Prestopino. Music by Benny Carter.

The Tender Game
(John Hubley, USA, 1958)
Stylized human figures in the form of colors in motion court each other to the voice of Ella Fitzgerald singing the ballad "Tenderly," accompanied by the Oscar Peterson trio. One of the most important jazz cartoons of all.

Date with Dizzy
(John Hubley, USA, 1958)
The first collaboration between Gillespie and the great American animator. Others will follow.

Tal Farlow
(Len Lye, UK, 1958)
White lines cross on a black screen. One of the most famous abstract works in animated film history, accompanied by Tal Farlow's jazz guitar. (*Tal Farlow* is a sort of work in progress completed by Steve Jones in 1972.)

1960s

Full-Length Features and Short Films

À bout de souffle/Breathless
(Jean-Luc Godard, France, 1960)
Godard reinvents the movies, relying on the jazz beat of the peerless Martial Solal orchestra. Jean-Paul Belmondo and Jean Seberg's bodies come to life in sound.

Cinderfella
(Frank Tashlin, USA, 1960)
Jerry Lewis as an irresistible crooner descends a sweeping staircase with, at its feet, Count Basie in person and his orchestra that swings like never before. Unforgettable.

The Rat Race
(Robert Mulligan, USA, 1960)
The adventures of a jazz musician (Tony Curtis) and a dancer (Debby Reynolds), on Broadway, put to music by the great Elmer Bernstein.

The Subterraneans
(Ranald MacDougall, USA, 1960)
Based on Jack Kerouac, with appearances by Carmen McRae, Art Pepper and Art Farmer, with a bit part played by Gerry Mulligan.

The Connection
(Shirley Clarke, USA, 1961)
"It's music that makes emotions. People listen to the movie and react to the music" (Shirley Clarke). The Jackie McLean quartet improvises while awaiting a drug dealer named Cowboy. Features a ghost that haunts the movie's only set: Charlie Parker.

Too Late Blues
(John Cassavetes, USA, 1961)
The tale of how Ghost, a talented jazz pianist, sells his soul to a strange countess, while at the same time Cassavetes tries to keep his own countess in Hollywood.

Paris Blues
(Martin Ritt, USA, 1961)
Sidney Poitier and Paul Newman, jazzmen, friends and fellow Americans in an idealized, racially tolerant Paris. Music by Duke Ellington, with an appearance by Louis Armstrong. Too beautiful to be true.

The Ladies' Man
(Jerry Lewis, USA, 1961)
For Jerry, as for Woody in *Stardust Memories* (1980), paradise is peopled with jazzmen all dressed in white (here, with the Harry James orchestra).

The Errand Boy
(Jerry Lewis, USA, 1961)
Features a fabulous miming act based on a Count Basie tune, by a jazzman named Jerry Lewis.

Nóz w wodzie/Knife in the Water
(Roman Polanski, Poland, 1962)
Bold music by Krzysztof Komeda, influenced by the John Coltrane quartet in this, Polanski's first feature film.

Eva
(Joseph Losey, UK/France, 1962)
Jeanne and jazz: after Miles Davis' trumpet, the amazing voice of Billie Holiday singing *Willow Weep Me* and *Loveless Love*.

The Cool World
(Shirley Clarke, USA, 1963)
The streets of black Harlem, featuring Mal Waldron's excellent music played by the Dizzy Gillespie quintette, with James Moody and Kenny Baron. An exemplary collaboration between a great moviemaker and a jazz giant.

Prima della rivoluzione/
Before the Revolution
(Bernardo Bertolucci, Italy, 1964)
The movie of a generation, music by Gino Paoli and Ennio Morricone, and featuring the outstanding participation of Gato Barbieri.

Mickey One
(Arthur Penn, USA, 1965)
Eddie Sauter's fine music, with Stan Getz as an inspired solist.

Repulsion
(Roman Polanski, UK, 1965)
Chico Hamilton and the stridence of free jazz, somewhat redundant in an already-tormented world.

A Man Called Adam
(Leo Penn, USA, 1966)
Fine melodrama about racism in the jazz milieu. Music by Benny Carter, with Louis Armstrong, Sammy Davis, Jr. (with Nat Adderley as stand in) and Mel Tormé singing *All That Jazz*.

Blow-Up
(Michelangelo Antonioni, UK, 1966)
Very little music, as always with Antonioni, but what there is is by Herbie Hancock.

Les Cœurs verts/Naked Hearts
(Édouard Luntz, France, 1966)
Delinquency, black leather, prison and difficult comebacks, set to the free jazz of Jean-Louis Chautemps, Daniel Humair, Henri Renaud, Bernard Vitet and Guy Pedersen. A tough movie with hard music. Dated but moving.

Sweet Love, Bitter
(Herbert Danska, USA, 1967)
Inspired by the death of Charlie Parker. Wonderful musical score by Mal Waldron.

Big Ben: Ben Webster in Europe
(Johan van der Keuken, Holland, 1967) SM
A poignant portrait of Ben Webster by one of the most jazz-inspired of filmmakers.

In the Heat of the Night
(Norman Jewison, USA, 1967)
Anti-racist movie with Sidney Poitier and Rod Steiger (going by the name "Gillespie"!) and a nice score by Quincy Jones, as always greatly inspired by the jazz of his early years (Basie, Gillespie).

Le Départ
(Jerzy Skolimowski, Belgium, 1967)
Krzysztof Komeda's best movie music, the jazziest, too, played by Don Cherry, Gato Barbieri and René Urtreger... for a strange yet enticing film with a perfectly cast Jean-Pierre Léaud.

Bullitt
(Peter Yates, USA, 1968)
Among Lalo Schifrin's (many) fine scores, it draws skillfully on a jazz story he knows well.

Faces
(John Cassavetes, USA, 1968)
Cassavetes' "free" movie, as free and as densely layered yet controlled as "Free Jazz," Ornette Coleman's LP manifesto.

Change of Mind
(Robert Stevens, USA, 1969)
One of Duke Ellington's rare movie scores, set against a background of anti-racism.

Cartoons/Animated Films

Liquid Jazz
(Joseph Kramer, USA, 1962)
A triumph of color and light with a Dixieland soundtrack in this example of an American independent animated production.

The Interview
(Ernest Pintoff, USA, 1962)
An apology for mass media society: this is among Pintoff's most important animation experiments (early on Pintoff was a jazz trumpet player and, later, a director of "live action" TV programs). Soundtrack by Stan Getz.

The Hole
(John Hubley, USA, 1962)
A black man and a white man in the depths of a mine talk about the possibility of a nuclear war. Music by Quincy Jones, with Dizzy Gillespie's voice, in this Oscar-winning cartoon.

Sul ritmo di ogni spiritual
(Roberto Laganà, Italy, 1963)
One of the rare examples in the Italian animated film industry of a successful marriage of the cartoon medium and Afro-American music.

The Hat
(John and Faith Hubley, USA, 1964)
This pacifist apologia is another classic of animation by the Hubley husband-and-wife team. Once again, music and voice-over by Gillespie.

Concerto erotico
(Jannik Hastrup, Denmark and Flemming Quist Møller, 1964)
The most famous work by Hastrup, a jazz trumpet player and master of Danish animated film drawing.

Particles in Space
(Len Lye, USA, 1966)
The great animator's abstract extrapolations are in lockstep with a score based on tribal rhythms from Nigeria and the Bahamas. (*Particles in Space* was completed by Len Lye's staff in 1979.)

Rondo
(Miroslaw Kijowicz, Poland, 1966)
One of the most successful examples of the collaboration between Krzysztof Komeda and Miroslaw Kijowicz, maestro of the "philosophical" trend in Polish animation during the 1960s.

1970s

Full-Length Features and Short Films

Appunti per un'Orestiade Africana/ Notes Towards an African Orestes
(Pier Paolo Pasolini, Italy, 1970)
Free jazz performances by Gato Barbieri, Don Moye, Marcello Melis, Yvonne Murray and Archie Savage, perfectly matched with the *Oriestade* project, "halfway between tradition and innovation, the Africa of the founding myth, and America as a tragic present-day reality" (Hervé Joubert-Laurencin).

Jack Johnson
(William Cayton, USA, 1970)
Documentary on the great black boxer, with an excellent score by Miles Davis in his "electric" period.

Le Souffle au cœur/Dearest Heart
(Louis Malle, France, 1971)
1954: an adolescent's first sexual stirrings… Music by Charlie Parker and Sidney Bechet. Bespeaks Louis Malle's passion for jazz.

Play Misty for Me
(Clint Eastwood, USA, 1971)
Eastwood's first movie. The title reveals his interest in jazz: *Misty* is a famous jazz standard by Erroll Garner. Several scenes were filmed during the Monterey Jazz Festival, with Cannonball Adderley's quartet playing.

Sweet Sweetback's Baad Asssss Song
(Melvin Van Peebles, USA, 1971)
A great raging, clear-eyed, music-filled movie-manifesto. This is Melvin with his clenched fist raised. Black.

Dagboek
(Johan van der Keuken, Holland, 1972)
"Van der Keuken films the way people say Charlie Parker or Bud Powell played: all the notes, sure, but unbelievably fast" (Serge Daney). The first part of Johan van der Keuken's triptych, dedicated to the memory of Charlie Parker.

Ultimo tango a Parigi/Last Tango in Paris
(Bernardo Bertolucci, Italy/France, 1972)
Gato Barbieri's theme songs as orchestrated by Oliver Nelson, the perfect musical match for Maria Schneider and Marlon Brando's performances.

Lady Sings the Blues
(Sidney J. Furie, USA, 1972)
The first film biography of a great black female vocalist, but Billie Holiday would no doubt have preferred to be left in peace up there in heaven… with Lester Young.

The Hot Rock
(Peter Yates, USA, 1972)
Quincy Jones' sophisticated, unexplored sound universe with, among others, Clark Terry, Gerry Mulligan and Ray Brown.

The Sting
(George Roy Hill, USA, 1973)
And Scott Joplin becomes a movie star.

The Conversation
(Francis Ford Coppola, USA, 1974)
Gene Hackman as a wire-tap sound engineer and amateur tenor sax player, with a superb score by David Shire that includes *Sophisticated Lady*, played by Duke Ellington's orchestra.

Lacombe Lucien
(Louis Malle, France/Italy/Germany, 1974)
A young man makes his way during the Occupation, with music by "Hot Club de France" (*Minor Swing*, *Nuages*, *Douce ambiance*…)

Les Valseuses/Going Places
(Bertrand Blier, France, 1974)
The score is by Stéphane Grappelli, with (fine) backup by Maurice Vander, Philippe Catherine, Marc Hemmeler, Guy Pedersen and Daniel Humair.

Le Gitan/The Gypsy
(José Giovanni, France, 1974)
Jazz and the movies, French-style: a score by Claude Bolling based on theme songs by Django Reinhardt.

La Cecilia
(Jean-Louis Comolli, France/Italy, 1975)
A filmmaker crazy for jazz and a great composer of movie music: Michel Portal, with Bernard Lubat, Joseph Déjean and Maurice Vander.

Next Stop Greenwich Village
(Paul Mazursky, USA, 1976)
An actor's dream, with music by Bill Conti.

Sven Klangs Kvintett/Sven Klang's Combo
(Stellan Olsson, Sweden, 1976)
Harsh critique of an inward-looking society, freely inspired by the life of the great Lars Gullin, an alto and baritone sax player, pianist, composer and arranger.

The Gauntlet
(Clint Eastwood, USA, 1977)
Eastwood as an alcoholic cop who rediscovers a lust for life and… love, with music by Jerry Fielding, and the great Art Pepper playing solo.

La Menace/The Threat
(Alain Corneau, France, 1977)
A very fine score by Gerry Mulligan, with magnificent Canadian scenery as a backdrop; very skillful direction by Alain Corneau.

New York, New York
(Martin Scorsese, USA, 1977)
Robert De Niro plays a white saxophonist who discovers be-bop… and the unbridgeable gap separating him from black musicians. Scorsese, fascinated by the white big bands but dazzled by the energy of the little black jazz ensembles. Clear-eyed.

Passing Through
(Larry Clark, USA, 1977)
A young sax player, initiated by an elderly musician, tries to affirm his artistry in a milieu where a bunch of gangsters represent showbusiness. Black filmmaker Larry Clark's militant agenda expressed here is to "improvise with the artistic form."

Remember My Name
(Alan Rudolph, USA, 1978)
Roberta Hunter's blues in the ever-musical universe of Alan Rudolph.

Série noire
(Alain Corneau, France, 1979)
A pathetic, laughable Frank Poupart (Patrick Dawaere) dances to the improbable sound of Duke Ellington and Juan Tizol's *Moonlight Fiesta*. Jazz as paradise lost.

The Last of the Blue Devils
(Bruce Ricker, USA, 1979)
Excellent documentary on the heyday of Kansas City jazz, recounted by Count Basie, Jay McShann, Jimmy Forest, Jesse Price and company.

Cartoons/Animated Films

Voyage to Next
(John and Faith Hubley, USA, 1974)
The last Dizzy Gillespie-Hubley film.

1980s

Full-Length Features and Short Films

Gloria
(John Cassavetes, USA, 1980)
Gena Rowlands battles the mafia, protected by Tony Ortega's sax – perfection.

Heart Beat
(John Byrum, USA, 1980)
The creative process seen through the relationship between Jack Kerouac and Neal Cassidy, far from Hollywood biopics. Music by Jack Nitzsche.

Stardust Memories
(Woody Allen, USA, 1980)
Django Reinhardt, Duke Ellington's orchestra, Louis Armstrong's voice: for Woody Allen, happiness is jazz.

Le Choix des armes/Choice of Arms
(Alain Corneau, France, 1981)
The thriller, as revisited by Corneau, with two greats of the acoustic bass: Ron Carter and Buster Williams.

L'Ombre rouge
(Jean-Louis Comolli, France, 1981)
Comolli, his accomplice Yvan Jullien, and a flawless representation of jazz's romantic potential. With Claude Barthélémy, Christian Escoudé, Faton Cahen, Daniel Humair, Jean-François Jenny-Clark, Emmanuel Roché and Louis Sclavis.

Mississippi Blues
(Bertrand Tavernier and Robert Parrish, France, 1983)
Along the bank of this legendary river a nostalgic walk towards the origins of blues.

Mortelle randonnée/Deadly Circuit
(Claude Miller, France, 1983)
Carla Bley composed the extremely taut score for this strange cop movie.

The Cotton Club
(Francis Ford Coppola, USA, 1984)
Forget the conventions of the crime genre and admire the musical numbers, masterfully filmed by Coppola.

Autour de minuit/'Round Midnight
(Bertrand Tavernier, France/USA, 1986)
Dexter Gordon's massive presence, an irreproachable musical cast, and all of Tavernier's nostalgia.

She's Gotta Have It
(Spike Lee, USA, 1986)
Spike Lee's first full-length feature movie definitely has a jazz beat.

Bird Now
(Marc Huraux, Belgium, 1987)
The life and music of Charlie Parker, with moving testimonials. A fine homage to Bird.

Radio Days
(Woody Allen, USA, 1987)
1930s jazz in a highly nostalgic evocation of Allen's childhood dreams.

Street Smart
(Jerry Schatzberg, USA, 1987)
An ambitious journalist quickly undone by diabolical manipulation. Musical sequences played and acted by Miles Davis.

September
(Woody Allen, USA, 1987)
Woody's other side, but always with jazz close to heart: the sweetness of an amorous encounter, Ben Webster's sax entwining Art Tatum's piano.

Yeleen/Brightness
(Souleyman Cissé, Mali, 1987)
Michel Portal in Cissé's poetic universe: one of his finest movie music scores.

Bird
(Clint Eastwood, USA, 1988)
Eastwood makes the first biography of a black music giant while trying to capture be-bop on film: heartfelt and stirring.

Chocolat
(Claire Denis, France, 1988)
The first movie by Claire Denis, the most musical of filmmakers, with some fine work by Abdullah Ibrahim: "We filmed the entire movie with *Namhanje* playing in our heads" (Claire Denis, "Jazz Magazine," December 2001).

Stormy Monday
(Mike Figgis, USA, 1988)
Worth it for the movie's theme song, sung by BB King.

Let's Get Lost
(Bruce Weber, USA, 1988)
A romanticized portrayal of the great Chet Baker's life.

Les Baisers de secours/Emergency Kisses
(Philippe Garrel, France, 1989)
Just a few notes audible here and there, with Barney Wilen's signature.

Straight, No Chaser
(Charlotte Zwerin, USA, 1989)
Thelonious Monk's musical backbone continuously eludes the camera in this, the only film ever to show this genius' opaque mystery.

Cartoons/Animated Films

Buddy Bolden Blues
(Claes-Göran Lillieborg, Sweden, 1981)
Buddy Bolden's spirit flutters around this Swedish cartoon centered on the history of jazz and its origins.

The Technology of Tears
(Pierre Hébert, Canada, 1987)
Image distortion following the sound distortion of John Zorn's sax and Fred Frith's music. This film is a graphical elaboration based upon a dance performance of the choreographer Rosalind Newman.

Ko-Ko
(George Griffin, USA, 1988)
Short animated film using collage technique, with improvised riffs by Charlie Parker.

Knick Knack
(John Lasseter, USA, 1989)
Computer animation short film produced by Pixar, built around vocals by Bobby McFerrin.

1990s

Full-Length Features and Short Films

Taksi-Blyuz/Taxi Blues
(Pavel Lounguine, USSR, 1990)
Lounguine's virtuoso directing and Vladimir Chekassine's haunting music.

The Hot Spot
(Dennis Hopper, USA, 1990)
From a novel by Charles Williams (1952), a *noir* related to *Double Indemnity*, not always filmically inspiring, but with jazz that is both excellent and quite multicolored: from Miles Davis to John Lee Hooker, Taj Mahal to Roy Rogers.

Mo' Better Blues
(Spike Lee, USA, 1990)
The jazz is very (perhaps too) clean, a keepsake of the black community, with Denzel Washington playing a sanitized Miles Davis.

Step Across the Border
(Nicolas Humbert and Werner Penzel, Germany/Switzerland, 1990)
One of the most convincing looks at music in the movies, with Fred Frith playing a congenial inventor of sounds.

Tune in Tomorrow
(Jon Amiel, USA, 1990)
Peter Falk is fantastic in this crazy comedy with music by Winton Marsalis.

Bix
(Pupi Avati, Italy, 1991)
A new, highly romanticized biography of Bix Beiderbecke, a fascinating personality who died of pneumonia in 1931 aged 27. The young man with a horn still finds ways to inspire moviemakers.

Naked Lunch
(David Cronenberg, Canada, 1991)
Cronenberg "dares" Ornette Coleman, the man who blew jazz to pieces in 1959, the year *Naked Lunch* came out.

Malcolm X
(Spike Lee, USA, 1992)
Highly ambitious movie with disappointing music played by the Malcolm X Orchestra (!) under the baton of Terence Blanchard. This is a far cry from the angry young turks of jazz.

Just Friends
(Marc-Henri Wajnberg, Belgium, 1993)
A portrayal of the European jazzmania of the 1950s, inspired by the eventful life of Flemish sax player Jack Sells.

A Great Day in Harlem
(Jean Bach, USA, 1994)
The legendary photo of Art Kane comes to life before our very eyes, and it's jazz's Golden Age that is slowly reborn.

On Animal Locomotion
(Johan van der Keuken, Holland, 1994) SM
With a dozen films in common, van der Keuken draws inspiration from Willem Breuker's music. Two musicians, together.

Le Nouveau monde/The New World
(Alain Corneau, France, 1995)
The memories of an adolescent Corneau as he discovers jazz, rock and the movies back in 1959.

Kansas City
(Robert Altman, USA, 1996)
James Carter and Joshua Redman (among others) in this evocation of the historic Kansas City jam sessions, with a *film noir* backdrop.

Wild Man Blues
(Barbara Kopple, USA, 1997)
Moving portrait of Woody Allen, the musician.

Sweet and Lowdown
(Woody Allen, USA, 1999)
Fictional biography of Emmett Ray, "the best guitarist in the world after Django Reinhardt." Bursting with Woody Allen's love for jazz.

Cartoons/Animated Films

Moaning Lisa
(Wesley Archer, USA, 1990)
Lisa Simpson, sax player for personal pleasure and vocation, gets up close with jazz and blues thanks to her friend Murphy, an old black sax player who reminds her that "the blues isn't about feeling better. It's about making other people feel worse..." One of the most memorable episodes of "The Simpsons," the television cartoon pro-

duced by Matt Groening. And the title refers to a famous Nat King Cole song.

Round Springfield
(Steven Dean Moore, USA, 1995)
The last days of Murphy, the black sax player and friend of Lisa who already appeared in the *Moaning Lisa* episode. One of the most tear-jerking episodes of "The Simpsons." And the title obviously refers to Thelonious Monk's *Round Midnight*.

Bridgehampton
(John Canemaker, USA, 1998)
The seasons go by on Long Island to the piano playing of Fred Hersch in this cartoon by Canemaker, one of the most famous American historians of animated films.

2000s

Full-Length Features and Short Films

Quatre jours à Ocoee
(Pascale Ferran, France, 2001)
Pascale Ferran films a recording session of *Winter* by Tony Hymas and Sam Rivers in a studio in Ocoee. Four trying, cloistered days. The work of jazz musicians, the creative act, and the interplay of two jazzmen (captured as the jazz sparks to life suddenly and miraculously) have never been filmed better.

**Ma femme est une actrice/
My Wife Is an Actress**
(Yvan Attal, France, 2001)
A light-hearted comedy about a young, jazz-loving filmmaker, with music by Brad Mehldau.

Our thanks to Philippe Carles, Baptiste Piégay and Bernie Uhlmann.

Mo' Better Blues (Spike Lee, 1990)
Spike Lee

CONTRIBUTORS

Giampiero Cane, a refined music scholar, is Professor of African-American Musical Civilization at the University of Bologna, Department of Art, Music and Performing Arts (DAMS), a course that is offered exclusively at this University. He has written a number of fundamental critical works on spirituals, the blues, Duke Ellington, free jazz, Monk and Cage and other topics. A journalist in his own right, he regularly contributes to the national daily newspaper "il manifesto."

Philippe Carles, editor-in-chief of "Jazz Magazine" and radio producer (France-Musiques) since 1971, was born in Algiers on March 2nd, 1941. He is co-author with Jean-Louis Comolli of *Free Jazz/ Black Power* (Champ Libre, 1971, Folio/Gallimard, 2000) and of the *Dictionnaire du Jazz* (published under the direction of P. Carles, J.-L. Comolli, André Clergeat – Laffont, Bouquins, 1988, 2001). Discography (interviews published on CD): "Aldo Romano, Intervista" (Universal), "Jimmy Giuffre Talks and Plays" (Celp/Harmonia Mundi).

Jean-Louis Comolli wrote for "Cahiers du Cinéma" from 1962 to 1978 and was the magazine's editor-in-chief from 1966 to 1971. He teaches at the FEMIS in Paris, and also in Barcelona and Buenos Aires. He writes for "Trafic," "Images documentaries," "Jazz Magazine," "L'Image," and "Le Monde." He has made the following films and documentaries: *La Cecilia* (1976), *L'Ombre rouge* (1981), *On ne va pas se quitter comme ça* (1981), *Tous pour un* (1988), the series "Marseille" (1989-2001), *Le Concerto de Mozart* (1996), *Jeux de rôles à Carpentras* (1998), *Buenaventura Durruti, anarchiste* (1999), *L'Affaire Sofri* (2001). He has also published the following books: *Free Jazz/Black Power* (Champ Libre, 1971, with Philippe Carles; republished Folio/ Gallimard, 2000); *Regards sur la ville* (BPI, 1994); *Arrêt sur Histoire* (BPI, 1997); *Cinéma et politique, 56-70* (BPI, 2001). He was co-director of the *Dictionnaire du Jazz* (published under the direction of P. Carles, J.-L. Comolli, André Clergeat – Laffont, Bouquins, 1988, 2001).

Ermanno Comuzio, a well-known Italian film critic and journalist, is senior writer for newspapers and film magazines and has written extensively on music and film. Among his titles in this field are a Filmlexicon of film music and an impressive dictionary on film musicians. He has also written on the work of Cukor, Walsh, the American musical and several other topics.

Michele Fadda has just completed his specialization in Comparative Literature at the University of Bologna with a dissertation on cinema and literature. A film critic for sometime, one of his fields of interest includes cartoons. In recent years he edited, with Fabrizio Liberti, a book on Tex Avery and another on Chuck Jones.

Krin Gabbard, Professor of Comparative Literature at the State University of New York, Stony Brook, editor of *Jazz Among the Discourses* and *Representing Jazz* and author of *Psychiatry and the Cinema* and *Jammin' at the Margins. Jazz and the American Cinema*, is a major world authority on jazz and cinema.

Bill Krohn has been the Los Angeles correspondent of "Cahiers du Cinéma" for 25 years. He is the author of the award-winning *Hitchcock au travail*, which has appeared in French, English and Italian editions. He previously edited *Hollywood Boulevard – Joe Dante e l'altro cinema indipendente* (Italian edition) and *Feux croisés* (French edition) for the Locarno Film Festival. He is the co-director/writer/producer of *It's All True: Based on an Unfinished Film by Orson Welles*, which had its European première at Locarno Film Festival in 1994.

Franco La Polla, for 30 years Professor of American Literature and Culture in Italian universities, now teaches American Film at the University of Bologna, Department of Art, Music and Performing Arts (DAMS). Author of more than a dozen books, mostly on Hollywood cinema, he has edited an equal number of essay collections (including on Joseph L. Mankiewicz and Joe Dante for the Venice and the Locarno Film Festivals, respectively). Curator of the 1996 Retrospective on the Beat Generation and Film for the Venice Film Festival, his most recently published critical work is *Stili americani* (2003).

Franco Minganti teaches Anglo-American

literature at the University of Bologna. He is often involved in research regarding Afro-American culture, jazz and the relationship between literature and music. He is co-author of the *Storia della letteratura americana* (1991), author of *X-Roads. Letteratura, jazz, immaginario* (1994) and *Modulazioni di frequenza. L'immaginario radiofonico tra letteratura e cinema* (1997) and editor of *Jazztoldtales. Jazz e fiction, letteratura e jazz* (1997). In 2002 he published the afterword to *Mumbo Jumbo* by Ishmael Reed.

Antonio Monda, Assistant Professor of Film and Television at New York University, has directed numerous documentaries and a full-length film entitled *December*. He collaborates with the Italian newspaper "La Repubblica" (culture section) and is a film critic for the "Rivista dei Libri." He has organized exhibitions for the Guggenheim, the MoMA, Lincoln Center and the Academy of Motion Picture Arts and Sciences.

Gilles Mouëllic is Maître de Conférences at the University of Rennes 2, where he teaches jazz and cinema. He is the author of *Jazz et cinéma* (Editions Cahiers du Cinéma, 2000) and of *Le jazz, une esthétique du Xxe siècle* (Presses Universitaires de Rennes, 2000), and also of numerous articles devoted to the relationship between music and film. He writes for the periodicals "Jazz Magazine" and "Africultures."

Baptiste Piégay, a critic for "Cahiers du Cinéma," is co-author with Serge Toubiana of the volume *Exil et terrritoires, le cinéma d'Amos Gitaï* published by Editions Cahiers du Cinéma (2003).